[redacted]

D1520233

APPROPRIATING HEIDEGGER

Although Martin Heidegger is undeniably one of the most influential philosophers of the twentieth century, among the philosophers who study his work we find considerable disagreement over what might seem to be basic issues: why is Heidegger important? What did his work do? This volume is an explicit response to these differences, and is unique in bringing together representatives of many different approaches to Heidegger's philosophy. Topics covered include Heidegger's place in the "history of being," Heidegger and ethics, Heidegger and theology, and Heidegger and Nazi concepts of race. More generally, the contributors also address their respective visions of the nature of philosophy and the presuppositions which guide their understanding of Heidegger.

JAMES E. FAULCONER is Professor of Philosophy at Brigham Young University. He is co-editor (with Richard Williams) of *Reconsidering Psychology: Perspectives from Contemporary Continental Philosophy* (1990).

MARK A. WRATHALL is Assistant Professor of Philosophy at Brigham Young University. He is co-editor (with Jeff Malpas) of *Heidegger, Authenticity, and Modernity* and *Heidegger, Coping, and Cognitive Science* (forthcoming).

APPROPRIATING HEIDEGGER

EDITED BY

JAMES E. FAULCONER

Brigham Young University

MARK A. WRATHALL

Brigham Young University

CAMBRIDGE
UNIVERSITY PRESS

PUBLISHED BY THE PRESS SYNDICATE OF THE UNIVERSITY OF CAMBRIDGE
The Pitt Building, Trumpington Street, Cambridge, United Kingdom

CAMBRIDGE UNIVERSITY PRESS
The Edinburgh Building, Cambridge CB2 2RU, UK www.cup.cam.ac.uk
40 West 20th Street, New York, NY 10011-4211, USA www.cup.org
10 Stamford Road, Oakleigh, Melbourne 3166, Australia
Ruiz de Alarcón 13, 28014 Madrid, Spain

© James E. Faulconer and Mark A. Wrathall 2000

This book is in copyright. Subject to statutory exception
and to the provisions of relevant collective licensing agreements,
no reproduction of any part may take place without
the written permission of Cambridge University Press.

First published 2000

Printed in the United Kingdom at the University Press, Cambridge

Typeset in Baskerville 11/12.5pt [VN]

A catalogue record for this book is available from the British Library

Library of Congress Cataloguing in Publication data

Appropriating Heidegger/edited by James E. Faulconer, Mark A. Wrathall.
p. cm.
Includes index.
ISBN 0 521 78181 7 (hardback)
1. Heidegger, Martin, 1889–1976. I. Faulconer, James E. II. Wrathall, Mark A.

B3279.H49 A77 2000
193–dc21 99-087094

ISBN 0 521 78181 7 hardback

Every confrontation of . . . different interpretations of a work . . . is in reality a mutual reflection on the guiding presuppositions: it is the discussion of these presuppositions – a task which, strangely, is always tolerated only marginally and covered up with empty generalizations.

Martin Heidegger, *What Is Called Thinking?*

Contents

List of contributors *page* ix
Acknowledgments x

1 Appropriating Heidegger 1
James E. Faulconer

PART I THINKING OUR AGE

2 Philosophy, thinkers, and Heidegger's place in the history of being 9
Mark A. Wrathall

3 Night and day: Heidegger and Thoreau 30
Stanley Cavell

4 Heidegger's alleged challenge to the Nazi concepts of race 50
Robert Bernasconi

5 Heidegger and ethics beyond the call of duty 68
Albert Borgmann

PART 2 HEIDEGGER IN CONTEXT

6 People of God, people of being: the theological presuppositions of Heidegger's path of thought 85
John D. Caputo

7 Heidegger for beginners 101
Simon Critchley

8 The critique of anthropologism in Heidegger's thought 119
Françoise Dastur

PART 3 READING *BEING AND TIME*

9 In respectful contempt: Heidegger, appropriation, facticity 137
Rudi Visker

10 Could anything be more intelligible than everyday intelligibility? Reinterpreting division I of *Being and Time* in the light of division II 155
Hubert L. Dreyfus

11 Another time 175
John Sallis

12 Intentionality, teleology, and normativity 191
Mark Okrent

Index 207

Contributors

ROBERT BERNASCONI
University of Memphis

ALBERT BORGMANN
University of Montana

JOHN D. CAPUTO
Villanova University

STANLEY CAVELL
Harvard University

SIMON CRITCHLEY
University of Essex

FRANÇOISE DASTUR
University of Nice Sophia-Antipolis

HUBERT L. DREYFUS
University of California, Berkeley

JAMES E. FAULCONER
Brigham Young University

MARK OKRENT
Bates College

JOHN SALLIS
Pennsylvania State University

RUDI VISKER
Catholic University of Leuven

MARK A. WRATHALL
Brigham Young University

Acknowledgments

The editors wish to thank Brigham Young University for its generous financial support of the conference that gave rise to this volume, particularly General Education and Honors, the Departments of Philosophy, Political Science, English, and German and Slavic Languages, and the Colleges of Humanities and Family, Home, and Social Sciences. We wish also to thank Tammy Krebs for her unflagging efforts in keeping us organized and Julie Murdock and Jennifer Hodge for their help in editing and source-checking. Finally, our gratitude to Hilary Gaskin at Cambridge University Press for encouraging this project.

CHAPTER I

Appropriating Heidegger

James E. Faulconer

In Britain and North America today we find a division between "analytic" and "continental" philosophy. To be sure, the division is an unequal one, with most philosophers in each region to be found on the analytic side of the divide. However, the near absence of this division in continental Europe suggests that it is as much political as anything else, often a quarrel over whose students will get jobs and which work will be recognized as genuinely philosophical.[1] Whatever the rationality of the analytic/continental distinction, one of its oddities is that in recognizing the division or even in overcoming it (as may be happening today), we often neglect the diversity within each side of the division. There is nothing that could properly be called either continental or analytic philosophy. At best, those terms designate family resemblances or constellations or even clusters of constellations.

In continental philosophy, one such constellation in the cluster is that of the "Heideggerians," philosophers with research programs based in the work of Martin Heidegger. Within that constellation we find considerable difference over what might seem to be basic issues: why is Heidegger important? What did his work do? What should we do with it? – and the differences on these issues sometimes carry with them considerable philosophical suspicion. No one is surprised when John Searle says, "most philosophers in the Anglo-American tradition seem to think that Heidegger was an obscurantist muddlehead at best or an unregenerate Nazi at worst."[2] However, many would be surprised to hear similar, though usually more guarded and less caustic, remarks of one Heideggerian about another: there is little consensus among Heideggerians as to what Heidegger's work does or how we are to deal with it.

This volume is an explicit response to that situation, though the essays in it are not attempts to overcome the supposed problem of those differences. James E. Faulconer and Mark A. Wrathall brought the philosophers in this volume together in May 1999, in Park City, Utah, to provoke an encounter between several different and important ways of talking about and using Heidegger. Some of the writers reflect explicitly on their relation to Heidegger and the relation of their work to the work of others. Other writers show those relations in the juxtaposition of their essays rather than in explicit reflection. That itself says something about the difference in approaches.

In *A Companion to Continental Philosophy*, Simon Critchley discusses the difference between analytic and continental philosophy by picking out a number of the distinguishing features of continental philosophy, including its focus on particular thinkers rather than on problems, its refusal to dissociate philosophical problems from their historical origin and context, and its insistence on the primacy of practice (and, therefore, crisis) rather than technical analysis.[3] To Critchley's list one could at least add a consideration of the connection between rhetoric and argument (an interest indissociable from the primacy of practice) and a focus on important texts. However, whatever list one would draw up would also more or less describe the differences *between* the approaches to philosophy taken by continental philosophers, including Heideggerians, as the pieces in this volume illustrate.

Each philosopher in this collection appropriates Heidegger differently, but each shares with the others that he or she does *appropriate* Heidegger. They share the belief that a philosophical response to Heidegger's work – or the work of any philosopher, for that matter – is always more than a scholarly reconstruction of the best interpretation of the philosopher's texts. Scholarly work is the spadework that makes appropriation possible; it makes it possible to think with Heidegger, the goal of the philosophers who take Heidegger's work seriously. And, the ambiguity of *with* in "think with Heidegger" – Heidegger as tool? Thinking alongside him? – marks one of the differences in how these writers have appropriated Heidegger's work. In no case, however, does their appropriation result in an uncritical attitude toward that work. "Thinking with" means neither simple repetition nor discipleship, but there is nothing that all agree constitutes an appropriation of Heidegger.

Besides the differences between these philosophers as to what it means to think with Heidegger, there are other differences. Some of their essays focus on texts more than on problems, and between the essays that focus on problems, there is wide divergence as to what constitutes an important philosophical problem. Some Heideggerians are less insistent on the historical dimension of Heidegger's thinking than the rest. The work of some looks more like the technical work of analytic philosophy than the work commonly associated with continental philosophers (at least associated in the minds of most English-speaking philosophers). For some of the writers, one's style is critical to one's philosophical thought, part and parcel of it. To others, style is a matter of saying straightforwardly what one wishes to say and no more (though the philosophers in the other parts of the constellation might well argue about what constitutes straightforwardness). For some, it is impossible to understand Heidegger without incorporating his destruction of the history of ontology. For others, that destruction is only important insofar as it is relevant to the particular philosophical problems in which they have an interest.

Besides the fact that they begin with Heidegger's work, these essays are held together by the Heideggerian project itself: attention to the enigmatic character of the everyday. The task of *Being and Time* was to retrieve the question of being by loosening up, destroying, the history of ontology, a destruction to be accomplished by attending to the enigmatic character of the everyday – exposing the unnoticed metaphysical presuppositions by means of which we understand the everyday and behind which the everyday is concealed. Heidegger's observation is that the obvious and given character of supposedly everyday objects and practices conceals a great deal. It conceals that what it means to be a thing is not easy to explicate. It conceals the character of our involvement with things. It conceals our being and how the world, an "environing world," as Heidegger reminds us (*Sein und Zeit* paragraphs 14–16), is constituted. It conceals the character of time and the temporality of being. It conceals what it means to be a person, a people, and to be in relation to others. The Heideggerian constellation can be said to cluster around attention to this observation, though there is a multiplicity of ways that one can think the enigma of the everyday. Some writers in this volume stress its character, focusing on the enigma. Without wishing merely to undo the enigmatic, others stress the understanding that Heidegger's analysis of the everyday brings to a variety of philosophical problems.

This collection brings together essays that attend to Heidegger's thinking about the everyday and its enigma, and they reflect on how they do so. We hope they will open a discussion between the various sorts of Heideggerians as well as show those outside the circle of Heidegger scholarship the variety of ways in which Heidegger is read and the variety of discussions to which his work is germane.

Although there are many ways in which the essays in this volume could have been organized, we have divided them into three rough groups. The contrast between the essays within each part can give readers a feel for the distinctive ways in which Heideggerians of different stripes approach the related problems.

In the first part, each essay addresses Heidegger's attempt to think through the nature of the modern age and the technological understanding of being that shapes contemporary philosophy, the sciences, and indeed all human practices. Mark Wrathall asks how Heidegger's thinking can help us understand the historical situatedness of philosophy without, on the one hand, making philosophical problems merely historically contingent, or on the other hand, ignoring the historical character of the problems with which philosophers deal and the responses they make to those problems. By juxtaposing Heidegger and Thoreau, Stanley Cavell suggests a uniquely American, rather than German, response to the call to philosophize, a call understood in a Heideggerian fashion as the call to "dwell in what is one's own." Robert Bernasconi asks what we might learn from Heidegger's encounter with early twentieth-century race science, particularly what we might learn about how philosophers can respond to contemporary racism. And Albert Borgmann looks at Heidegger's work to understand the failure of standard ethics and the need for an ethics of obligation, arguing that only the latter can help us face contemporary ecological and social problems.

The second group of thinkers, John D. Caputo, Simon Critchley, and Françoise Dastur, examine the context of Heidegger's work. Caputo examines the effects on that work of Heidegger's willingness to return to the Greeks combined with his inability to see the contribution that biblical thinking made to his understanding: Heidegger's sharp distinction between philosophy and religion will not hold, but his insistence on it undermines his work. Critchley seeks to understand Heidegger's work from out of its background in Husserlian phenomenology, arguing that on Heidegger's view the natural attitude is neither natural nor an attitude. The result of Heidegger's attack on the natural attitude is an alternative that avoids the twin problems of scientism and obscurantism. Dastur argues that the anthropologism of *Being and Time* must be understood as a necessary part of the ontological project rather than as anthropologism as such, and she shows how that discussion of human being plays out in Heidegger's later thought as the "appropriating mirror-play of the simple one-fold of earth and sky, divinities and mortals."[4]

In the final section, Rudi Visker, Hubert Dreyfus, John Sallis, and Mark Okrent each offer an essay based on Heidegger's first major work, *Being and Time.* Visker uses the phenomenon of philosophical styles – styles of the sort that separate various appropriations of Heidegger's work – to call into question the adequacy of Heidegger's account of facticity and everydayness in *Being and Time.* Dreyfus also begins with the question of everydayness, arguing that everyday public practices ground everyday forms of intelligibility and using that to try to clarify Heidegger's claim, from division II of *Being and Time,* that there is a higher form of intelligibility. He concludes by briefly reviewing some of the implications for ethics and politics of this higher intelligibility. Sallis's essay begins with the often neglected second division of *Being and Time* and its focus on temporality. He asks what time it is that gives us our ordinary understanding of time (both as the time of concern and as world time), what relation that "other time" has to the temporality of Dasein, and what it would mean to think that time. Sallis's answer is that "time cannot take place without also referring – or rather, submitting – to the gift of light bestowed by the heaven, preeminently by the sun" (p. 188). Finally, Okrent exploits the arguments made in *Being and Time* to articulate a pragmatist solution to the problem of intentionality.

NOTES

1 See John McCumber, "Time in the Ditch: American Philosophy and the McCarthy Era," *Diacritics* 26.1 (1996), 33–49, for a provocative analysis of the origins of the conflict between analytic and continental philosophy in the United States.
2 "The Limits of Phenomenology," in *Heidegger, Coping, and Cognitive Science,* ed. Mark A. Wrathall and Jeff Malpas (Cambridge, MA: MIT, forthcoming).
3 Simon Critchley, "Introduction: What Is Continental Philosophy," in *A Companion to Continental Philosophy,* ed. Simon Critchley and William R. Schroeder (Oxford: Blackwell, 1998), pp. 8–13.
4 Martin Heidegger, *Zur Seinsfrage* (Frankfurt a.M.: Klostermann, 1959), pp. 30–1.

PART I

Thinking our age

CHAPTER 2

Philosophy, thinkers, and Heidegger's place in the history of being

Mark A. Wrathall

THE END OF PHILOSOPHY

The response to Heidegger in the analytical world is, to a considerable degree, a paraphrase of Rudolf Carnap's 1932 essay "Überwindung der Metaphysik durch Logische Analyse der Sprache." To the extent Heidegger intends to make philosophical claims with assertions like "the nothing nothings," Carnap charges, his writings are utterly meaningless; to the extent that Heidegger is creating art, he does it poorly. Or, more likely, Heidegger's work, like that of all metaphysicians, confounds art and philosophy:

> Metaphysicians are musicians without musical ability. Instead they have a strong inclination to work within the medium of the theoretical, to connect concepts and thoughts. Now, instead of activating, on the one hand, this inclination in the domain of science, and satisfying, on the other hand, the need for expression in art, the metaphysician confuses the two and produces a structure which achieves nothing for knowledge and something inadequate for the expression of attitude.[1]

To respond to such charges with a defense of the meaningfulness of Heidegger's claims about "the nothing" would, however, miss the deeper point. Carnap's analysis of Heidegger's alleged "pseudo-sentences" is really ancillary to the project of rehabilitating philosophy as a discipline – a project driven by Carnap's view of language. For Carnap, assertions are meaningless unless they have empirical content. And if they have that, they belong properly to the empirical sciences. Thus, for Carnap and many others in the analytical tradition,[2] philosophy (at least, when properly done) has no substantive content; instead, it is "only a *method*: the method of logical analysis."[3]

This narrow view of philosophy – philosophy as a method of analysis – is grounded in a profound skepticism regarding our ability to discover truths about ourselves and our world through reason alone. Thus, even analytical philosophers like Dummett – philosophers who "no longer regard the traditional questions of philosophy as pseudo-questions to which no meaningful answer can be given" – believe that "philosophy can take us no further than enabling us to command a clear view of the concepts by means of which we think about the world, and, by so doing, to attain a firmer grasp of the way we represent the world in our thought."[4] Philosophy, the analytical philosopher concludes, ought to abandon metaphysics (thereby leaving the empirical sciences in charge of the pursuit of substantive knowledge) and restrict itself to conceptual analysis.

Heidegger's response to this view of philosophy can be seen in a concentrated form in a series of notes which draw their title, "Überwindung der Metaphysik," from Carnap's, and which Heidegger began writing shortly after the publication of Carnap's essay. Indeed, the notes cannot be understood except as articulating an alternative to Carnap's view of the failings of the metaphysical tradition. Like Carnap, Heidegger believes in the need to criticize and, eventually, overcome the metaphysical tradition, but Heidegger denies that Carnap's approach is competent for that task. Heidegger explains: "this title ['The Elimination of Metaphysics'] gives rise to a great deal of misunderstanding because it does not allow experience to get to the ground from which alone the history of Being reveals its essence."[5] That is to say, Carnap's conception of metaphysics (as something which can be eliminated simply through the logical analysis of metaphysical claims) will prevent us from understanding that to which the metaphysical tradition has been a response – the background understanding of being. If we are genuinely to overcome or eliminate the metaphysical tradition, Heidegger believes, we can only do so by thinking through the history of metaphysical efforts to understand the being of what is and, in the process, owning up to the task of thinking being non-metaphysically.

Thus, in Heidegger's way of understanding the task of eliminating metaphysics, "elimination does not mean thrusting aside a discipline from the scope of philosophical 'education.' "[6] Instead, the response to metaphysics begins, for Heidegger, with an understanding of metaphysics "as the destiny of the truth of beings, i.e., of beingness, *as* a still hidden but distinctive Event, namely the oblivion of Being."[7] On this view, two things characterize metaphysical thinkers. First, metaphysical thinkers manifest in their works an understanding of the being of everything that is – i.e., "beingness," the one character or feature of things in virtue of which they are. Second, metaphysical thinkers are unaware of this understanding *as* a background understanding – that is, they work out of an "oblivion of Being." If we see metaphysics in this way, Heidegger argues, it will become apparent that "metaphysics cannot be dismissed like an opinion."[8] One cannot simply change one's mind about metaphysics, simply decide to stop treating it as a serious and worthwhile branch of philosophy, because eliminating metaphysics in this way will, in fact, only heighten our oblivion to the way our understanding of the world is based on a background understanding of being and, in the process, make us more subject to it than ever.

In fact, Heidegger believes, the desire to eliminate metaphysics in the way Carnap proposes is itself a sign of the "technological" understanding of being. The elimination of metaphysics, he writes, might more appropriately be called the "Passing of Metaphysics," where "passing" means the simultaneous departing of metaphysics (i.e., its apparently perishing, and hence being remembered only as something that is past), even while the technological understanding of being "takes possession of its absolute domination over what is."[9] I take this to mean that, in the technological age, the understanding of the being of what is becomes so completely dominant that metaphysical reflection seems superfluous. Even philosophy itself no longer worries about the nature of what is, but simply works out a view of language and mind on the basis of the current understanding of being.[10] In fact, Heidegger would agree that the method of analysis is the "end" or "completion" of philosophy. Philosophy is able to restrict itself to conceptual analysis, and to cede all questions of theory and ontology to the empirical sciences, precisely because the scientific–technological understanding of being is so completely dominant: "philosophy is ending in the present age. It has found its place in the scientific attitude of socially active humanity."[11]

In short, Heidegger sees the effort to restrict philosophy to conceptual analysis, thereby ignoring or dismissing metaphysics, as a sign not that metaphysics is something past, but that philosophy is more subject than ever to the errors of the metaphysical past. Like the metaphysicians, contemporary philosophy works under the dominance of an understanding of being which is, for it, unquestionable. And like the metaphysicians, contemporary philosophy is oblivious to the need to think the background. The task of thinking at the end of philosophy is to overcome this oblivion, and to do this, we must become aware of our own place in the history of being. But we can arrive at such an historical awareness only through an engagement with the metaphysical past that Carnap and analytical philosophers in general would as soon ignore.

PHILOSOPHY AND ITS HISTORY

At this point, it might sound as if the disagreement between Heidegger and the analytical philosophers is shaping up as a familiar argument over the place of history in philosophy. On the one hand, there are those who see philosophy, like science, as a rigorous and timeless pursuit of truth, abstracted from any particular cultural and historical locus. From this perspective, philosophy's history is an accidental feature of philosophy properly understood. We might, out of a kind of curiosity, review the history of philosophy as if it were a catalogue of opinions once held on current philosophical issues. But in the final analysis, philosophy's concern is solving its current problems – problems for which historical figures have no authority, and can offer at most a little insight into an answer.

Against ahistoricism in philosophy are those who see philosophy as an ineliminably historical endeavor, and argue that the problems philosophers tackle and their approach to those problems are themselves dictated by their culture. To do philosophy is thus to work through the problems inherited from the past, problems made pressing by the philosopher's current historical situation. On this view, an effort to abstract philosophical problems and forms of reasoning from their history will misunderstand the philosophical past and, more importantly, obscure contemporary philosophy's most pressing task – that of responding to the tensions and crises of our age.

From what I have said so far, one might see Heidegger as advocating the historical picture of philosophy in opposition to the ahistorical. And there is some truth to that, provided that "history" is properly understood. But it would be a very crude misreading of Heidegger to attribute to him the view that philosophy is simply a cultural/historical phenomenon. To be more precise, cultural changes and crises are governed by a background understanding of being, and it is to this ontological background that philosophy is first responsible. To the extent that philosophers are responsive to the call to think being, they and their work are removed from ordinary historical and cultural influences. Heidegger thus argues that it is a mistake to explain the thought of a thinker in "terms of the influences of the milieu and the effects of their actual 'life' situation."[12] Heidegger's view of the role of history in philosophy hangs, then, on a distinction between *Geschichte* and *Historie* – between history and historiology (or historiography – *Historie* is translated both ways). We'll return to this distinction later; for now, a brief introduction to the distinction must suffice.

All thoughts, words, experiences, deeds, and rules – in short, all the stuff of ordinary history – are, according to Heidegger, determined by a background understanding which shapes and constitutes foreground activities. Heidegger refers to this background as "the *open region* of ends, standards, motives, possible results, and powers"[13] – namely, of everything that constitutes any particular action or experience as what it is. Here, incidentally, is where to look to see what Heidegger means by "the nothing." It is not, of course, meant in any straightforward sense as a negative existential quantification (although it entails a negative existential quantification: there is no thing that grounds our foreground activities). To call the background "nothing" is to point out that it is not a thing, and does not operate in the same way that things in the foreground do.

Metaphysics, as I indicated above, is the attempt to think and name the being of what is. But because metaphysicians do not understand that there is a background constituting the foreground as what it is, they interpret the unity of the foreground in terms of some uniform thing or feature in virtue of which everything is what it is; that is, metaphysics "thinks what is as a whole – the world, men, God – with respect to Being, with respect to the unity of what is in Being."[14]

The history of the West and of metaphysics on Heidegger's interpretation consists in a series of ways in which the being of what is – that characteristic or feature in virtue of which anything is what it is – has been given or "unconcealed" to human beings. With each "unconcealment of being," human beings have become progressively oblivious to the fact that their everyday thoughts, activities, identities, etc., are grounded in a background understanding of being that is neither necessary in its structure nor contingent in the sense of being within human control. While Heidegger believed that the metaphysical tradition has failed to think the background or "clearing" within which everything is what it is, he also believed that philosophers have nevertheless played a privileged role in opening up for their culture the possibilities given by the understanding of being. The history of being, a history traceable in the work of the metaphysicians, falls, according to Heidegger, into four distinct periods: the Greek (in which what is was primarily understood as *phusis*), the Medieval (in which what is was understood as "God's creation"), the Modern (where "beings became objects that could be controlled and penetrated by calculation"),[15] and finally an intensification of the Modern, the Technological (in which what is is understood as standing reserve – i.e., as being constantly available for flexible reconfiguration and re-evaluation).

Metaphysics, on this view, affects much more than philosophy. The metaphysical thinkers actually help open a space of possibilities for a culture by articulating, and thus making available to our practices in general, the understanding of being which characterizes (or is coming to characterize) the age. The best way to explain what Heidegger means is to review one of his examples of the way in which a philosopher, by responding to a new understanding of being, articulated it and, in the process, made it possible to experience the world in a new way.

Heidegger agrees with traditional historiological accounts that an important distinction between the modern and the medieval ages lies in the extent to which modern man "disengages himself from the constraints of biblical Christian revealed truth and church doctrine."[16] But what historiology misses, Heidegger contends, is the way that this change was itself only possible against the background of an altered understanding of being. What gave medieval life its coherence was a pursuit of salvation. The idea of salvation, however, was understood on the basis of a background understanding of being: "the truth of salvation does not restrict itself to a relation of faith, a relation to God; rather the truth of salvation at the same time decides about beings. . . Beings in their sundry orders are the creation of a creator God, a creation rescued from the Fall and elevated to the suprasensuous realm once again through the redeemer God."[17] An ideal of intellectual freedom would be nearly incoherent against the medieval background understanding, for it would appear as, at best, a rejection of not just the saving ordinances offered by the Church, but also as a departure from the God-given intelligibility inherent in things. Consequently, political and intellectual liberation was impossible for the medievals, because science and politics had to operate in harmony with God's order.

In modernity, however, there is a gradual shift away from understanding what is in terms of its relationship to God, and toward a sense that beings are what they are in virtue of being representable to a perceiving subject. This, in turn, made man responsible for himself and his thoughts in a way not possible so long as man was a child of God in the midst of God's creation. This background shift is first discernible in Descartes's work: "Descartes' metaphysics is the decisive beginning of the foundation of metaphysics in the modern age. It was his task *to ground the metaphysical ground of man's liberation in the new freedom of self-assured self-legislation*."[18] For example, when Descartes declares that the first rule of his philosophic method is "never to accept anything as true if I did not have evident knowledge of its truth,"[19] he does so not because he is a skeptic, Heidegger argues, but rather because the emerging modern style required man to take responsibility for his own knowledge and situation. The method of doubt – i.e., that I am "to include nothing more in my judgments than what presented itself to my mind with such clarity and distinctness that I would have no occasion to put it in doubt"[20] – is justified by Descartes through analogizing human understanding to a building. Noting that "buildings undertaken and completed by a single architect are usually more attractive and better planned than those which several have tried to patch up," Descartes argues that we should become our own architects, dispensing with the "old walls" inherited from teachers and past scholars, and rebuilding ourselves from the ground up.[21] In so doing, Descartes is responding to an emerging background understanding of us and our place in the world: "man becomes that being upon which all that is, is grounded as regards the manner of its Being and its truth. Man becomes the relational center of that which is as such."[22] In articulating his philosophical project in accordance with the new understanding, Descartes creates a pattern of thought which is then used to justify other shifts in the practices of the age, thereby ushering in a new understanding of being.

To summarize, the new possibilities available to modern man, including the possibility of becoming the "architect" of his own thoughts, are opened up by a fundamental shift in the metaphysical background. The task of the history of philosophy, for Heidegger, is to uncover such fundamental shifts.

We can now return to the questions with which this section began – what is the nature of Heidegger's disagreement with analytical philosophers? And what does Heidegger mean in saying that the task for thinking is necessarily historical? As to the latter question, we can see why Heidegger would reject both the views discussed in the beginning of this section on the role of history in philosophy. Both undoubtedly have a degree of truth to them. Insofar as a philosopher is a thinker, however, both views fail to capture what is most essential to the philosopher's task. A metaphysician's historical and cultural inheritance is at most the departure point for articulating a new understanding of being. Consequently, the content of the metaphysical thinker's thought cannot be reduced to its cultural setting. Likewise, while advances are certainly made in philosophy, to focus on the advances as an ahistorical march of progress is to ignore the question of the historical constitution of the problematics, facts, etc., with which philosophers as logical or conceptual analysts deal.

This leads us, then, to the nature of Heidegger's disagreement with a concept of philosophy as restricted to conceptual analysis. To begin with, philosophy as a mere method of analysis doesn't genuinely eliminate the metaphysical, it merely ignores it. It fails to account adequately for the back-groundedness of our concepts, even while it, as a human endeavor, is intrinsically shaped by current background sensibilities. This is why, in the passages quoted above, Heidegger sees Carnap's essay as itself more proof of the need for a genuinely historical reflection on metaphysics – Carnap is himself oblivious to the need to think about the background which shapes him as much as the metaphysical past. This oblivion, Heidegger believes, poses a unique threat to our historical essence as human beings. As Heidegger understands it, ever since the earliest Greek thinkers, human action in the world has been shaped and guided by a unified, background understanding of what it means to be. We are now in a technological age which has completely occluded the fact that our foreground activities are grounded by a background understanding of being. And this makes it almost impossible to own up to the way we are, in all our activities, essentially responsible to a background.[23]

Heidegger believes that metaphysics can only genuinely be overcome if we can somehow recover a sensibility for the background, and if we can learn to see how it constitutes the present and opens up futural possibilities. And this, Heidegger insists, requires an historical inquiry for two main reasons.

First, because the background is so completely entrenched as to escape our notice, it is only an historical thought which can loosen the grasp that our metaphysical understanding of being has on us. If we immerse ourselves in an historical reflection on the understanding of a past age, our current presuppositions and practices may come to seem strange and ungrounded. And if that happens, we will be prepared to confront the fact that we ourselves are thoroughly shaped by an understanding of the being of beings – an understanding which, while once revolutionary, is now so commonplace as to go unnoticed. As Heidegger notes, "in order to rescue the beginning, and consequently the future [i.e., the background understanding of being that shapes our current practices and future possibilities], from time to time the domination of the ordinary and all too ordinary must be broken." History, by giving us a "genuine relation to the beginning," brings about just such an "upheaval of what is habitual."[24]

Second, historical thought calls to our attention what Hubert Dreyfus has called "marginal practices" – that is, ways of relating to what is that draw their intelligibility from a different background understanding of being than now prevails. By learning to take these practices seriously, something we can only do when we see them against the background of the understanding of being which first grounded them, we can foster a readiness that will allow us to respond differently to the people and things we encounter in our everyday world. As Heidegger puts it, historical thought is "preparatory" in the sense that it prepares us for an escape from the metaphysics of our current age.

HISTORY AND HISTORIOLOGY

Now the question is, how is a genuinely historical reflection to proceed?

Heidegger is notorious for his "violent" interpretations of figures in the history of philosophy. His interpretive method is often quite disconcerting to the classical philologist as well as the historian of philosophy. Mourelatos, for instance, objects to Heidegger's "capricious use of etymology in 'hermeneutic' interpretations of the pre-Socratics,"[25] complaining that Heidegger and his followers have given etymology a bad name. Heidegger's interpretations of the presocratics, Mourelatos explains dismissively, "are correctly appreciated (as it is now generally conceded) not as contributions to the history of Greek philosophy, but as dialectical, rhetorical, and heuristic devices for the development of Heidegger's own philosophy."[26] Mourelatos's conclusion, I would argue, overstates the issue. There are in fact standards for judging Heidegger's histories beyond whether they successfully articulate his own philosophy. But he is quite right that Heidegger's work is not meant as a contribution to philological or historiological accounts of the philosophical past.

Of course, Heidegger's notoriety as a bad interpreter of historical philosophers is not something of which he was unaware. Already in 1935 he wrote: "In the usual present-day view what has been said here [in an interpretation of Parmenides] is a mere product of the farfetched and one-sided Heideggerian method of exegesis, which has already become proverbial."[27] And in the preface to the second edition of Heidegger's Kant book, he noted that "readers have taken constant offense at the violence of my interpretations. Their allegation of violence can indeed by supported by this text."[28] But there was a reason behind his approach – one which he was careful to explain and defend.

Heidegger's response to his critics consists in emphasizing the difference between the historiological study of what we have been calling the foreground events and activities in our past, and an historical reflection on the open region within which those events transpire, "that from which all human happenings begin."[29] As a result, the stuff of ordinary history – historical actors and events – are not the principal objects of Heidegger's history, although it would be a mistake to say that Heidegger's history is unconcerned with them.

The subsidiary role accorded to ordinary historiology in Heidegger's accounts brings with it the risk that his history will lose touch with reality, and critics like Richard Rorty have been quick to charge that Heidegger's histories are vacuous and mystical.[30] Rorty argues that Heidegger's history of being is nothing but the history of what philosophers have said about being. But because these pronouncements cannot be understood without seeing them in their connection to the "plain history" of peoples and things, Rorty argues that Heidegger fails to give content to his history of philosophy: "Without the reference to the history of nations, we should obviously have only what Versenyi suggests is all we get anyway: 'an all too empty and formal, though often emotionally charged and mystically-religious, thinking of absolute unity.'"[31] Along similar lines, Bernasconi argues that Heidegger's account of the history of philosophy deconstructs itself because every time Heidegger tells the history of philosophy, he does so in historiological terms. As a result, he concludes that "The distinction between *Geschichte* and *Historie* is here, as always, impossible to maintain."[32]

Such critiques fail to appreciate Heidegger's own explanation of history, historiology, and their interdependence. Bernasconi, for instance, interprets the distinction between historiology and history as the distinction between accounts that follow "the guiding thread of a story," and those that do not.[33] But this is a misunderstanding. It is quite right to say that historiology provides a "journalist's" account, describing things in terms of a series of passing events.[34] And such an account might even follow "the guiding thread of a story," but this is not what is determinative of historiology as historiology. Rather, historiology is what it is because in it the past is treated as a series of events, without regard for the background understanding of being which constitutes these events as the events that they are.

So, where historiology understands the passage of time in terms of "years and days," history investigates the passage of time in terms of changes in the "age" – i.e., "the situation of human things and man's dwelling place therein."[35] History traces the "movement of being," that is, changes in the background norms of intelligibility and the general style of the practices most central to an age. History thus seeks to uncover the ways in which identities and objects have been constituted and experienced, and the general kinds of constraints working on the field of possibilities open to historical actors. The goal is

> to draw nearer to what is "happening" in the history of the modern age. What is happening means what sustains and compels history, what triggers chance events and in advance gives leeway to resolutions, what within beings represented as objects and as states of affairs basically is *what is.* We never experience what is happening by ascertaining through historical inquiry what is "going on." As this expression tells us very well, what is "going on" passes before us in the foreground and background of the public stage of events and varying opinions. What happens can never be made historiologically cognizable. It can only be thoughtfully known by grasping what the metaphysics that predetermines the age has elevated to thought and word.[36]

Thus, Heidegger's distinction between history and historiology is not a distinction between the history of nations and peoples on the one hand, and the history of philosophy on the other. Rather, it is a distinction between ways of approaching the history of all human phenomena – namely, a historiological reporting on past events, a reporting which "touches only the foremost of the foreground"[37] – versus historical recovery of the understanding of an age which constituted what happened as the event it was. Heidegger believes that, at least within the history of philosophy, his history is a prerequisite to doing Rorty's "plain history":

> Since historiographical considerations are always subordinated to historical reflections, the erroneous opinion can arise to the effect that historiography is altogether superfluous for history. But from the order of rank just mentioned the only conclusion to be drawn is this: historiographical considerations are essential only insofar as they are supported by a historical reflection, are directed by it in their very way of questioning, and are determined by it in the delimitation of their tasks. But this also implies the converse, that historigraphical considerations and cognitions are indeed indispensable.[38]

Historiological considerations are indispensable, I take it, precisely because an investigation of the background understanding of being only makes sense as an investigation of the way the background grounds the foreground.

If history is properly conceived as the movement in background understandings of being, we can see why one ought to reject the historiological approach to philosophy, which proceeds by tracing the influence of foreground events on one another. A historiology will inevitably read our own understanding of being back into the events of the past. A foreground event, as we noted earlier, is constituted as the event it is only by fitting it into a context of ends or goals, standards of performance, motives or intentions, possible results, etc., and these all have the determinate shape they do given an understanding of what it is for something to be at all. Unless we are aware that we understand the world only in virtue of a background sense for things, we will drag along our own background as we confront the historiological record. As Heidegger explains in the context of a discussion of the history of the concept of truth, "we find only what we seek, and in historiography we are seeking only what we [already] may know."[39] Or, as he observes elsewhere, historiology necessarily works with "images of the past determined by the present"[40]: "Historiographical research never discloses history, because such research is always attended by an opinion about history, an unthought one, a so-called obvious one, which it would like to confirm by this very research and in so doing only rigidifies the unthought obviousness."[41]

This tendency is compounded, in Heidegger's view, when we approach philosophers historiologically. Philosophers not only work out of a different background understanding of Being, but they respond to that background. To the extent that they are doing metaphysics, their writings need to be seen as alethic rather than assertoric – that is, as tending to open up, clarify, and articulate the understanding of being rather than as making assertions about foreground events and objects. If we interpret philosophers as performing foreground acts – as saying things about occurrent beliefs, thoughts, concepts, etc. – and in addition interpret those foreground acts on the basis of our own background, we doubly obscure their true import.

For instance, the historiology of philosophy is dependent on philological research into how certain terms were used in the surviving literature of the philosopher's linguistic community. It also relies on the transcultural tracing of dependencies between philosophers. But both of these methods have their shortcomings if our aim is the ontological background.

Philology is limited by its reliance on non-philosophical sources as a basis for interpreting philosophical texts. Philology will fail to shed light on the ontological background to the degree that it depends on an everyday vocabulary, which draws its meaning from foreground events and objects. Consequently, unless the philologist employs metaphysical reflection to illuminate her reading of past texts, rather than relying on conclusions about language drawn from other sources, she will make little progress in understanding metaphysical discourse. Thus, where one seeks to understand the most fundamental underpinnings of a metaphysical position, Heidegger argues, one will require a thinker's insight into being.

In addition, the discovery of dependencies and philosophical influences is itself only illuminating if we comprehend the reason for those dependencies. Historiology of ideas, Heidegger explains, is no more than "scholarly historical detective work, searching out dependencies, [with which] we do not advance a step; we never get to what is essential, but only get stuck in external associations and relations."[42] The point is that, unless we are capable of an independent inquiry into the background, and thus capable of comprehending a philosopher's place in the history of being, we will not understand the significance of the fact that philosophers appropriate one another's work: "To search for influences and dependencies among thinkers is to misunderstand thinking. Every thinker is dependent – upon the address of Being."[43] The illuminating question to ask is thus not what problem or answer one philosopher borrowed from another, but rather why did certain philosophical predecessors and problems show up as relevant sources in the first place? Exploring this question, Heidegger argues, would lead us to ask about the understanding of being that governed those works.

Heidegger's defense of his use of history, then, consists of a reminder that what needs to be understood is the background understanding of a thinker. This understanding will seem violent by the historiologist's lights for two reasons. First, since metaphysical thinkers themselves are unaware of the background which makes it possible for them to think the things they do, a historical interpretation may even run contrary to the things they explicitly say. In addition, the violence of his appropriation is a result of an attempt to think independently of contemporary standards of understanding – something made necessary by the goal of overthrowing the complacency with which we inhabit our own background and project it on the philosophers of the past.

Abandoning, as he did, traditional approaches to the interpretation of philosophy, Heidegger's readings bear little of the sort of support often advanced within traditional historiology. He acknowledged this fact: "We cannot demonstrate the adequacy of the translation by scholarly means." But this was not to say that "scholarly means" were irrelevant; rather, that they would "not carry us far enough," since at best they could only point to the surface phenomena supported by a background understanding of being.[44] Or, as he explained elsewhere, the "doctrinal systems and the expressions of an age" tell us something, insofar as they are an "aftereffect or veneer" supported by the understanding of being of that age.[45] But to read the philosophical veneer correctly, one must be well versed in the thought of being.

This does not mean, as Rorty charges and Mourelatos suggests, that Heidegger has rendered his account of the history of philosophy immune to challenge. But it does mean that a challenge conducted at the level of an interpretation of what philosophers have said, without any sensitivity to the background which makes that interpretation plausible, will miss the mark. It is the background which is Heidegger's primary concern. Thus, a debate with Heidegger's reading ought to be addressed to showing how he has misunderstood this background.

HEIDEGGER'S USE OF HISTORY

We can now say more clearly what it means to be a metaphysical thinker – a philosopher – in Heidegger's sense and, as a result, what Heidegger's historical thinking is meant to accomplish.

The history of philosophy is, Heidegger tells us, the "thinker's struggle for a word for beings as whole."[46] The great philosophers, in Heidegger's way of understanding things, are those who receive an understanding of the being of the age, and struggle to articulate that understanding. Often, in the process, thinkers contribute to changing the background. This, in turn, makes possible a whole new range of foreground activities and events: "the thinker," Heidegger claims, "stands within the decision concerning what *is* in general, what beings are."[47] Another way of putting this point is to say, like Carnap, that the metaphysical thinker is a kind of artist – provided, however, that one does not understand art as Carnap does (i.e., as a means of "expression" for the artist's "emotional and volitional reaction to the environment, to society, to the tasks to which he devotes himself, to the misfortunes that befall him"[48]). Heidegger, following Nietzsche, argues that art, rather than serving as mere subjective expression, actually "creates and gives form" to our experience of the world. The metaphysician is an artist in the sense of "giv[ing] form to beings as a whole."[49] Metaphysical thought, in short, reflects and gives expression to the background understanding of being that determines, in any given age, the way things are. This thought concerning the essence of an age opens up a space of possibilities, or in the case of creative thinkers, anticipates a new space of possibilities.

But it would be a mistake to look for a philosopher's influence in the foreground events. Philosophy has, Heidegger notes, an "historically ascertainable yet irrelevant influence."[50] I take this to mean that the philosopher as a thinker of being does not affect any particular practice or activity in any demonstrable way at all, but instead gives room for a change in all the practices of an age. The classical case of this is, in Heidegger's view, that of Descartes as articulated above. The direct influence of Descartes's writings on any particular scientist, politician, or other historical figure is irrelevant compared to the influence on the modern age that the whole new background sensibility for man's place in the world had. As Heidegger explained with reference to Nietzsche, a thinker's thought "needs neither renown nor impact in order to gain dominance."[51] Instead, the thought the thinker experiences – that is, the changed being of beings in the age – works itself out in the practices of the age as a whole.

Now, how does Heidegger conceive of his place in this history? In particular, how does Heidegger conceive of the difference between himself and metaphysical thinkers?

Heidegger conceives of himself as a preparatory thinker – that is, as being concerned with preparing us for a transformation of the current age of being, rather than himself participating in changing the understanding of being: "the thinking in question remains unassuming, because its task is only of a preparatory, not of a founding character. It is content with awakening a readiness in man for a possibility whose contour remains obscure, whose coming remains uncertain."[52] To do this, he tries to show how, despite the oblivion of being that marks the present age, there is a coherence and unity to our practices given by the technological understanding of being. But this attempt to "name" the background understanding of being does not itself open up a clearing for a new metaphysics, nor does it articulate the understanding of being in order to help establish it. Instead, Heidegger hopes that by showing us the understanding of being which forms the background of modern technological practices, he can encourage us to reflect on the nature of the "open region" itself which harbors any given understanding of being: "What matters to preparatory thinking is to light up that space within which Being itself might again be able to take man, with respect to his essence, into a primal relationship. To be preparatory is the essence of such thinking."[53] Indeed, the most vital task in the technological age, in order to prepare for its overcoming, is the historical task of showing the ungroundedness of its understanding of being. And this will not happen without awakening an awareness of the background itself, and our reliance as human beings on a background understanding of the Being of beings.

HEIDEGGER'S PLACE IN THE HISTORY OF BEING

In response to persistent questioning on the role of philosophy and of his own thought in dealing with the problems of the technological age, Heidegger finally responded: "It is not for me to decide how far I will get with my attempt to think and in what way it will be accepted in the future and transformed in a fruitful way."[54] Of course, there is an obvious sense in which Heidegger is unable to control his reception – he has no say over what use readers will make of his work. But Heidegger meant more than just this with the claim. As we have learned from Heidegger's view of history, the appropriation of historical works in philosophy is always driven by a background sense of the task for thought (as determined by the understanding of being that prevails in our age). Heidegger's comment, then, should be seen as recognition of the fact that he cannot decide how useful his work will prove for the task of thought. For instance, as I have suggested in the discussion of Carnap's response to Heidegger, the perceived uselessness of Heidegger's work is a function of a prior decision about the nature of philosophy, a decision shaped by the ontological background of the age. The same holds true of all the ways in which Heidegger's thought has been accepted and transformed.

Using the categories Heidegger has provided us, we can ask of any use of Heidegger whether it treats his work historically, historiographically, or analytically.[55] Is he taken as providing useful analyses at the conceptual level? *Being and Time*, with its detailed phenomenological and conceptual analyses of various problems in intentionality, is a rich source of such philosophical work.[56] Along these lines, one could articulate Heidegger's response to analytical philosophy rather differently than I have here. Rather than seeing it as an argument over the role of historical reflection in philosophy, one could cast the disagreement in terms of different views about the philosophy of mind and language.[57] But to isolate wholly Heidegger's conceptual analyses from his destruction of western metaphysics would be to deny the importance of what Heidegger took to be central to his work (at least following the "Kehre") – the need to respond to the call of being.

One might also approach Heidegger and his work as a product of the cultural and historiological forces operating in Germany in the first half of this century – a particularly sensational issue in Heidegger's case. Indeed, one can read Heidegger's mythological account of the history of being as itself a historiological event.[58] Likewise, a considerable amount of scholarship is devoted to discovering and articulating Heidegger's dependence on, for instance, Husserl.[59] But, once again, to limit one's reading of Heidegger to historiographical considerations – that is, to situate him wholly within his culture, his age, and his place in the philosophical tradition – would be a denial of one of the central elements of his work. Namely, it would be a tacit rejection of Heidegger's own assessment of his place in the history of philosophy, as well as of his claim to be responding to the call of being.

The most faithful appropriation of Heidegger, then, would be one in which we confront the problems with which Heidegger was most concerned – the nature of our background understanding of being, the meaning of the oblivion of being, and the task of preparing a way to overcome that oblivion. But even with a commitment to the project of historical reflection as Heidegger articulated it, further decisions are in order. Do we accept his description of the background, his account of the history of being? It would, of course, be possible to treat the details of his readings of Anaximander, Parmenides, Heraclitus, Plato, Aristotle, Augustine, Descartes, Kant, Nietzsche, and so on, as dispensable or indeed as fundamentally mistaken. For instance, one might agree that the history of philosophy needs to be understood in terms of the prevailing background understanding which shaped each thinker, but nevertheless reject his unified account of that background.[60]

Another pressing issue that arises from Heidegger's history is the question of what to make of his diagnosis of the ills and dangers confronting the current age, and of the need to prepare for the overcoming of the metaphysical age. Here again, there is a range of responses to Heidegger which, while broadly sympathetic to his analysis of the dangers of technology, nevertheless depart from that analysis in important ways.[61] One might, for instance, find his enigmatic claims about the "saving power" useless in coming to terms with the problem of technology. Thus, even if one accepts the task of Heidegger's preparatory thinking, there remains the question of how best to carry on that task.

Other related issues arise in any thoughtful reception of Heidegger's work. For example, one inescapable but central element of Heidegger's work was his particularity as a thinker. Heidegger explicitly saw himself as preparing for the overcoming of metaphysics on the basis of the resources inherent in the German language and culture. This presents a constant obstacle in working with Heidegger's writings, as one must decide how much weight to give to the often archaic, German-based terminology/jargon that Heidegger employs. Heidegger's particularity gives rise, in turn, to sometimes heated disagreements over the appropriateness of different translations of Heidegger's thought – into, for instance, a vocabulary more accessible to analytical philosophers.

Viewed from the perspective of "the history of being," however, it becomes clear that what, at least for the past few decades, have seemed to be the most divisive dimensions of Heidegger scholarship are, in fact, not so important. Differences between schools of Heidegger interpretation have, to a considerable degree, been defined in terms of literary style and the canon of other philosophical works typically consulted (for example, does one refer to Levinas and Derrida, or Wittgenstein and Searle for illuminating comparisons with Heidegger's work?). While the question of style is, on Heideggerian grounds, something to take seriously,[62] neither it nor the authors one reads are, in and of themselves, determinative of one's fidelity to the Heideggerian project. To the extent that divisions between schools of Heidegger studies are premised on a historiological assessment regarding intellectual dependencies, they are based on the kind of factors that Heidegger's approach to history has taught us to look beyond. For even a similarity of style and shared intellectual dependencies can easily mask a wide diversity of approaches to a problem. More importantly, a diversity of styles and influences can obscure a more fundamental agreement in thoughtful reflection on the matter to be thought. This kind of agreement, if Heidegger himself is to be believed, is what marks the continuation of the Heideggerian project in the fullest sense. Afraid that his work would be taken, in historiological or analytical fashion, as a set of doctrines, Heidegger urged his readers to instead treat his writings "as directions for the road of independent reflection on the matter pointed out which each must travel for himself."[63] Thus, appropriating Heidegger's thought is, from Heidegger's own perspective, a matter of taking his project as one's own.[64]

NOTES

1 Rudolf Carnap, "The Elimination of Metaphysics Through Logical Analysis of Language," in *Logical Positivism*, ed. A. J. Ayer (Glencoe, Illinois: Free Press, 1959), p. 80.

2 See, for instance, Ludwig Wittgenstein, *Tractatus Logico-Philosophicus*, trans. C. K. Ogden (London: Routledge, 1922), paragraph 6.53.
3 "The Elimination of Metaphysics Through Logical Analysis of Language," p. 77.
4 Michael Dummett, *The Logical Basis of Metaphysics* (Cambridge, MA: Harvard University Press, 1991), p. 1.
5 "Überwindung der Metaphysik," in *Vorträge und Aufsätze* (Stuttgart: Gunther Neske, 1954), p. 67.
6 Ibid.
7 Ibid.
8 Ibid., p. 68.
9 Ibid., p. 67.
10 Heidegger frequently makes offhand remarks to the effect that analytical philosophy is thoroughly enmeshed in the technological understanding of being. He notes, for instance, that analytical philosophy (which he typically refers to as "logistics") is "in many places, above all in the Anglo-Saxon countries, . . . today considered the only possible form of strict philosophy, because its result and procedures yield an assured profit for the construction of the technological universe." *What Is Called Thinking?* trans. J. Glenn Gray (New York: Harper & Row, 1968), p. 21.
11 Martin Heidegger, "The End of Philosophy and the Task of Thinking," in *Basic Writings*, rev. edn., ed. David Farrell Krell (San Francisco: Harper, 1993), p. 434.
12 Martin Heidegger, *Nietzsche*, vol. 4, trans. David Farrell Krell (San Francisco: Harper, 1991), p. 22.
13 *Grundfragen der Philosophie: Ausgewählte "Probleme" der "Logik", Gesamtausgabe*, vol. 45 (Frankfurt a.M.: Klostermann, 1984), p. 36.
14 "The End of Philosophy and the Task of Thinking," p. 432 (translation modified).
15 "The Origin of the Work of Art," in *Basic Writings*, p. 201.
16 *Nietzsche*, vol. 4, p. 97.
17 *Nietzsche*, vol. 3, trans. Joan Stambaugh, David Farrell Krell, and Frank Capuzzi (San Francisco: Harper & Row, 1987), pp. 239–40.
18 *Nietzsche*, vol. 4, p. 100.
19 Descartes, *Discourse on Method*, in *The Philosophical Writings of Descartes*, vol. 1, trans. John Cottingham, Robert Stoothoff, and Duguld Murdoch (Cambridge: Cambridge University Press, 1985), p. 120.
20 Ibid., p. 120.
21 Ibid., p. 116.
22 Martin Heidegger, "The Age of the World Picture," in *The Question Concerning Technology and Other Essays*, trans. William Lovitt (New York: Harper & Row, 1977), p. 128.
23 For a perspicuous discussion of Heidegger's understanding of the danger of our oblivion to metaphysics, see Hubert L. Dreyfus, "Heidegger on the Connection Between Nihilism, Art, Technology, and Politics," in *The*

Cambridge Companion to Heidegger, ed. Charles Guignon (Cambridge: Cambridge University Press, 1993), pp. 289–316.

24 *Basic Questions of Philosophy: Selected "Problems" of "Logic"*, trans. Richard Rojcewicz and André Schuwer (Bloomington: Indiana University Press, 1994), p. 38.

25 Alexander P. D. Mourelatos, *The Route of Parmenides* (New Haven: Yale University Press, 1970), p. 197.

26 Ibid., p. xiv.

27 Martin Heidegger, *Introduction to Metaphysics*, trans. Ralph Manheim (Garden City, NY: Anchor Books, 1961), p. 176.

28 Martin Heidegger, *Kant and the Problem of Metaphysics*, trans. Richard Taft (Bloomington: Indiana University Press, 1962), p. xviii.

29 *Basic Questions of Philosophy*, p. 38.

30 For a more detailed response to Rorty, see Mark B. Okrent, "The Truth of Being and the History of Philosophy," in *Heidegger: A Critical Reader*, ed. Hubert L. Dreyfus and Harrison Hall (Oxford: Blackwell, 1992), pp. 143–59.

31 Richard Rorty, "Overcoming the Tradition: Heidegger and Dewey," *Review of Metaphysics* 30 (1976), 297.

32 Robert Bernasconi, "Descartes in the History of Being," *Research in Phenomenology* 17 (1987), 94.

33 Ibid., p. 87.

34 Martin Heidegger, *Parmenides*, trans. André Schuwer and Richard Rojcewicz (Bloomington: Indiana University Press, 1992), p. 64.

35 Ibid., p. 7.

36 *Nietzsche*, vol. 3, p. 8.

37 *Basic Questions of Philosophy*, p. 40.

38 Ibid., p. 46.

39 Ibid., p.184.

40 Martin Heidegger, "The Anaximander Fragment," in *Early Greek Thinking*, trans. David Farrell Krell and Frank A. Capuzzi (San Francisco: Harper & Row, 1975), p. 17.

41 *Parmenides*, p. 96.

42 *Nietzsche*, vol. 3, p. 31.

43 "The Anaximander Fragment," p. 55.

44 Ibid., p. 57.

45 *Nietzsche*, vol. 3, p. 188.

46 Ibid., p. 19.

47 Ibid., p. 6.

48 "The Elimination of Metaphysics Through Logical Analysis of Language," p. 79.

49 *Nietzsche*, vol. 1, p. 73.

50 *Nietzsche*, vol. 3, p. 8.

51 Ibid., p. 4.

52 "The End of Philosophy and the Task of Thinking," p. 436.

53 Martin Heidegger, "The Word of Nietzsche: 'God is Dead'," in *The Question Concerning Technology and Other Essays*, p. 55.

54 " 'Only a God Can Save Us': *Der Spiegel's* Interview with Martin Heidegger," trans. Maria P. Alter and John D. Caputo, *Philosophy Today* 20 (1976), 281.

55 Of course, these are not mutually exclusive approaches to Heidegger. The historical question is given traction by the historiography. The historiography, in turn, should be guided by our sense for history. And using Heidegger's analysis of contemporary problems to counteract mistaken philosophical views, particularly when those views contribute to the "oblivion of Being," may in some ways be as fitting a tribute to him as is possible.

56 See, for example, the essays in the third part of this volume.

57 I suggest such a critique in my "Intentionality without Representation: Heidegger's Account of Perception," *Philosophy Today* 42 (supplement) (1999), 182–9.

58 See John Caputo's essay in this volume.

59 This, of course, occurs in quite different ways. Compare, for instance, Dagfinn Føllesdal, "Absorbed Coping, Husserl and Heidegger," in *Heidegger, Authenticity, and Modernity*, ed. Mark A. Wrathall and Jeff Malpas (Cambridge, MA: MIT Press, 2000), and Simon Critchley's, and Françoise Dastur's essays in this volume.

60 See, for instance, Jacques Derrida, *Spurs: Nietzsche's Styles*, trans. Barbara Harlow (Chicago: University of Chicago Press, 1978).

61 See Albert Borgmann's contribution to this volume.

62 See Rudi Visker's contribution to this volume.

63 Martin Heidegger, "Preface," in William J. Richardson, *Heidegger: Through Phenomenology to Thought* (The Hague: Martinus Nijhoff, 1974), p. viii.

64 I am indebted to James Faulconer and Hubert Dreyfus; they have saved me from a variety of errors through their careful attention to earlier drafts of this paper and their willingness to discuss the matters addressed herein. I have also benefitted from many conversations with James Siebach, in which I have taken advantage of his knowledge of the history of philosophy.

CHAPTER 3

Night and day: Heidegger and Thoreau

Stanley Cavell

In the preface to my little book on *Walden*, published in 1972, I say that "I assume the rhyming of some of the certain concepts I emphasize – for example, those of the stranger . . . of the everyday, of dawning and clearing and resolution – with concepts at play in Nietzsche and in Heidegger."[1] I had then read of Heidegger only *Being and Time*, and I say nothing about what it might mean to "assume" this connection, nor why I invoke a metaphor of "rhyming" to mark it – as if the connections will, or should, by the end become unmistakable but at the beginning are unpredicted. Since then I have periodically gone somewhat further in various connections with each of these writers, but what has brought me to another stop with Heidegger, specifically in conjunction with Thoreau, are two lecture courses of Heidegger's published posthumously in the 1980s and recently translated into English, most obviously the volume entitled *Hölderlin's Hymn "The Ister,"* given in 1942 (imagine), and behind it *The Fundamental Concepts of Metaphysics* (from 1929–1930, the years almost immediately after the appearance of *Being and Time*). The Hölderlin text is an obvious cause for stopping given that "Ister" is the name of a particular river (or of a significant part of the river Danube) and "Walden" is the name of a particular woodland lake. But while we will find each writer talking about fire and earth and sky as well as about water, we will not reach here certain matters in *Walden* that are not among Heidegger's, or Hölderlin's, concerns in their related texts, for example, how *Walden* places smoke after fire, nor how in it the earth inspires a vision of excrement, nor what gives voice to the sky, nor can we here follow the significance of bubbles within the ice, although we cannot, in connection with water, ignore its transformation into ice. All in all, I leave open the time Thoreau takes for a hundred details concerning his pond that a single ode or hymn has no room for, and so leave open any bearing this difference may have on a difference in the willingness to recognize Hölderlin and Thoreau as inspiring or requiring philosophy.

Indeed, in my book I mostly left out, or open, the question of what is called, or calls for, philosophy. But the difficulty of determining what philosophy is, or rather of recognizing who is and who is not philosophizing, is something that both Thoreau and Heidegger insist upon. *Walden's* crack on the subject was once famous enough, in its early pages: "There are nowadays professors of philosophy, but not philosophers" (I, 19).[2] One suggestion is that nowadays philosophers may well not be recognized by that title, hence more than likely not at all. Heidegger rather implies as much when he says, in *The Fundamental Concepts of Metaphysics,* that "[Ordinary understanding] . . . does not reflect upon the fact and cannot even understand that *what philosophy deals with only discloses itself at all within and from out of a transformation of human Dasein.*"[3] It is a good guess that this connection has something to do with the fact that *Walden is* a text about crisis and metamorphosis. ("Our moulting season, like that of the fowls, must be a crisis in our lives. The loon retires to solitary ponds to spend it." This is one of a number of Thoreau's declared identifications with the loon [I, 36]).

What Heidegger refers to as the "preparation" for this transformation (which is the most, according to him, that philosophy can provide) he speaks of as awakening, also a fundamental term for *Walden,* heralded in the sentence from itself that *Walden* takes as its epigraph: "I do not propose to write an ode to dejection, but to brag as lustily as chanticleer in the morning, standing on his roost, if only to wake my neighbors up" (II, 7). Nothing short of *Walden* itself could give what it calls a faithful account of what is strung in such a sentence, of the relations among the concepts of awakening, hence dawning and morning, dejection or melancholy, bragging, roosting, standing, singing, neighboring, writing; and then tell why the audience of this writing must be addressed in such a fashion, meaning why thus allegorically, let's call it, or duplicitously, and why through just these concepts. But what I ask attention to here is that these are all concepts – variously inflected, together with associated others – at work in Heidegger's texts as well.

Since Thoreau's epigraph begins his book's narrative with its declaration, so with a proposed instance, of his powers of awakening, and Heidegger's *Fundamental Concepts of Metaphysics* announces and later re-announces "the task of awakening a fundamental attunement in our philosophizing,"[4] we might take a bearing or two here at the outset. I note additionally that in *Being and Time,* Heidegger's epigraph from Plato, preceding, indeed calling for, his Introduction, or rather his adjoining comment upon this epigraph, had spoken of the task of awakening, or rather reawakening. But there what we must be awakened to is said to be an understanding for the meaning of the question of being, or rather for the question of the meaning of being. *The Fundamental Concepts* formulates awakening as "letting whatever is sleeping become wakeful,"[5] where this "letting" names the relation to being that forms a world, the distinct privilege of the human.

Now a specific linking of awakening precisely with sleeping and with questioning is what Thoreau finds at the moment he actually depicts himself awakening at Walden, in the opening sentences of chapter XVI, "The Pond in Winter":

> After a still night I awoke with the impression that some question had been put to me, which I had been endeavoring in vain to answer in my sleep, as what – how – when – where? But there was dawning Nature, in whom all things live, looking in at my broad windows with serene and-satisfied face, and no question on *her lips*. I awoke to an answered question, to Nature and daylight. . . Nature puts no question and answers none which we mortals ask. She has long ago taken her resolution.

Heidegger's problematic of the question comes under repeated suspicion in Derrida's recent text entitled *Of Spirit,* which asks "Why 'Why?,'"[6] I gather because making the existential analytic of being a function of human questioning (being *is* what is under question in Dasein's being stirred) hands metaphysics over to humanism (which turns out to mean over to a carefully selected band, or species, of human beings of western consciousness). Derrida's text will come back briefly. I note here that in this late chapter of *Walden,* Thoreau is gently enough mocking the questions which his opening page had cited as "very particular inquiries . . . made by my townsmen concerning my mode of life . . . Some have asked what I got to eat; if I did not feel lonesome; if I was not afraid; . . . how many poor children I maintained." Having initially taken these inquiries as his justification for "obtrud[ing] my affairs so much on the notice of my readers," he now declares that his attempt to answer such questions as they stand has been undertaken in a sleeping state; accordingly, as he achieves a state of awakening, he is to awaken from the sense of such questions (from, let us say, their moralism). This is not to deny that he owes his townsmen an earnest effort to make himself intelligible. *Walden* is what he precisely calls his account, the terms in which he finds himself accountable, called upon to settle his accounts. If this is a moral task why does it look so unlike what academic philosophy understands as moral philosophy? Why, for example, does Thoreau insist on emphasizing his book's autobiographicality, declaring in the second paragraph of his book that "we commonly do not remember that it is, after all, always the first person that is speaking." Again, if this is some kind of philosophy of nature, why does it continuously strike one as a work of moral imagination?

When we spoke of "letting whatever is sleeping become wakeful" (or, as Heidegger inflects the matter of "letting" in *What Is Called Thinking?*, namely as letting-lie-before-us, identified as the task of thinking), we did not remark the pointed role of letting in *Walden*. For instance: Thoreau's second chapter, "Where I Lived, and What I Lived for," continues having a good time with the doubtfully countable economic terms he has put in play in his first chapter (doubtfully countable because such terms as "means," "interest," "speculation," "exchange," "class," "terms," do not always announce themselves as economic concepts in the contexts Thoreau sets them in). He is, in the opening paragraph of the chapter, as it were, following, or initiating, Heidegger's well-known requirement that dwelling precede building, namely by determining a possible site for his house.

> Wherever I sat, there I might live, and the landscape radiated from me accordingly . . . There I did live, for an hour, a summer and a winter life . . . An afternoon sufficed to lay out the land into orchard, woodlot, and pasture, and to decide what fine oaks or pines should be left to stand before the door . . . and then I let it lie, fallow perchance, for a man is rich in proportion to the number of things which he can afford to let alone. (II, I)

The parody of Locke's labor theory of value is obvious enough, here as elsewhere in *Walden,* and he is no less in deadly earnest about it than he is about what "letting lie" requires, as when he adds the unobtrusive "perchance" to "I let it lie, fallow perchance." This is to say that letting the land lie might, as it happens, mean leaving it fallow, if, let us say, it actually is fallow; but might it equally mean leaving it seeded, if it actually is seeded? What would count as plowing it is his earlier problem. What kind of problem? I note that plowing (like carving, hammering, warbling, settling, and so forth) are concepts of Thoreau's for writing; and since settling, along with the rest, is preparation for leaving, for departure, so for death, he is writing in view of his death, which is to say, he is writing a testament.

One line and a little of the next in Hölderlin's seventy-three lines on the Ister river says: "For rivers make arable the land" (that is, plowable).[7] Heidegger's word for what Hölderlin is doing is "poetizing." Thoreau's word for what he is doing is "revising mythology." Poetizing means something to Heidegger that he strenuously denies is "concerned with images in a symbolic or metaphysical sense" (*HH* 18). What is at stake for him is this:

In every employment of symbolic images we presuppose that this distinction [namely between a sensuous and a nonsensuous realm] has been made. The decisive drawing of this distinction, its unfolding and its stucturing, which are normative for the Western world, occurred in Plato's thought. What emerges as essential in that thought is that the nonsensuous, the realm of the soul and of the spiritual, is the true actuality, and that the sensuous realm [the "physical"] is "a preliminary and subordinate stage". (*HH* 17)

In *Of Spirit*, Derrida is concerned to show that in the years following *Being and Time* Heidegger gave up once for all on deconstructing this distinction, signaled by his no longer keeping "Spirit" in quotation marks, what the English interestingly call "scare quotes." In the first years I studied philosophy I was taught to free myself from such a distinction by showing its assertion and its denial to be meaningless – or perhaps we can say, in non-positivist terms, to be replaced by the cultural cataclysm represented by the advent and installation of the new science in the sixteenth and seventeenth centuries. Heidegger and Thoreau evidently regard their writing as addressing different times of further cultural cataclysm. These are not the terms in which I propose now, perhaps not ever, to link their writing. A common moment between their worlds of difference is a perception or vision that, for the most part, the others they encounter (not alone philosophers) do not realize what they are saying, that they endlessly mean (unlike their words) essentially nothing. Wittgenstein, according to me, understands them to mean to (that is, to want to mean nothing). (Why would they? And what happens to their words? These are issues concentrated in *The Claim of Reason.*)

Needing myself to continue assessing what it is in philosophy that I can say, or can mean, I shall, I trust, take a practical lead from a thought I expressed some years ago in proposing that Emerson and Thoreau might be said to be their own Hölderlins, deriving concepts from sources beyond philosophy's traditional store of responsibilities. Then the question becomes how or must or can philosophy, as I inherit it, take an interest in them? For Emerson and Thoreau their words have, somewhat like the case of the prophets, been put in their mouths, and they are bound to show themselves variously assaulted, we might say deranged, by their words.

This is hard to demonstrate within a polite span of time, since the best way to show what I mean is to take a concentration of sentences from *Walden* and prove that you must give up hope in reaching the end of their reverberances, as precise as mountainous echoes, I mean even within this text. It is a reason I have spoken of the book as sometimes seeming immeasurably long and boring; I might equally have said, immeasurably slow. We might, for a glimpse, skip to the last but one paragraph of the chapter whose beginning I previously quoted, about sitting as appropriation, where he comes to say: "Be it life or death, we crave only reality. If we are really dying, let us hear the rattle in our throats and feel cold in the extremities; if we are alive, let us go about our business." An obvious and correct reading of this takes it to ask that we not die before our deaths, earlier than necessary as it were; another reading finds it to suggest that we live out our mortality, in which we must die earlier and earlier, to each moment that denies us life unnecessarily. In which case "the rattle in our throats" is, or should be, every word that comes from us, shaken by matters of life and death, craved for his pages by the writer of *Walden*. And in that case to "feel cold in the extremities" is to know the state of your hands and feet. What constitutes such knowledge? The following paragraph, for example, concluding the chapter, observes "My head is hands and feet," one summary of who knows how many of his observations, past and to come, concerning what his extremities are. But let's go further.

The opening sentence of *Walden* contains hands: "When I wrote the following pages . . . I lived alone, . . . in a house which I had built myself . . . and earned my living by the labor of my hands only." An obvious register, or one that soon becomes obvious, is that writing is a privileged mode of something he calls earning his living; a less obvious register is the declaration that he is showing his hand in it throughout, not alone to take pride in his possession, but to exonerate anyone else from it, as if some crime is in the offing. This becomes explicit in the second half of the first chapter, where, giving an openly comic, that is, comically literal version of an account – "account" being one of his characteristic predicates for what he is writing, or giving, or keeping, or settling – he names his earnings for his first ten months of life at Walden, $13.34 (through surveying and carpentry primarily), and then lists the price of everything he ate during that period, down to the quarter of a cent, including three cents worth of salt. (He is – is he not? fulfilling the words of St. Matthew:

"Till heaven and earth pass, one jot or one tittle shall in no wise pass from the law, till all be fulfilled,"[8] which is to reaffirm Matthew's report of the words: "Think not that I am come to destroy the law, or the prophets: I am not come to destroy, but to fulfil."[9] This passage is the one that contains, three or four verses earlier, the image of "A city that is set on an hill,"[10] which the Puritans took as the destiny of their departure from England, and whose present understanding by their descendants [whatever the original sought] Thoreau mocks, by, let us say, showing that fulfilling is a question of destroying.)

His first comment, after a list of fourteen items of food, is: "Yes, I did eat $8.74 all told [that is, all counted; writing, like adding, and unlike adding, is counting]; but I should not thus unblushingly publish my guilt, if I did not know that most of my readers were equally guilty with myself, and that their deeds would look no better in print." I am willing to pass by the somewhat surrealist suggestion of eating eight actual dollars and a fraction, presumably using a country idiom to ask what money is and what eating is, or should be, of. "Unblushingly" to publish his guilt suggests that there is something he is blushingly publishing, namely everything he is printing, writing as such for consumption, which presumably would not need confessing if it were not guilty, indebted beyond any thanks or excuse it is fit offer, taking more than giving, concealing more than showing, conditions that the comedy of economy would make liveable. But why is the taking of food the unblushing moment (suggesting a reprieve from shame) in his accounts? One could say that, unlike writing, eating, the sustaining of human existence, is not a choice, though Thoreau goes far to show how much and how fateful a choice each of them is. This sustenance, this self-preservation (Schopenhauer had called it the will to life), in any and all cases, demands justification, a settling of accounts. It is a question whether we do, or do not, have the means to provide it, a question Thoreau explicitly takes on its comic side, as though we would claim to be certain that our existence, like our speech, is not depriving others of theirs. (Emerson puts the point similarly: "[Ours is an] expensive . . . race living at the expense of race."[11] This does not quite say that we are wolves to man. It says we are cannibals.)

But I let myself be taken aside by hands. In that last paragraph of chapter II, where his head is hands and feet, the writer of *Walden* says he does "not wish to be any more busy with my hands than is necessary." Take that as a suggestion to attend to what he is saying about his feet. In the preceding paragraph, the invitation to settle ourselves is continued by the direction to "work and wedge our feet downward through delusion, and appearance, that alluvion which covers the globe," which includes going "through poetry and philosophy and religion" to get to the reality he finds we crave. And since in the paragraph before that he had said: "God himself culminates in the present moment, and will never be more divine in the lapse of all the ages," and since he has already said that "The present was my next experiment" (II, 7), namely his writing but at the same time his investigation of what the present moment is, he cannot mean by "going through religion" less than what you may call the study of God, though his way of composing a theology is to write a bible, as is the claim of that early book of mine I have cited.

The paragraph about hands and feet begins, speaking of the present: "Time is but the stream I go a-fishing in. I drink at it; but while I drink I see the sandy bottom and detect how shallow it is. Its thin current slides away, but eternity remains." That is, I internalize time, separating and integrating past, present, and future; but I am also beyond these constructions. "I would drink deeper; fish in the sky, whose bottom is pebbly with stars. I cannot count one, I know not the first letter of the alphabet." In this assault of thirst, or say divine desire, the universe is upside down, and he has not one syllable or integer with which to say what he senses. Later, in winter, in the chapter "The Pond in Winter," that is, the time when anyone will feel the cold in his or her extremities, he repeats, differently, this scene of drinking. After, as cited earlier, he has awakened to an answered question, he continues:

> Then to my morning work. First I take an axe and pail and go in search of water, if that be not a dream. . . I cut my way first through a foot of snow, and then a foot of ice, and open a window under my feet, where, kneeling to drink, I look down into the quiet parlor of the fishes . . . with its bright sanded floor the same as in summer. . . Heaven is under our feet as well as over our heads.

At some stage, writing of this kind carries its weight with you or it does not. Even when it does in general, we cannot count on it in particular, that is, count on its making sense, say waking us up as to an answered question, at any moment one of us would speak of it to another. (Depicting himself interrupted in meditating a passage of Confucius, he looks up to ask himself "I know not whether it was the dumps of a budding ecstasy. Mem. There never is but one opportunity of a kind" [XII, 5].)

It is perhaps a good moment, after hearing just now of the possibility that the search of water is perhaps, or is conducted through, a dream, and hearing about some connection between time and a stream, or river, and recalling that *Walden*'s first chapter ends with a sentence that contains the question of a hand, of what it is you have to give and take, and contains a river, the Tigris, this time not standing for the transitory but for the perpetual, continuing to flow "after the race of caliphs is extinct" – a good moment for me to get closer to the other of Heidegger's texts I mentioned as motivating these present remarks, with the title *Hölderlin's Hymn "The Ister."*

Heidegger, early and unblushingly, announces that "The poem poetizes a river" (*HH* 6) and more specifically, in the heading of the next section: "Hymnal poetry as poetizing the essence of the rivers" (*HH* 11). In crossing to this I am encouraged by such passages as these:

> From the first strophe of the Ister hymn, . . . and likewise from the sixth strophe of the Rhine hymn, we also learn that the rivers are a distinctive and significant locale at which human beings, though not only human beings, find their dwelling place. (*HH* 12)

and more particularly:

> The flow of the rivers does not simply run its course "in time," as if the latter were merely an indifferent framework extrinsic to the course of the rivers. The rivers intimate and vanish into time and do so in such a way that they themselves are thus of time and are time itself. (ibid.)

But my encouragement is quite at once sorely tested by the following, closing paragraph of this first section of Heidegger's study, which begins: "Yet we wander around in errancy if we proceed to bring together, in an extrinsic and disjointed manner, suitable 'passages' about rivers and waters from Hölderlin's various poems in order then to construct for ourselves some general idea of what Hölderlin might have 'meant' by 'rivers' and 'waters' " (ibid.). Here is one of those signature, condescending pedagogical asides of Heidegger's that I still cannot always take in stride, with its insinuation of depths to come (a place not "extrinsic and disjointed," and guess who alone knows the measure of what is intrinsic and joined), and a description of where, if I fail it, I will be helplessly left, looking for some general idea of what a great writer might have meant by his focal themes – as if I must enter into this new teaching by savoring an abject tactlessness I have never thought to question in myself. True, Heidegger does say that we wander in errancy, and there is that in his philosophy that requires him not to exempt himself from his insinuations. Do I trust it? Here I am.

Let me recover myself a bit by going on to the following explicitly pedagogical section – Heidegger calls it a "Review" – which speaks of the Greek word for hymn, "humnos," which Heidegger notes "means song in praise of the gods, ode to the glory of heroes and in honor of the victors in contests" and then goes on to say: "The humnos is not the 'means' to some event, it does not provide the 'framework' for the celebration. Rather, the celebrating and festiveness lie in the telling itself" (*HH* 13). This familiar Heideggerean performative turn (away, as it were, from the extrinsic), speaks directly to the duplicitous tone in Thoreau's epigraph, something I did not stop over when I introduced it a while ago: "I do not propose to write an ode to dejection, but to brag . . ." Now leaving open what relation Thoreau is proposing of his work to Romanticism (whether the allusion to Coleridge's ode to dejection is meant as invoking an example to avoid or to reconstitute), why does he caution that he does not propose to write such an ode? Is it because it may turn out, whatever he thinks his purpose is, that he has written some such thing notwithstanding, or several hundred times one ode? Is it, before that, to ask why, or how, one could do such a thing as write a song, as of praise, to the victory of spiritual loss? Is it to raise some further question of the relation of dejection to bragging, for example that what he is manic about – his poverty, his civil disobedience, his isolation, his "revising of mythology" (most specifically, of Christianity) – will strike others as causes for depression? I am reminded here of Heidegger's citing "melancholy" as the mood of philosophizing,[12] for which one can imagine the mood of an ode to promise a certain relief, as it were before philosophy actually catches up with it.

Walden's paragraph about wedging our feet downward implicitly contrasts a river, or rather a stream, with a pond. When the writer asks, "Why should we knock under and go with the stream?," that is, hurry along with the transitory things others institutionalize as necessities (Thoreau cites here the institution of the dinner), which bear little resemblance to the ways and means by which he shows himself sustaining himself, he contrasts this image of a rushing stream with what he calls, in the preceding paragraph, "the perpetual instilling and drenching of the reality that surrounds us," the image of which is quite evidently a pond. While Heidegger cautions, still early, that "The rivers belong to the waters. Whenever we make remarks on such poetry, we must ponder what is said elsewhere concerning the waters" (*HH* 6), he does not, as I recall, make anything of enclosed bodies of water, such as the lakes dear also to Wordsworth.

There is no likelihood of knowing, in our few minutes here, how far the contrast of Hölderlin's river and Thoreau's pond may take us. It may well seem unpromisingly banal, or irremediably obvious. Both offer these bodies as instructions in where and how to live, or dwell, and as bound up with the fate of their nations – Heidegger, in 1942, takes Hölderlin's Ister as marking a hopeful, privileged destiny for Germany, as well as for German; Thoreau, ten decades earlier, fighting despair, takes his Walden as revealing the failures of America to become itself, to find its language in which to rebuke its pretensions in the Mexican War, in the forced migration of its natives, in its curse of slavery. These contradictory perspectives seem to arise at once from the one taking rivers as marking "the path of a people" (*HH* 31), and from the other taking the pond as "the perpetual instilling and drenching of the reality that surrounds us" (II, 21). Instilling and drenching are concepts that articulate the individual's mode of what the writer calls "apprehending," that is, thinking, and thinking specifically of whatever is culminating in the present. It is when the writer is kneeling alone on the ice that he shows himself to drink from Walden, that is, to be drenched by it, to receive what it gives to drink.

But how different are these differences? The difficulty, here as elsewhere, is not that there are so many apparent attractions and repulsions in play, but that it seems both imperative and unfeasible to weigh them.

Take the opening line of the Ister Hymn: "Now come, fire," to which Heidegger devotes much of the first section of his text. He notes: "Were it not for this most everyday event [taking it as sunrise], then there would be no days. Still, to explicitly call out 'Now come' to one thus coming, to the rising sun, is a superfluous and futile act" (*HH* 7). And you know that Heidegger is about to offer his reader exemption from being so superfluous and futile as to concede that. Compare Hölderlin's invocation to the sun and Heidegger's gloss with the moment at which Thoreau, early in his first chapter, in "attempt[ing] to tell how I have desired to spend my life," lists, among other attempts (for example, "trying to hear what was in the wind"), the work of "[Anticipating], not the sunrise and the dawn merely, but, if possible Nature herself!" (I, 22–5). Later in that paragraph he concedes: "It is true, I never assisted the sun materially in his rising, but, doubt not, it was of the last importance only to be present at it." ("To assist" at a social event, for example, a theater performance, is precisely an old-fashioned term for making oneself present, or attending. An importance of his observance, as elsewhere, is his showing that he can make sunrise a communal event even when what is called religion has forgotten how. I observe that "assistance" etymologically contains the idea of standing beside, hence helping. This will find further resonance.) "Assisting the sun" participates in Thoreau's theme of "making a day of it," of refusing to live what he will not call his life, so that, in Thoreau's tone, it would be true to say that "Were it not for this most everyday event [namely, now, of Thoreau's assistance at the sun], then there would be no days" (*HH* 7).

Heidegger says about Hölderlin's line, "Now come, fire," that it is a call, and "The call says: we, the ones thus calling, are ready. And something else is also concealed in such calling out: we are ready and are so only because we are called by the coming fire itself" (ibid.). (I pass by here the recurrent concept of calling as questioning the given names of things in *Walden.*) Thoreau's work of anticipating is a case of being ready, something he thematizes as being early, and earlier, and earliest. Heidegger reads the tint of earliness in the ideas of anticipation and of dawning and morning more elaborately out of the poetry of Georg Trakl, from which (in connection with Heidegger's essay, "Language in the Poem") Derrida takes it up in *Of Spirit*, where he refers to the idea as one of seeking a more matutinal morning, something he emphasizes,[13] but does not, I believe, pursue. How far a fuller occasion should take us is marked in *Walden*'s great concluding lines: "There is more day to dawn. The sun is but a morning star." – his rewriting of Emerson's having said, "there is always another dawn risen on mid- noon."[14] (thus quoting, as Wordsworth had quoted in *The Prelude*, Milton's *Paradise Lost*). But we must move.

I quoted a moment ago Heidegger's saying "the river determines the dwelling place of human beings upon the earth." Substituting "pond" for "river," it might be an epigraph for *Walden.* It is Heidegger's gloss more specifically on Hölderlin's line: "Here, however, we wish to build" (*HH* 4). Comparably early in *Walden*, Thoreau writes, somewhere around the pond, "Here I will begin to mine," namely to prepare the ground for his house. Thoreau's context is the paragraph in which he has declared his head to be hands and feet and adds: "My instinct tells me that my head is an organ for burrowing, . . . and with it I would mine," another identification of his writing with the details of his building and his preparations for building. Hölderlin precedes his naming of his site with the lines, "Not without pinions may/Someone grasp at what is nearest/Directly" (ibid.). The "however" (in "Here, however, we wish to build"), modifying the wish to build, suggests that, however it may be with things with wings, with human beings and their hands and feet, nearness is a matter of dwelling. Now it is when a couple of chapters later Thoreau recurs to the moment of discovering "the place where a wise man will dig his cellar" that he asks, "What sort of space is that which separates a man from his fellows and makes him solitary?" (raising the question of the existence of the other's existence in terms of the Emersonian theme of the distance and the point at which souls touch), and declares: "Nearest to all things is that power which fashions their being. *Next* to us the grandest laws are continually being executed. *Next* to us is not the workman whom we have hired, with whom we love so well to talk, but the workman whose work we are" (v, 6). This is brought on as his response to the sense that "For the most part we allow only outlying and transient circumstances to make our occasions" (shall we say, to provide the events of our appropriation?), make our day, make our living, make our excuses, make our escapes, make our friends and our enemies. In Heidegger's formulation: "one's own is what is most remote" (*HH* vii).[15]

Nextness is a task then, a poise or stance of existence, as of assistance, not assignable or measurable from any given place, for it is the sign that you are at home in the world, such as home might be for the essentially strange creatures Thoreau has visions of at the opening of his book (where he, as it were, hallucinates his townsmen in tortured ecstacies of repentance). He is not there speaking alone of others, but confessing his own strangeness, and first of all to the way others confess or express theirs. Heidegger's book on the Ister hymn takes Hölderlin's text to be locating the work of becoming at home, namely as "the encounter [of] the foreign and one's own as the fundamental truth of history" (*HH* v). The river poetizes the human being because, in providing "the unity of locality and journeying" (ibid.), it conceals and reveals Dasein's being and becoming "homely," homelike, I would say homebound. Thoreau's word for maintaining something like this unity is sojourning, living each day, everywhere and nowhere, as a task.

Heidegger's term for the stance of maintaining the unity of locality and journeying is "to be in the between between gods and humans."[16] This is to be what Heidegger names demigods, and since both poets and rivers are in the between, both are demigods (ibid.). Thoreau's word for being between is being interested. And Heidegger too, elsewhere, takes up this registering of what is "inter-"; but in Thoreau the word takes its part in the immensity of economic terms his text puts in motion, and, in a counter-move within what is commonly called economics, Thoreau's "interest" names a withholding as well as a placing of investment. I went so far in my book about *Walden* as to relate its concept of interest to what, in translations of the Bhagavad-Gita, is called unattachment.

When Heidegger, nearing his conclusion, says "Mourning pervades the Ister," he qualifies it as "a knowing of the necessity of patient whiling 'near the origin.' "[17] If translation is, as Heidegger claims, an exploration of the resources of one's own language, a translation that attempts to make "whiling" some sort of generalization of spending a while or staying for a while or whiling away seems to me to have given up the game. Maybe it means to. (Two of Thoreau's concepts in this neighborhood are worked out in terms of "being seated" and of "sojourning," learning how to spend a day, hence how to stay, but equally how to leave – let alone.)

Does it take a demigod to learn the interval of being between? Let's at least note that the writer of *Walden* as surely identifies himself with the pond as Heidegger's poet does with the river. In chapter IX, called "The Ponds," he records that, having seen Walden almost daily for more than twenty years, he is struck again by its sheer existence, that it is the same woodland lake, still drenching, reviving, its surroundings; and he continues: "I see by its face that it is visited by the same reflection; and I can almost say, Walden, is it you?" (IX, 25). He sees his reflection in the pond. Is it him? He finds that he can almost say, but perhaps he is still unsure of his right to praise, or perhaps he is at the moment stripped of words.

I have to find some place to stop for the moment. Perhaps I have said enough to make us want to know what point there may be in these, and untold further, comparisons between such thinkers. What relation do I propose between Heidegger and Thoreau in calling Thoreau his own Hölderlin? This apparently takes for granted that Thoreau is also his own philosopher, which accordingly would, according to Heidegger, imply both that he poetizes and that he philosophizes what he poetizes. Are there in *Walden* what Heidegger calls philosophical concepts, as examples of which, in *The Fundamental Concepts of Metaphysics,* he takes "death, freedom, and the nothing"?[18] But when Heidegger speaks of how philosophical concepts are to be understood he says this:

> The thoroughgoing character of philosophical concepts . . . [is] that they are all formally indicative concepts. That they are indicative implies the following: the meaning-content of these concepts does not directly intend or express what they refer to, but only gives an indication, a pointer to the fact that anyone who seeks to understand is called upon by this conceptual context to undertake a transformation of themselves into their Dasein.[19]

This joins with Heidegger's various affirmations that philosophy calls one out of the realm of the ordinary, outside everyday understanding; this may, or may not, be another story. Heidegger's attention to how the concepts in question are to be taken does not invoke a systematic listing of philosophical or metaphysical concepts. Do the terms "nearest" or "earliest" or "dwelling" or "building" name peculiarly philosophical concepts? Suppose what makes them philosophical is the controlling feature in Heidegger's account, that understanding them requires a transformation of some kind. Then in principle any concept used in such a way as to require such a transformation might count as philosophical. Then perhaps, if *Walden* is, as it seems everywhere to insist, an account of transformed understanding, then any and every word in it is perhaps philosophical. The transformation would be of our relation to our language and therewith – or because of – a transformation in our relation to the world. When Wittgenstein says in *Philosophical Investigations,* "What we do is return words from their metaphysical to their everyday use,"[20] he is speaking of such a transformation in our relation to words, one that requires us, in his image, to turn ourselves around, in a transformed sense. But in his case, as in J. L. Austin's, it follows that there are no peculiarly philosophical concepts, none requiring, or entitled to, super-ordinary understanding; which in a sense means that there are no ordinary concepts either, none exempt from philosophical strain.

A person portrayed by Wittgenstein as striking himself on the chest and saying "Another person cannot have *this* pain"[21] has been called from the everyday by philosophy, and after further philosophy has, to its satisfaction, rid him of his illusion, which is to say, returned the demonstrative pronoun to its circulation, the one for whom it had become frozen has vanished from philosophy's notice. When Emerson defines thinking as transfiguring and converting our words, traditional philosophical words notably rub elbows with civilian words, words familiar in philosophy such as "experience," "impression," "form," "idea," "necessity," "accident," "existence," "constraint"; here the idea is not so much to deny that there are philosophical concepts as to assert, if somewhat in irony, that Americans can handle them, their way. Wittgenstein says that in philosophy concepts sublime themselves. Derrida says they haunt themselves. Whom do you believe?

If there can be religion without religion, can there be philosophy without philosophy? Do not both Wittgenstein and Heidegger in a sense desire it? Is this a reasonable proposal for what Thoreau enacts?

Go back hurriedly to a couple of earlier spots. I aligned Hölderlin's "Here we wish to build" with Thoreau's "Here I will begin to mine." Apart from further comparisons of context, I ask myself whether I should speculate about that verb "mine" as Thoreau has placed it, recalling (and perhaps resisting recalling) Heidegger's familiar instruction, as in *Being and Time* that "In each case Dasein is mine to be in one way or another."[22] Shall we put it past Thoreau to be proposing the verb "to mine" to name the act of making things mine, say appropriating them, given that his entire book is about what he is determined to own and what to disown, and given how much play he and Emerson make with terms of getting and having and so forth. – But would one see this without Heidegger's example? – Why not, if Thoreau saw it?

And how about the crossing of Heidegger with Thoreau on the matter of letting things lie as a condition of knowing them? I have elsewhere linked with them Wittgenstein's claim, or challenge, that "Philosophy leaves everything as it is,"[23] a claim blatantly, to most ears, conservative. But if Wittgenstein is naming a philosophical task here, then in the light of the other claims for leaving or letting, Wittgenstein may be seen as detecting and resisting philosophy's chronic tendency to violence, principally toward ordinary language, against letting it speak, having decided time out of mind that it is vague and misleading, to say the least. Wittgenstein should here be somewhat grateful for Heidegger's company. But elsewhere not. In *The Fundamental Concepts of Metaphysics,* Heidegger goes at length, in the effort to characterize the human and what he calls world, into the differences between man as world-building, animals as poor in world, and stones as worldless. Early along this path he observes: "There is . . . [an] important and quite fundamental question here: *Can we transpose [versetzen] ourselves into an animal at all?* For we are hardly able to transpose ourselves into another being of our own kind, into another human being. And what then of the stone – can we transpose ourselves into a stone?"[24] Heidegger calls this fundamental question a methodological one. How is it fundamental? How can we locate it? Compare this with Wittgenstein's *Investigations*:

> What gives us so much *as the idea* that living beings, things, can feel? Is it that my education has led me to it by drawing my attention to feelings in myself, and now I transfer the idea to objects outside myself? . . . I do not transfer [*ubertrage*] my idea to stones, plants, etc. . . . And now look at a wriggling fly and at once these difficulties vanish and pain seems able to get a foothold here, where before everything was, so to speak, too smooth for it.[25]

In Wittgenstein the idea of getting over to the other is shown as motivated by a non-neutral prior step in which we take our own case as primary. What makes that step, seemingly so obvious, in turn fundamental? An importance of making this issue explicit is that taking one's own case as the given from which to transfer concepts to others is a moment in the progress of skepticism with respect to other minds. The idea of transfer here, or of transposition in Heidegger's discussion, should accordingly come under philosophical suspicion. Heidegger's pleasantry about our being "hardly able to transpose ourselves into another being of our own kind, another human being," is part of what is suspicious. It seems to me an indication, as of a somewhat guilty intellectual conscience, of avoiding the issue of skepticism, something phenomenology, as in Husserl, is perhaps made to do.

And what shall we say of Thoreau, as when, for example, he depicts himself for more than an hour, in what he calls a pretty game with a loon on the pond, trying to predict this fowl's sailings out and to anticipate his divings, a pastime the writer describes by saying, among many things, "While he was thinking one thing in his brain, I was endeavoring to divine his thought in mine" (XII, 17). Here one is taking the problem of the other in rather the reverse direction from the way philosophers tend to conceive the matter, letting it provoke him to learn something about himself from the encounter: it is not the other that poses the first barrier to my knowledge of him or her, but myself. The direction is confirmed early in Thoreau's recounting of his "business" prospects at Walden (anticipating Nature, assisting the sun, waiting for the sky to fall), when, finding that his fellow-citizens were not likely to offer him a living, "I turned my face more exclusively than ever to the woods, where I was better known" (I, 32). Do I trust these sallies of speculation in Thoreau? I treasure them.

But what are these native notes, or local gems (however many of them we might go on to unearth) worth – let's say on the international market? What good is this testament, or legacy, or what bad is it, compared with the legacies, Heidegger's principally among them, that, in the text I mentioned earlier, Derrida gestures at inheriting and disinheriting at the close of *Of Spirit*? Well, for one thing, since Heidegger's political record should not on the whole inspire the democratically inclined, or let's say, the immigrant, with perfect confidence, a thinker such as Thoreau who matches, I would say uncannily, so many of the philosophical configurations of Heidegger, while reversing his political sensibilities – shall we call them? – is a notable curiosity.

And besides, Thoreau speaks English, if heavily accented. I mean, as he puts it, he dearly loves to talk it, to one or to all. It is almost justification enough for the love of English merely to have the sounds of morning in it, I mean the double sound in morning of dawning and of grieving, which colors every thought in the book of Walden. So I like it, thinking of Heidegger's rivers that carve the historical path of a people, for Thoreau to say, "Every path but your own is the path of fate" (IV, 10), having said, "I would fain be a track-repairer somewhere in the orbit of the earth" (IV, 6), meaning of course that he would repair how his townsmen think about paths and destiny, not that he wishes to repair the track they are on. And I like it that in his "Conclusion" he remembers that "I had not lived there [at Walden] a week before my feet wore a path from my door to the pond-side; and though it is five or six years since I trod it, it is still quite distinct. It is true, I fear that others may have fallen into it, and so helped to keep it open." No doubt this humbleness is part of his bragging, and his double English is in its way as easy to misunderstand as Heidegger's German. To have shown that convincingly, as a cause for philosophy, would be achievement enough for any efforts of mine with him.

One further uncanny encounter before a closing thought. Heidegger's text on the Ister ode enacts an all but obsessive play with the idea of the essence of Dasein as "homely" (*Heimischsein*), and hence with the human as *Unheimlich*, uncanny, in the way it is always and never, let's say, homebound. This serves to invite the incorporation of a reading of the *Antigone,* focusing on the Ode to Man, whose opening lines are familiarly known in English as something like "Many the wonders but nothing walks stranger than man."[26] Heidegger translates the lines by inserting *Unheimlich* at the place others have "wonders" or "strange." He relates to this beginning the closing words of the ode, which "pronounce a rejection and expulsion of this most uncanny being that the human being is . . . thereby indeed confirm[ing] the opening words, which state that nothing is more uncanny than the human being" (*HH* 92): "Such shall not be entrusted to my hearth) nor share their delusion with my knowing, / who put such a thing to work." That the human is such that its rejection is an expulsion from the hearth prompts a series of questions from Heidegger about who is rejected and who is rejecting, culminating in the question "And what is the hearth?" (*HH* 93).

One answer is: "The hearth is the site of being-homely [*Heimischseins*]. . . . What is essential to the hearth, however, is the fire in the manifoldness of its essence, which essentially prevails as lighting, illuminating, warming, nourishing, purifying, refining, glowing" (*HH*

105). An eventual answer is: "Being is the hearth" (*HH* 112) – that from which and to which the homewardness of Dasein is bound. In the next-to-last section of *of Spirit*, Derrida summarizes Heidegger's "*negative* approaches to the essence of spirit. In its most proper essence, as the poet and thinker allow it to be approached, *Geist* (spirit) *is neither* Christian *Geistlichkeit* (spirituality) *nor* Platonic-metaphysical *Geistigkeit* (intellectuality). What is it, then? . . . In order to reply to this question in an affirmative mode, still listening to Trakl, Heidegger invokes the flame"[27] (one of the guiding themes of Derrida's book). Then in the final section Derrida finds that "It is with reference to an extremely conventional and doxical outline of Christianity that Heidegger can claim to de-Christianize Trakl's *Gedicht*."[28] Without comment, I juxtapose a sentence from chapter XIII of *Walden*, called "House-Warming," in which the writer builds his hearth: "I was surprised to see how thirsty the bricks were which drank up all the moisture in my plaster before I had smoothed it, and how many pailfuls of water it takes to christen a new hearth" (XIII, 10). Since baptizing bricks is not likely to be included in a doxical outline of Christianity, the question whether Thoreau is de-Christianizing the spirituality, or transcendentality, of his fireplace will turn on whether his ecstatic playfulness here is granted, as elsewhere, its due seriousness.

I should perhaps add that I do not recall finding the mood of uncanniness present in *Walden*. Its perpetual doubleness (to say the least) suggests a different shade of wonder or strangeness, engaging the perpetual task of converting mourning into morning, grieving into dawning, dejection into the discovery of praise, turnings in which neither position denies the causes of its other. Is this a secret of America, I mean one it keeps also from itself?

NOTES

1 Stanley Cavell, *The Senses of Walden* (San Francisco: North Point Press, 1972), p. xiv.
2 To make my references to *Walden* independent of any particular edition, I shall give citations parenthetically by chapter and paragraph, roman numerals for the former, arabic for the latter, unless otherwise mentioned in the text.
3 Martin Heidegger, *The Fundamental Concepts of Metaphysics*, trans. William McNeill and Nicholas Walker (Bloomington: Indiana University Press, 1995), p. 292.
4 Ibid., pp. 59, 352.

5 Ibid., p. 60.
6 Jacques Derrida, *Of Spirit* (Chicago: University of Chicago Press, 1989), p. 9.
7 Martin Heidegger, *Hölderlin's Hymn "The Ister,"* trans. William McNeill and Julia Davis (Bloomington: Indiana University Press, 1996), p. 4. Hereafter parenthetically referenced as *HH.*
8 Matt 5:18 King James Bible.
9 Matt 5:17 King James Bible.
10 Matt 5:14 King James Bible.
11 *Ralph Waldo Emerson*, ed. Richard Poirier (Oxford: Oxford University Press, 1990), p. 347.
12 *The Fundamental Concepts of Metaphysics*, p. 183.
13 *Of Spirit*, pp. 92, 94, 107, 110, 113.
14 *Ralph Waldo Emerson*, p. 166.
15 Thoreau and Emerson endlessly rehearse the idea of America as, initially, foreign and as endlessly unable to make itself sufficiently foreign from the lands of its departure. So in them the dialectic of nearness and distance equally plays itself out in terms of the old and the new.
16 *The Fundamental Concepts of Metaphysics*, p. 166.
17 Ibid., p. 163.
18 Ibid., p. 300.
19 Ibid., p. 297.
20 Ludwig Wittgenstein, *Philosophical Investigations*, trans. G. E. M. Anscombe (Oxford: Blackwell, 1958), paragraph 116.
21 Ibid., paragraph 253.
22 Martin Heidegger, *Being and Time*, trans. John Macquarrie and Edward Robinson (New York: Harper and Row, 1962), p. 68.
23 *Philosophical Investigations*, paragraph 124.
24 *The Fundamental Concepts of Metaphysics*, p. 209.
25 *Philosophical Investigations*, paragraphs 283–4.
26 *Antigone*, ed. David Grene and Richard Lattimore, trans. Elizabeth Wyckoff (New York: Washington Square Press, Inc., 1968), line 332.
27 *Of Spirit*, p. 96.
28 Ibid., p. 108.

CHAPTER 4

Heidegger's alleged challenge to the Nazi concepts of race

Robert Bernasconi

To present Heidegger's views on race in a forum dedicated to a dialogue between the different ways of appropriating Heidegger might look at first sight like an attempt to short circuit the task at hand. To many people, Heidegger's appropriation of National Socialism is a reason for not appropriating him at all. Those people would most likely say the same about Heidegger's account of race. However, without defending Heidegger, I want to argue that his treatment of race provides an additional and important reason for studying his writings from the 1930s. In keeping with the theme of "Appropriating Heidegger," I do not intend to use this occasion to elaborate all the facets of Heidegger's account of race, so much as indicate the kinds of inquiries that would need to be made if the discussion is to pass beyond the question of whether one is "for" or "against" Heidegger. The main task here is to see what can be learned from Heidegger's encounter with the race-science of his day. A subsidiary task will be to take advantage of the recent publication of hitherto unavailable sources for the study of Heidegger's account of race. I will argue that they call for a serious revision of previous discussions of the topic.

The basis of Heidegger's defense after the war, readily adopted by his advocates and even by many of his critics, is that he attacked racial biology and proposed in its place a spiritual conception of the German *Volk*. Already in his letter to the Rector of Freiburg University of 4 November 1945, Heidegger juxtaposed his own "fundamental spiritual position" with "the spiritual, or rather unspiritual, basis of the National Socialist movement."[1] In the same letter he wrote: "In the first semester after the resignation of the office [as Rector of the University of Freiburg], I lectured on logic and dealt with the essence of language under the title *The Doctrine of Logos*. It was necessary to show that language is not an object of expression of the biologically and racially conceived human being, but conversely that the essence of man is grounded in language as the fundamental actuality of spirit" (AAR 540–1).[2] However, we should beware taking these comments at face value, particularly if our interest is not limited to the more extreme forms of National Socialism but extends to racism more generally. In his lectures on language, Heidegger repeated the longstanding idea that the Negro has no history.[3] This familiar trope of European racism was made worse when, the following semester, Heidegger drew the consequence that "Only a historical people is truly a people" (*GA* 39: 284). Similarly in the Nietzsche lectures which he himself subsequently characterized as "a confrontation with National Socialism,"[4] presumably for their attack on biologism, Heidegger wrote that "historical Western man can also be overwhelmed by a lack of reflectiveness, a disturbance of lucidity" as "a destiny that is thoroughly spared an African tribe" (*N* III 69).[5] Western humanity alone is shaped by reflection (*Besinnung*) and so can have that reflection disturbed. It is irrelevant to the essential issue whether or not one could use Heidegger's unpublished manuscripts to introduce a technical sense of *Besinnung* that might make the remark less offensive. Heidegger's students would not have been familiar with that sense. Furthermore, the fact that these remarks are found in texts that, after the fact, Heidegger presented as combatting racism suggests either that Heidegger had a faulty memory or that he was not particularly sensitive to racial issues. Nevertheless, to appreciate the character of Heidegger's remarks on race, it is important to understand how outrageous were the things being said by his contemporaries, including some of those who opposed the Nazi regime.

Heidegger claimed that, even at the time, his Rectoral Address was criticized for not being constructed on the basis of racial thought.[6] Whether Otto Wacker, Staatsminister for Education in Baden, who was alleged to have made this objection, had heard every word of the Address is not clear because there is a passage in which race is clearly evoked, even though the term race is not used.[7] Heidegger wrote:

> the *spiritual world* of a people is not the superstructure of a culture any more than it is an armory [*Zeughaus*] filled with useful information and values; it is the power that most deeply preserves the people's earth- and blood-bound strengths as the power that most profoundly shakes the people's existence. Only a spiritual world guarantees the people's greatness. (*SU* 14; *HC* 9)

When in 1934 Heidegger sought to explicate the concept of race, he explained it in terms of "the bodily, blood-bound connection of the members of the *Volk*" (*GA* 38: 65). This confirms that the phrase "the people's earth- and blood-bound strengths" from the Rectoral Address is a reference to race.[8] However, when in his letter to the Rector of Freiburg University of November 1945 Heidegger launched his self-defense, he quoted these sentences from the Rectoral Address for their emphasis on *Geist* but omitted the compromising phrase. According to his own account, this passage from the Rectoral Address was not only an expression of his concern for the crisis of the western spirit, but also an attack on Alfred Rosenberg:

> For every knowledgeable and thoughtful person, these sentences decisively express the opposite of the Rosenbergian doctrine and worldview, according to which, conversely, spirit and the spiritual world remain only an "expression" and exudation of the racial predisposition and physical condition of the person. (AAR 536–7)

Heidegger did not actually say that he had proposed an exclusively spiritual idea of the *Volk*. He merely insisted that he opposed "the dogmatic hardening and primitivity of the biologism promulgated by Rosenberg" (AAR 538–9). Heidegger's efforts at this time were not directed to excluding "the racial element," but rather to attacking the idea that race was primary. This is what Heidegger objected to in Rosenberg, for example, and this is why Heidegger insisted that it is "the spiritual world of a people" – and not, for example, its racial purity – "that most deeply preserves the people's earth- and blood-bound strengths." If one misses the reference to race in the Rectoral Address, as many commentators do, its argument about race is effaced.

Some of the same commentators have built a defense of Heidegger on the basis that there is no racism and no nazism without biologism and that Heidegger was opposed to biologism.[9] If the claim is that one could not be a National Socialist without being committed to biologism then this is an empirical argument that is false. Although there were National Socialists, like Hans Weinert, who insisted that biology was the core of the National Socialist worldview,[10] many prominent supporters of National Socialism were not committed to its racial doctrines.[11] Nor did National Socialism operate with a single conception of race. My interest here is not the broad question of Heidegger's relation to National Socialism, but specifically the question of where Heidegger stood with reference to race, given his attack on biologism. Julian Young maintains that, because race is exclusively a biological notion, "spiritual racism" is a self-contradiction, with the consequence that Heidegger cannot be said to be guilty of it.[12] He even goes so far as to insist that there is no necessary link between cultural antisemitism and the gas chambers.[13] The argument is as unimpeccable in its logical form as it is offensive in its deliberate neglect of how historically a cultural antisemitism has sustained and continues to sustain a racialized antisemitism. Another of Heidegger's apologists, Pascal David, dissociates Heidegger's conception of *Volk* from that of race by identifying it as spiritual, but the question of the relation between spirit and race, which is the issue, is left unclear. "A people is not a 'racial group,' but a spiritual community. And this spiritual community has its apex in the life of the mind, not in the 'struggle for life.'"[14] Elsewhere, David writes of Heidegger: "this thinker's understanding of 'people' opens the possibility for grasping 'people' as a non-racial and non-biological entity."[15] However, although there had been a widespread tendency early in the twentieth century to dissociate the idea of race from that of culture, thereby rendering race an exclusively biological concept, this movement had had relatively little impact in Germany or Europe generally. This tendency was most prominent among intellectuals in the United States, where Franz Boas had been one of its most powerful advocates. North Americans were also more inclined than Europeans to see race in terms of four or five basic groups, whereas in Europe the tendency was to posit a multiplicity of races thereby bringing the notion of race closer to that of a people. Of course, these were only tendencies, but in Germany in the 1920s and 1930s the concepts *Rasse* and *Geist* were as readily thought of as complimentary as in opposition. One will not get very far reading the race literature of the time working on the assumption that they are as separate as mind and body within Cartesianism, and yet attempts to reconstruct Heidegger's position often seem to take it as axiomatic that they are. It is even more extraordinary to find that assumption at work in attempts to read Heidegger's discussions of race, given his consistent opposition to Cartesianism.

The publication of Heidegger's 1934 lectures "Logic as the Question of the Essence of Language" has made it possible to judge his claim that in them he opposed biological and racial conceptions of the human being in favor of a conception founded on spirit.[16] It is clear that Heidegger rejected as inadequate any attempt to reduce the idea of the *Volk* to a biological notion, a gesture he associated with the *völkische Bewegung* with its goal of returning the *Volk* to the purity of its lineage (*GA* 38: 61 and 65).[17] It is clear too that he located his discussion of race in the context of a discussion of bodily features rather than in terms of soul and spirit, which were the two other categories to which he referred *Volk* (*GA*

38: 65–70). But Heidegger did not reject the notion of *Volk* as body in favor of *Volk* as spirit. Nor did Heidegger disassociate the concept of *Volk* from that of race. He argued that both terms share the same level of ambiguity because they belong together (*GA* 38: 65).

Although Heidegger, in the lecture course, opposed an exclusively racial conception of *Volk*, it is nevertheless not an easy task to summarize the positive conception that he sought to leave in its place. Indeed, his references to the *Volk* in subsequent writings, such as the *Beiträge*, tend to focus on how the term is locked in ambiguity, evoking a variety of senses including the communal, the racial, the base and inferior, the national, and the permanent (*GA* 65: 117). At the end of the 1930s Heidegger was less concerned to redefine the *Volk* in terms of *Da-sein*, although such efforts continued (e.g. *GA* 65: 319), than to emphasize that the ambiguity of the term is evidence in favor of the diagnosis that we are suffering from the abandonment of being (*GA* 65: 117).[18] According to Heidegger, the concept of *Volk*, like the concepts of "community," "nation," "continent," and "planet," does not cancel metaphysical subjectivity, but rather only becomes historically relevant on its basis (*GA* 54: 204 and 247). Unless new evidence becomes available to the contrary, the 1934 lecture course is the place where Heidegger did most to develop his own conception of *Volk*. Toward the end of the course, Heidegger explicitly rejected the bodily, and thus usually racial, conceptions of the *Volk* in favor of one developed, following *Being and Time*, in terms of temporality and historicality (*GA* 38: 157).[19] But he did not embrace a spiritual conception of *Volk*.

Heidegger's strategy in the lecture course seems to have been to critique the widespread popular notions of *Volk* in terms of body, soul, and spirit in their partiality, but without rejecting them totally. Rather he proceeded with the task of reconceptualizing them by trying to think them in their unity (*GA* 38: 67–8), just as the idea of the human being as the composite of body, soul, and spirit must be radically rethought (*GA* 20: 207). After a radical rewriting of the existential analytic of *Being and Time*, Heidegger identified the historical being of the *Volk* with the state (*GA* 38: 165).[20] The text of the 1934 lecture course thus supports Heidegger's subsequent claim that he opposed biological racism, but not that he proposed in its place an account of language framed in terms of *Geist*.[21] Indeed, the decisive characterization of language is with reference to the temporalizing of the historical Dasein of the *Volk* (*GA* 38: 169). Although Heidegger employed the phrase *die Geistigkeit unseres Dasein* (*GA* 38: 153), it was not to exclude the body, but in the context of recouping the body on terms made possible by *Being and Time*. He proclaimed: "Blood and bloodline [*Geblüt*] can be an essential determination of human beings, only if blood and bloodline are determined by moods and never simply on their own. The voice of blood comes from the fundamental mood of human beings" (*GA* 38: 153). The language of *Geist* that had been prominent in the Rectoral Address was submitted to reconceptualization, as were the other terms widely used to characterize the *Volk*, specifically *Leib* and *Seele*. Indeed, Heidegger is quite specific in his diagnosis that the problem that needed to be addressed derived from Descartes's attempt to liberate "the subject" from Church dogma, the body, and the community (*GA* 38: 143). It is in terms of modernity's reconceptualization of nature in terms of the mechanical that the body is reduced to a machine over which *Geist* governs. Heidegger identified this conceptual scheme as providing the basis of liberalism. He sought to overcome it by avoiding individualism and seeking a new experience of the being of human beings (*GA* 38: 149).

If in the following year, in *Introduction to Metaphysics*, Heidegger presented *Geist* as sustaining and governing, the first and the last, this must be seen in the context of an attack on, among other things, the proposal that the race of a people be taken for its authentic reality. Although it is somewhat shocking to see the extent to which Heidegger in these pages embraced the language of *Geist*, it was in large measure in an effort to offer a favorable interpretation of German Idealism in contrast with the situation in Europe at that time (*GA* 40: 49). In any case, Heidegger is clear that the reconceptualization of *Geist* cannot be accomplished by opposing it to its rivals, because this is the source of the problem. Hence in opposing the subordination of *Geist* to *Leib*, he takes care to say that the force and beauty of the body is grounded in the spirit (*GA* 40: 50–1). In fact, three years later in *Besinnung*, Heidegger argued that attempts to think the permanent in "Man," in terms of body-soul or spirit, are equivalent because they reduce the justification of "Man" to the present-at-hand, be it matter, life, or spirit (*GA* 66: 234). But prior to the publication of this text, even Heidegger's critics have tended to attribute to him a spiritual conception of race.[22] They had lost sight of the fact that the notion of *Geist* does not ultimately warrant a place in Heidegger's account of Dasein.

The publication of Heidegger's 1934 lectures with its correction of Heidegger's self-defense has implications for Derrida's understanding of Heidegger's use of the language of *Geist* as a tool to combat biological racism. Derrida's thesis with respect to this issue was that "one cannot demarcate oneself from biologism, from naturalism, from racism in its genetic form, one cannot be *opposed* to them except by reinscribing spirit in an oppositional determination."[23] The language of *spirit* is, like humanist teleology, part of "the price to be paid in the ethico-political denunciation of biologism, racism, naturalism, etc." (*E* 87; *S* 56).[24] Heidegger is therefore caught in a bind: he can no longer avoid the term "spirit" as he had announced he would in *Being and Time* (*SZ* 46). However, if one takes a broader perspective than Derrida appears to do, the options are even more constrained. It is not only recourse to the word *Geist* that is overdetermined, but also its renunciation. At that time the renunciation of the word "spirit" was already clearly associated with Ludwig Klages, the scholar against whom Heidegger directed his attack on biologism.[25] This highlights the problem with Derrida's interpretation, which like that of David, projects an opposition between race and spirit that is not reflected in Heidegger's texts of this period, just as it is not always reflected in contemporary usage. Although some of the most offensive discussions of race in Germany at that time were conducted with reference to *Seele*, as Heidegger himself noted when attacking Rosenberg,[26] race often played a role within the discourse of *Geist*.[27] Indeed, Heidegger seems to have remained suspicious of the notion of spirit. In a letter to Elisabeth Blochmann from 30 March 1933 Heidegger denied that he was putting any value in past spirituality (*Geistigkeit*) and cultivation (*Gebildetheit*), terms which he associated with Ernst Krieck.[28]

Derrida's *Of Spirit*, however, has left a further legacy for discussions of Heidegger's thoughts on race through his question, "Is a metaphysics of race more or less serious than a naturalism or a biologism of race?" (*E* 119; *S* 74). Derrida leaves the question suspended, but Berel Lang, apparently ignoring the difference between racial thought and racism, does not hesitate to provide his own answer that what he calls metaphysical racism is "in one sense . . . potentially even more dangerous" than biological racism on the grounds that "it comes unburdened by the pseudoscientific biological ground that makes the first so vulnerable to criticism."[29] This perhaps dismisses too quickly how ineffective criticism of Nazi pseudoscience was and how powerful that pseudoscience was in fashioning the "final solution." Furthermore, it is the biological conception of race that provides the basis for the arguments on race purity. However, Lang's book serves as a valuable corrective to those commentators who confine racism to biological racism: "Heidegger's thinking and writing nonetheless advocates an alternative version of racism that is no less pointed and severe in its implications" (*HS* 39).

Lang does not fully explain why he calls this "metaphysical racism," although he describes it as "not only beyond personal prejudice but beyond psychological or social categories more generally" (*HS* 68).[30] It could be that Lang was familiar with Moeller van den Bruck's reference to race as "almost a metaphysical concept," and yet one that is built "on a physiological basis."[31] But the internal evidence is that Lang borrows the term from Heidegger's own sentence in "Nietzsche's Metaphysics," even though it refers to a metaphysical thought of race and not a metaphysical racism: "Just as Nietzsche's thought of will to power was ontological rather than biological, even more was his racial thought metaphysical rather than biological" (*N* III 231). Whether or not Lang converts Heidegger's thesis that Nietzsche's racial thought was metaphysical into the idea of a metaphysical racism, the usage is widespread. Rockmore, for example, refers to the *Rektoratsrede* as having "a non-biological but metaphysical theory of racism."[32] Thus the idea of a Heidegger "stubbornly committed to the metaphysical racism he shared with Nazism" was adopted even by some of Heidegger's severest critics.[33] To understand what Heidegger meant when he attributed a metaphysical thought of race to Nietzsche will help determine whether one wants to attribute a similar thought to Heidegger. Heidegger's lectures on Nietzsche are the main site of his public confrontation with the extreme forms of Nazi racial thought in the late 1930s. It is to these that I will now turn in order to introduce the radically new approach that Heidegger took to the question of race at that time.

The extent to which Heidegger challenged biologism in *The Will to Power as Knowledge*, his lectures on Nietzsche from 1937–8, is controversial. One commentator declares Heidegger's alleged confrontation with National Socialism in his Nietzsche lectures to be "literally invisible."[34] Another commentator argues that Heidegger's Nietzsche lectures "represent a frontal attack on the traditional metaphysics of racism and biologism."[35] To address the question of Heidegger's challenge to National Socialism in the Nietzsche lectures, it is important to recall the context in which Heidegger gave the lectures. In Germany in the 1930s the emphasis on what we today would call Nietzsche's racism was a way of establishing his relevance to the National Socialist revolution. Irrespective of whether, as I believe, current Nietzsche scholarship should be more critical of Nietzsche's racial doctrines, it is undeniable that the biological reading of Nietzsche had been the dominant reading and was put to a political use.[36] There were relatively few dissenting voices among those who were sympathetic to Nietzsche. The German exile, Alfred Rosenthal, opposed the antisemitic character of most Nazi readings of Nietzsche, but still offered a highly charged reading where race remained a criterion on the global level.[37] It was primarily Nietzsche's opponents who argued against the use of Nietzsche by National Socialism.[38] What is one to make of the fact that Heidegger worked so hard to free Nietzsche from a biologistic reading at a time when euthanasia and sterilization programs were already in progress? Although some Nazis sought vindication for their racial programs from Nietzsche, Nietzsche's thought did not serve as the epistemological basis for those policies. One could be a Nazi without believing in Nietzsche. To that extent, Heidegger's attack leaves those policies untouched. Why was Heidegger so concerned to save Nietzsche from the Nazis when he appears to have been so unconcerned about their real victims?

Heidegger's reading of Nietzsche challenged the widespread attempt among his contemporaries to assimilate Nietzsche to Darwinism or, rather, Social Darwinism. This lends Heidegger's attack on Nietzsche's biologism a broader purpose beyond Nietzsche scholarship (*GA* 47: 75–6). Because the readings of Nietzsche that emphasized his Darwinism were often written in such a way that they contributed to a climate in which "racial hygiene" was practiced, attempts to contest those readings were a way of expressing opposition to the policies. Nevertheless, although Heidegger was certainly justified in opposing the distorted reading of his contemporaries in this regard, Nietzsche scholars today tend to concede that on the balance of the evidence Darwinism's influence was strongly felt by Nietzsche.[39] Heidegger argued that Nietzsche's tendency to view human beings in terms of the body and animality was distanced from all Darwinist explanations of the descent of man (*N* III 80. See also *N* III 92). Heidegger claimed: "Nietzsche does not see the essence of life in 'self-preservation' ('struggle for existence') as do the biology and the doctrine of life of his time influenced by Darwin, but rather in a self-transcending enhancement" (*N* III 15). What contributes merely to the preservation of life is thereby downgraded. The focus is shifted to life-enhancement, and thus to determining the essence of life anew (*N* III 17). Nevertheless, Heidegger somewhat undercut the force of his argument when he denied that the characterization of Nietzsche's thinking as biologistic that was current at that time was in a way correct; his point was that it was the main obstacle to penetrating Nietzsche's fundamental thought (*GA* 47: 60; *N* III 41). Heidegger's ambivalence is confirmed by a letter to Elizabeth Blochmann from 14 April 1937 in which he described it as extremely enigmatic that, although Nietzsche apparently sunk into the most crude biologism, his reckless exaggeration of this direction succeeded in turning it into something completely different, and that this happened in the notebooks and did not take shape in his standard works.[40]

Heidegger's initial criticism of biologism was that it transferred concepts from the field of plant and animal life to the field of human beings, for example, that of history (*N* III 45). This criticism was already sketched out briefly in *Being and Time*, thereby confirming the continuity of this aspect of his thought (*SZ* 49–50). In *The Will to Power as Knowledge*, in a lecture subsequently given the title "Nietzsche's Alleged Biologism," Heidegger explained further that this unfounded extension of concepts from their own field arises from a failure to recognize the metaphysical character of propositions concerning the field: "all biology that is genuine and restricted to its field points beyond itself" (*N* III 45).[41] Heidegger concluded that biological thinking can only be grounded from within the metaphysical realm and that the reason for the degeneration of scientific thinking, particularly in its popular forms, is that it fails to know this. The nature of the critique thereby subtly changes. The problem is no longer seen to lie in the unfounded extension of concepts beyond their realm, but applies to all scientific thinking that has failed to take the leap to metaphysical reflection (*N* III 43). The criterion for judging Nietzsche guilty of biologism is not whether he applied a concept beyond a given field, but whether he recognized that that use of the concept implied a metaphysical decision (*N* III 45–6). In spite of the fact that the characterization of Nietzsche's thinking as biologism is "in a way, correct" (*N* III 41), Nietzsche escaped the charge on what might look like the technicality that "Nietzsche is moving in the realm of thinking metaphysically" and doing so knowingly (*N* III 108). So when Nietzsche defined the human being as a "beast of prey" he was not thinking biologically but grounding this apparently merely biological worldview metaphysically (*N* III 46). By contrast, "the many writers who whether consciously or unconsciously expound and copy Nietzsche's treatises invariably fall prey to a variety of biologism" (*N* III 46).

However, there is a second sense in which Nietzsche's racial thought is metaphysical rather than biologistic, and it arises from Heidegger's locating Nietzsche's thinking at the consummation of western metaphysics (*N* III 46). Heidegger's point in the treatise "Nietzsche's Metaphysics" was that Nietzsche's thought belonged within western metaphysics as Heidegger characterized it in terms of the truth of beings (*N* III 187). The remarks on Nietzsche's racial thought were intended to show that it is only at a certain stage in the history of western metaphysics, specifically in the epoch of subjectivity, that the idea of eugenics becomes possible. Or, rather, necessary: "Only where the absolute subjectivity of will to power comes to be the truth of beings as a whole is the *principle* of a program of racial breeding possible; possible, that is, not merely on the basis of naturally evolving races, but in terms of the self-conscious *thought* of race. That is to say, the principle is metaphysically necessary" (*N* III 231). In a manuscript written at roughly the same time as "Nietzsche's Metaphysics" but only recently published, Heidegger developed this analysis by arguing that contemporary racial science with its projects of race breeding, race cultivation, and race ranking must be seen as a manifestation of western metaphysics (*GA* 69: 70–1).[42]

Both senses of metaphysics, metaphysics as the realm from which the decision about concepts are made (*N* III 40–7) and metaphysics as "the tradition of metaphysical thinking" (*N* III 73; see also *GA* 47: 90) are in play when Heidegger wrote that "Just as Nietzsche's thought of will to power was ontological rather than biological, even more was his racial thought metaphysical rather than biological" (*N* III 231). This passage has therefore nothing to do with an alleged attempt by Heidegger to supplant the Nazi biological idea of race with a spiritual idea of race. Furthermore, we now know, as Derrida did not, that the crucial sentence was not written in 1940 but in 1960, twenty years later. It is not to be found in the edition of "Nietzsche's Metaphysics" published in 1990 as volume 50 of the *Gesamtausgabe*, which presents the text as Heidegger left it in December 1940 on the basis of an initial draft written in August (*GA* 50: 101). On my reading Heidegger's sentence about Nietzsche's racial thought as metaphysical clarifies the argument of the 1940 text. It does not alter or try to alter its meaning. But even if one could interpret the sentence as part of an argument for a metaphysical or spiritual, rather than a biological, conception of race, because the sentence was written in 1960, not 1940, it cannot be used to support Heidegger's claim that under National Socialism he had sought to replace the Nazi biological notion of race with a cultural or spiritual notion of race.

When Heidegger employed the phrase "metaphysical thought of race," he did not mean a thought of race that was somehow altogether divorced from biology. He meant, in the first place, a thought of race that was engaged in metaphysical reflection and, secondly, one that belonged to western metaphysics. The ambiguity of the double concept of metaphysics is that, whereas the first sense seems to offer some relief from biologism, the second sense warns that there is no easy way out. By calling Nietzsche's racial thought "metaphysical," Heidegger did not seek thereby to defend or rescue that thought but to place it within the purview of the broader problematic of the overcoming of metaphysics. Nevertheless, this does not locate the metaphysical thought of race within the paradox Derrida identifies in *Of Spirit.* This is because, for Heidegger, the attempt to escape western metaphysics, difficult though it is, does not give rise to an aporetic structure, as it does in Derrida. Heidegger did not exclude the possibility of an opening beyond the metaphysics of race. In notes Heidegger made during the winter semester 1937–8, in connection with a working group drawn from the faculty of the natural sciences and medicine that met on the theme "The Threat of Science," Heidegger dismissed the Science of Folklore (*Volkskundewissenschaft*) as "the new form of an at once empty self-stupefaction and stupidity."[43] But in this context Heidegger claimed that because the crude, nonsensical, and naïve outburst of a "new national (*völkisch*) science" had gone fully astray, the counter-eruption must and can now readily succeed.[44]

With some help from texts published only recently and without addressing Lang's interpretation in its entirety, I have argued that Lang's conception of metaphysical racism has very little to do with what Heidegger meant by a "metaphysical thought of race." Nevertheless, the debate that Lang initiated can still help clarify what is at stake in Heidegger's discussions of race. Lang uses the notion of metaphysical racism to make the point that a specifically biological racism is of relatively recent origin and that biological racism has historically served as a justification of a racism already in place, a "cover" for racism's other varieties rather than the other way around (*HS* 25–6 and MR 22). In other words, it is false to assume that if one removes the biological grounds for racism, then the building block that sustains the Nazi ideology disappears (MR 220). Even if in his general assessment Lang underplays the fact that biological racism has been responsible for some of the most extreme forms of racism, he is right to insist that the history of racism should play a part in any analysis of racism. Most importantly, Lang has shown that the debate about race in Heidegger, by being fixated on the presence or absence of the term "race," strayed far from the real issues raised by race theory.[45]

To focus exclusively on Heidegger's use of the term "race" ignores the fact that it might also be implicit, for example, in the concept of *Volk.* When commentators attribute to Heidegger a concept of *Volk* as a spiritual community that has no reference to race, they seem to forget the role biological factors have played in most parts of the world in identifying populations and their cultures. The world will have to change before that changes. What is needed therefore is a deeper appreciation of the issues raised by race theory. One should not approach the topic with the assumption that all concepts of race belong to a racist ideology and thus are to be condemned on moral grounds, particularly when so many distinguished race theorists who supported some form of universal humanism – such as, Du Bois, Senghor, Sartre, Fanon, and Biko – have argued for the concept as a tool to combat racism. After judgment has been passed against Heidegger for his political and philosophical errors, as well as for his moral failings, the philosophical – and political – question remains about how one sustains a language of political community, particularly in the light of the individualism associated with the metaphysics of subjectivity.

The thrust of Heidegger's thinking on race during the war years is about the difficulty of avoiding racial thought not for ethical or political reasons, but because the concept of race is imposed on us by western metaphysics. This does not mean that we should not scrutinize the idea of race or try to reconceptualize it. For Heidegger, the reverse is true. To accept the necessity of talk about race does not mean that one cannot discriminate between certain discourses of races. It makes these kinds of discrimination more important. The anomaly is that those who seem to be least critical of Heidegger are least oblivious to this task, and they have been brought to this point because in their defensiveness they have been too quick to imagine that Heidegger in opposing biologism could attain a notion of *Volk* that was free from all reference to race. Heidegger's monolithic conception of metaphysics, albeit equipped with a conception of epochality, shows how positions that are often taken to be radically opposed operate within the same orbit. Over and beyond analytic arguments that try to show that a notion of a spiritual *Volk* is parasitic on a biological notion of *Rasse*, Heidegger argued that they are mutually supporting. If Heidegger in his self-defense after the war tried to suggest that he advocated the former against the latter, this was disingenuous on his part. It is true that in his public statements between 1933 and 1935 he sought to counter the primacy some theorists gave to race. But in his unpublished manuscripts at the end of the 1930s and the beginning of the 1940s he was more inclined to ascribe a certain necessity to race within the perspective of an analysis of western metaphysics.

In the context of his discussion of Nietzsche's relation to Darwinism in the Nietzsche lectures, Heidegger acknowledged that "Since even the greatest, even the most solitary, thinkers do not live in the supraterrestial space of a supraworldly place, they are always surrounded and touched – influenced, as one says – by contemporaries and traditions" (*GA* 47: 33; *N* III 23). The notion of "influence" can too readily be used as an excuse for laziness when it comes to determining the relations between one thinker and another or between a thinker and a current of ideas. Nevertheless, philosophers have recently also become adept at ignoring the impact of contemporaries, traditions, and also political events, in order to sustain the myth that thinkers live in a supraworldly place. The interpretation of Heidegger was long distorted by this fiction that was also on occasion promulgated by Heidegger himself. However, when one examines Heidegger's discussion of race breeding, race cultivation, and race ranking in his unpublished manuscripts and sees how he relates them to broader intellectual movements and ultimately to the history of being, it becomes apparent that any attempt to read his texts without reference to this context is to run counter to the direction of his thinking, as well as to invite the usual distortions that arise when context is ignored. And insofar as Du Bois's reflection that "the problem of the Twentieth Century is the problem of the color-line" has proved prophetic, and seems likely to retain its validity also for the twenty-first century, then it seems likely that choosing to ignore Heidegger's attempt to confront the racism of his situation will be just one more way in which we can choose to ignore the racism of our own situation.[46]

NOTES

1 Martin Heidegger, "An das Akademische Rektorat der Albert-Ludwig-Universität," dual-language version with translation by Jason M. Wirth, *Graduate Faculty Philosophy Journal*, 14.2 C 15.1 (1991), 538–9. Henceforth AAR.

2 The lecture course has been published under the title *Logik als die Frage nach dem Wesen der Sprache*, *Gesamtausgabe*, vol. 38 (Frankfurt a.M.: Klostermann, 1998). All references to Heidegger's *Gesamtausgabe* (Frankfurt a.M.: Klostermann, 1977–) are henceforth given as *GA* followed by the volume number and page number.

3 Heidegger began merely by entertaining the idea that Negroes and Kaffirs have no history as something that is sometimes said, thereby giving rise to a certain ambiguity in the notion of history, which is denied to part of humanity, even while at the same time it is acknowledged that the earth has a history (*GA* 38: 81, 83). However, once this is resolved by clarifying the nature of the historicality of a *Volk*, it seems clear that Heidegger is committed to the view not only that some peoples are without a history, but that they also lack a future (*GA* 38: 84). Heidegger prefaced the discussion

with the remark that "Only man has history, because he alone can be history, insofar as he is and according as he is" (*GA* 38: 78). In the transcript now attributed to Luise Grosse, the passage reads "Only man has history, insofar as he is and according to what level he is." This transcript is less reliable, but on this occasion may capture Heidegger's sense, if not his exact words. Martin Heidegger, *Lógica (Semestre verano 1934)*, ed. V. Farias (Barcelona: Anthropos, 1991), p. 34.

4 "Nur noch ein Gott kann uns retten," *Der Spiegel*, 31 May 1976, p. 204; "Only a God Can Save Us," trans. Maria Alter and John D. Caputo, in *The Heidegger Controversy: A Critical Reader*, ed. Richard Wolin (Cambridge, MA: MIT Press, 1993), p. 101. The latter volume is henceforth abbreviated as *HC*.

5 Martin Heidegger, *Nietzsche*, vol. 3, trans. Joan Stambaugh, David Farrell Krell, and Frank Capuzzi (San Francisco: Harper & Row, 1987). Hereafter abbreviated as *N* III.

6 Martin Heidegger, "Das Rektorat 1933/34," in *Selbstbehauptung der deutschen Universität* (Frankfurt a.M.: Klostermann, 1983), p. 30; trans. *HC* 23. The former volume is henceforth abbreviated as *SU*. For the debate about Heidegger's National Socialism, the absence of a clear reference to race, even if true, would not be decisive. See Endre Kiss, "Die Stellung der Nietzsche-Deutung bei der Beurteilung der Rolle und des Schicksals Martin Heideggers im Dritten Reich," in *Zur philosophischen Aktualität Heideggers*, ed. Dietrich Paperfuss and Otto Pöggeler (Frankfurt a.M.: Klostermann, 1991), vol. 1, p. 433.

7 This also contradicts those who speak of "the absence of racial and biological elements from the speech." For example, Parvis Emad, "Introduction," in H. W. Petzet, *Encounters and Dialogues with Martin Heidegger, 1929–1976*, trans. P. Emad and K. Maly (Chicago: University of Chicago Press, 1993), p. xxii and Pascal David, "New Crusades Against Heidegger (Part Two)," *Heidegger Studies* 14 (1998), 52.

8 For an interpretation of this phrase written prior to the publication of *GA* 38 that shows that it does not amount to a simple biological racism, see George Leaman, *Heidegger im Kontext* (Hamburg: Argument, 1993), pp. 128–30. However, in the light of *GA* 38 it seems clear that race in some sense is being evoked.

9 Emad, "Introduction," p. xxii.

10 Hans Weinert, *Biologische Grundlagen für Rassenkunde und Rassenhygiene* (Stuttgart: Ferdinand Enke, 1934), p. 165.

11 Historians readily acknowledge that the National Socialist worldview was a mishmash of ideas. See, for example, Martin Broszat, *Der Nationalsozialismus. Weltanschauung, Programm und Wirklichkeit* (Stuttgart: Deutsche Verlags-Anstalt, 1960), p. 21. Unfortunately, most writers on Heidegger's relation to National Socialism tend to treat the latter as a coherent philosophy.

12 Julian Young, *Heidegger, Philosophy, Nazism* (Cambridge: Cambridge University Press, 1997), pp. 36, 44.

13 Ibid., pp. 42, 137.

14 For example, Pascal David, "What does 'To Avoid' Mean? On Derrida's *De l'Esprit*," *Heidegger Studies* 8 (1992), 22. David cites *SU* 14, *GA* 39: 27 and *GA* 65: 19, 97, and 117.

15 Pascal David, "New Crusades Against Heidegger (Part Two)," p. 48. David offers no hint as to what he means by "grasping 'people' as a non-racial and non-biological entity" other than to refer to Heidegger's idea of *das Mitgegebene* and *das Aufgegebene*, a people's endowment and a people's task. He no doubt has in mind the 1934/35 lectures on Hölderlin (*GA* 39: 292), but that does not bring sufficient philosophical clarity to the idea.

16 The lecture course was originally called "The State and Science." The title was changed at the first meeting (*GA* 38: 172), but arguably the original title describes its contents just as well. Incomprehensibly, Rüdiger Safranski (on the basis of the Farias text) saw the course as evidence of a turning away from politics back to the spirit, thereby retaining the myth of Heidegger withdrawing from any interest in politics after resigning the Rectorate. *Martin Heidegger*, trans. Edward Osers (Cambridge, MA: Harvard University Press, 1998), p. 281.

17 Heidegger's public criticism of the *völkisch* movement is significant. *Völkisch* ideology was characterized by extreme nationalism, antisemitism, social Darwinism, and a romanticized conception of German history. Its conception of *Volksgemeinschaft* was constructed on the basis of a belief in racial purity. See George Mosse, *The Crisis of German Ideology* (New York: Grosset and Dunlap, 1964), pp. 97–107.

18 See, for example, Mouchir Aoun, *La polis heideggerienne* (Altenberge: Oros, 1996), p. 364.

19 See the reference to *Volk* in Martin Heidegger, *Sein und Zeit* (Tübingen: Max Niemeyer, 1967), p. 384. Henceforth *SZ*. For a valuable discussion which compares Heidegger's discussion of *Volk* from the first half of the 1930s to that of Oswald Spengler, see Sonya Sikka, "Heidegger's Concept of *Volk*," *The Philosophical Forum* 26.2 (1994), 101–26.

20 The relation of the *Volk* to the state arises in other writings from the same year. In a speech delivered on 22 February 1934 to a group of 600 former members of the unemployed, Heidegger extolled the way that knowledge unites the people into one great will of the State. In the same place Heidegger took up some strong political positions by lamenting urbanization and the fact that so many of the German *Volk* live beyond the boundaries of the *Reich*. "Nationalsozialistische Wissenschulung," in *Nachlese zu Heidegger*, ed. Guido Schreeberger (Bern: Suhr, 1962), pp. 200–1; trans. Dagobert D. Runes, "Follow the Führer," in *German Existentialism* (New York: Philosophical Library, 1965), pp. 38–41.

21 Although I am criticizing Heidegger's characterization of the lectures in his 1945 letter to the Rector, I would not make this the basis of a charge of distortion, given the difficulty of paraphrasing its positive doctrine in half a sentence.

22 For example, Rainer Marten, "Heideggers Geist," in *Die Heidegger Kontroverse*, ed. Jürg Altwegg (Frankfurt a.M.: Athenäum, 1988), pp. 227–8.

23 Jacques Derrida, *De l'esprit* (Paris: Galilée, 1987), p. 65; trans. Geoffrey Bennington and Rachel Bowlby, *Of Spirit* (Chicago: University of Chicago Press, 1989), p. 39. Henceforth *E* and *S* respectively.

24 This is why Julian Young misses the point when he reads Derrida's efforts as evidence of a "too-facile assumption that to 'spiritualise' a phenomenon is to simply provide an alternative grounding for its existing expression." *Heidegger, Philosophy, Nazism*, p. 137.

25 See Julius Deussen, *Klages Kritik des Geistes* (Leipzig: S. Hirzel, 1934). Heidegger singled out Klages as one of his targets in addressing Nietzsche's biologism (*GA* 47: 75–6).

26 Heidegger explicitly attacked Rosenberg and his language of *Rassenseele* and *Volksseele* in the first of his lecture courses on Hölderlin (*GA* 39: 26). Rosenberg praises Klages on the issue of a *rassisch-seelischen Begründung* in *Der Mythus des 20.Jahrhunderts* (Munich: Hoheneichen, 1935), p. 137. However, in 1938 Rosenberg drew his distance from Klages. See Hans Kasdorff, *Ludwig Klages* (Bonn: Bouvier, 1984), pp. 24–5 and 261–2. Much of the discussion of the association of race and soul in German in the 1930s was in connection with Ludwig Clauss, *Rasse und Seele* (Berlin: Büchergilde, 1939). See also R. Vierguss, "Rasse und Seele," *Volk und Rasse* 7.1 (January 1932), 40–4.

27 For example, Oswald Menghin, *Geist und Blut* (Vienna: Anton Schroll, 1934), p. 45.

28 Martin Heidegger and Elisabeth Blochmann, *Briefwechsel 1918–1969*, ed. Joachim W. Storck (Marbach: Deutsche Schillergesellschaft, 1990), p. 61.

29 Berel Lang, *Heidegger's Silence* (Ithaca: Cornell University Press, 1996), p. 39. Henceforth *HS.*

30 Subsequently, Lang published an essay "Metaphysical Racism (or: Biological Warfare by Other Means)," but it does not throw much additional light on Lang's choice of the term. Berel Lang, "Metaphysical Racism," in *Race/Sex*, ed. Naomi Zack (London: Routledge, 1997), pp. 17–27. Henceforth MR.

31 Moeller van den Bruck, "Rassenanschauung," *Der Tag*, 9 July 1908. Reprinted in *Das Recht der jungen Völker*, ed. Hans Schwarz (Berlin: Der Nahe Osten, 1932), p. 194. See also Fritz Stern, *The Politics of Cultural Despair* (New York: Anchor, 1965), p. 252n.

32 Tom Rockmore, *On Heidegger's Nazism and Philosophy* (Berkeley: University of California Press, 1992), p. 59.

33 Ibid., p. 242.

34 Tom Rockmore, "Philosophy or Weltanschauung? Heidegger on Hönigswald," *History of Philosophy Quarterly*, 16.1 (January 1999), 108.

35 Safranski, *Martin Heidegger*, pp. 301–2.

36 For example, in 1934 Baeumler quoted Nietzsche's call for the extinction of misfits, weaklings, and degenerates and argued that Nietzsche provided the foundations of a new policy that would ground the state on race. Alfred

Baeumler, "Nietzsche und der Nationalsozialismus," in *Studien zur deutschen Geistesgeschichte* (Berlin: Junker und Dünnhaupt, 1937), esp. p. 292.

37 Alfred Rosenthal, *Nietzsches "Europäisches Rasse-Problem"* (Leiden: A. W. Sijthoff, 1935).

38 See the excellent resource, Richard Frank Krummel, *Nietzsche und der deutsche Geist*, vol. 3 (New York: Walter de Gruyter, 1998).

39 See, for example, Werner Stegmaier, "Darwin, Darwinismus, Nietzsche," *Nietzsche-Studien* 16 (1987), 264–87. For the importance of Wilhelm Roux in this context, Wolfgang Müller-Lauter, "Der Organismus als innerer Kampf," *Nietzsche Studien* 7 (1978), 189–223.

40 Martin Heidegger to Elisabeth Blochmann, *Briefwechsel*, p. 90.

41 An example of the use of metaphysical reflection in the clarification of biological concepts is provided by Heidegger's discussion of organism in the 1929–30 lectures *The Fundamental Concepts of Metaphysics.* These lectures include a critique of Darwinism's concept of "adaptation" for its failure to think through the relation between the organism and its environment deeply enough (*GA* 29/30: 374–85).

42 See also *GA* 69: 223. I intend to address this aspect of Heidegger's account of race in more detail in a paper I am writing for a conference on Heidegger organized by Abraham Mansbach under the auspices of the Van Leer Jerusalem Institute in January 2000.

43 Martin Heidegger, "Die Bedrohung der Wissenschaft," ed. Hartmut Tietjen in *Zur philosophischen Aktualität Heideggers*, vol. 1, p. 23.

44 Ibid., p. 24.

45 Lang's work has on this very point played a part in contemporary race theory. See K. Anthony Appiah, "Race, Culture, Identity: Misunderstood Connections," in *Color Conscious* (Princeton: Princeton University Press, 1996), p. 82. In the original version of this essay I developed this connection, but the discussion had to be omitted because of space constraints.

46 W. E. B. Du Bois, *The Souls of Black Folk*, in *Writings*, ed. Nathan Huggins (New York: Library of America, 1986), p. 359.

CHAPTER 5

Heidegger and ethics beyond the call of duty

Albert Borgmann

Ethical norms and judgments are clearly implied in *Being and Time*, the book that established Heidegger's reputation.[1] Heidegger coyly insisted that it was all dispassionate analysis, but the language of authentic, resolute, ready-for-anxiety, running-ahead-into-death existence is no doubt morally charged, as is Heidegger's scathing account of the distracted busyness of everyday life. Heidegger's uneasiness with standard ethics became explicit in his 1931–2 course of lectures on Plato's allegory of the cave, where he concluded his discussion of the idea of the good as follows: "It is not at all a matter of ethics or morality, nor is it of course a logical or epistemological principle. Such distinctions – they already existed, to be sure, in antiquity – are those of scholars of philosophy, not of philosophy."[2]

Heidegger elaborated his rejection of ethics in the 1947 letter "On Humanism."[3] But, chastened perhaps by his hapless political involvement in a movement that violated everything that could be called ethical, he conceded the need for ethics, however unsatisfactory it appeared from the standpoint of his own thinking.[4] One may deplore Heidegger's determined move away from ethics.[5] Or one may try to discover a continuing ethical dimension in Heidegger's later thought.[6] But there is in fact something unsatisfactory and unrevealing in contemporary mainstream ethics.

In the modern period, standard ethics is concerned with obligatory principles of conduct, rules that tell you what you must do to be blameless. Most of these rules tell you that you ought to be honest, respect freedom of speech, keep your promises, and the like. Unlike many religious precepts, standard ethics does not tell you to welcome the sojourner or forgive your enemy. It is good to do such things, but you are not required to do them. They go beyond the call of duty. Philosophers call such acts *supererogatory*, duties of imperfect (i.e., less than absolute) obligation, or acts in keeping with the morality of aspiration rather than that of duty.[7] Supererogatory ethics, in short, tells you not how to remain blameless, but how to become praiseworthy. Heidegger no doubt would have taken such fine distinctions as evidence of the scholastic or derivative character of contemporary ethics. In any event, supererogatory ethics will be the crucial and vexing kind in the years to come, as I will try to show. The fact, however, that standard ethics, or to put it more invidiously, that "scholars of philosophy" are by and large unprepared for this challenge can be counted as evidence that Heidegger's doubts about standard ethics are justified.

But has not virtue ethics enjoyed a recent renaissance? And is it not devoted to the pursuit of moral excellence? The answer to both questions is yes, and one might add that virtue ethics has had a measure of popular acclaim, as shown by the bestselling success of William Bennet's *The Book of Virtues*.[8] I suspect, however, that the common applause was more dutiful than heartfelt and that *The Book of Virtues* was more often bought than read. Here too a Heideggerian suggestion as to the thin effect of ethics (virtue ethics in this case) is at hand. Virtues are in important part moral skills and hence specific to a certain setting, as skills are in general. The skill of identifying edible plants is one that lost importance when hunting and gathering yielded to agriculture and became useless when rural life was superseded by city life. Aristotle himself struggled with the meaning of courage because the stage of its exercise had changed from the heroic to the civic.[9] And what is the proper setting for the exercise of courage today? The search for an answer must begin with a consideration of the epochal changes the setting of settings, the world, has undergone in the modern period, and few thinkers have given this problem the incisive if programmatic attention Heidegger has devoted to it.

In connecting Heidegger with ethics beyond the call of duty, I am trying to discover norms of conduct that are appropriate to this moment in human history. I invoke Heidegger to determine the character of contemporary reality. I refer to supererogatory ethics to make clear that we must go beyond standard contemporary ethics to see how we ought to conduct ourselves here and now.

Technology is the title under which Heidegger has analyzed the contemporary condition most concretely. The crucial document is his 1949 lecture "The Question Concerning Technology,"[10] where he explains technology as the modern disclosure of being – reality is revealed as raw material for the aggressive transformation into resources. Technology as the modern dispensation of the history of being is more than a project humans have thought up. But since the eventuation of reality involves humanity, technology is also something other than an inevitable fate. In fact, out of technology and through human thought another, saving, dispensation of being may come to pass.

Putting matters more schematically, Heidegger's celebrated essay considers the rise and the possible overcoming of technology. What limits the force of this particular account for us today is its failure to say much of anything about the period we live in, the period *between* the establishment and the passing of technology. Heidegger's description of technology, namely as a setting upon all there is in order to process it into available resources, captures the massive material reshaping of the advanced industrial countries between roughly 1775 and 1975 – the modern period. Meanwhile the subordination of material reality is, in the advanced industrial countries, an accomplished fact, and we have moved into a period of refinement and dematerialization – the postmodern era. As it turns out, Heidegger has elsewhere scattered thought-provoking observations on what roughly corresponds to the postmodern condition.

Heidegger himself implied something like a postmodern era in his repeated remarks that the technological era will likely be of long duration.[11] Obviously the conquest of material reality does not take long in historical measures and in fact is taking less and less time as technological devices are becoming more powerful and sophisticated. Hence the period of aggressive transformation must be succeeded by another kind of technological culture.

Heidegger sensed the coming of the postmodern condition before he set down his analysis of the classical modern condition. Broadly put, the aggressive energy of modern technology is followed by a slackening and smugness of life. Heidegger had already touched on this condition in *Being and Time*, where he described the disengaged and distracted condition of everyday existence.[12] In *The Fundamental Concepts of Metaphysics*, of 1929–30, his language becomes more pointed in its condemnation of the desolation and vanity of contemporary life.[13] This critique was undoubtedly inspired in part by the broad current of reactionary romanticism that swept Germany between the world wars.[14] Often, however, this romantic condemnation of mass culture was joined with enthusiasm for modern technology. At least until the mid 1930s, Heidegger was undecided about the relation between the attitudes he condemned and the new technological reality. In his *Contributions to Philosophy* of 1936–8, however, he began to link the human condition to the rise of technology. The description of technology, carried out under the title of machination (*Machenschaft*), was in broad outline the one that attained its classic rendition in *The Question Concerning Technology*. Naturally this included the attitude of domination.[15] Thus in *Contributions*, we find the aggressive attitude of technological conquest and the desolation of slackness and superficiality side by side.[16]

We can summarize Heidegger's inclusive view of technology (in terms Heidegger would have rejected) as follows. What emerges first is the anthropology of postmodern technology, the condition of languor and aimlessness. When Heidegger proceeds to the ontology of technology, it comes to the fore as the structure of modern technology, the disclosure of reality as resource. The ontology brings in its train an anthropology of modern technology, the exploitation and domination of reality. This modern account remains canonic for Heidegger, and what remains missing is an explicit ontology of postmodern technology. What does the world look like once the technological conquest of reality has been accomplished in all essentials?

It has reached the end of history, we might say. In 1989, Francis Fukuyama raised the question, and in 1992 he titled his book affirmatively *The End of History and the Last Man*.[17] The end of history is a state of resolution where the contradictions of history have been answered definitively in favor of a ruling social regime. For Fukuyama, the end state consists of the amalgam of democracy and capitalism. Not all regions of the globe have reached this eventuality and its benign consequences: in all too many parts there is oppression, economic chaos, hunger, illness, and ignorance. Clearly the United States is closest to the end of history and most enjoys the fruits of liberty and prosperity. Yet even within the United States there is poverty, disease, lack of education, and social injustice. Still there must be some 200 million people in our society who live in peaceful, prosperous, and unencumbered circumstances.

Moreover, the United States has seen the resolution of contradictions that were internal to democratic capitalism and seemed stubborn and unyielding. One was the supposed incompatibility of low inflation and low unemployment. Another was the apparent impossibility of obliging the norms of both fiscal responsibility and political popularity. A third was the alleged inconsistency of economic growth and environmental prudence. No one will declare these problems solved fully or for all times. Yet enough progress has been made to leave the United States uniquely prosperous and powerful on the contemporary stage of history.

Thus the status of the middle and upper class in the United States constitutes the goal of global aspirations. Everywhere the industry of the gifted and determined is directed toward obtaining the affluence and prestige of the rich American. To be sure, individuals in Europe and Japan have attained that status too, and so have the rich in almost all countries. But only in the United States are individual prosperity, economic vigor, and political power woven into the unified fabric of the historical end state.

We can connect the end state of history with Heidegger's anthropology of postmodern technology by asking what sort of ontology would correspond to the anthropology. Winfried Franzen has given an indirect answer by noting the condition that Heidegger saw as the salutary opposite of the postmodern reality he deplored. Franzen speaks of "The Yearning for Hardness and Heaviness" on Heidegger's part.[18] John Caputo has pointed out that here again reactionary sentiments are at work.[19] But even if the pseudoheroic severity that surfaced in Heidegger's rectorial address of 1933 is the wrong answer to the question of postmodern ontology, the reply nevertheless adumbrates the unsatisfactory condition it responds to.[20]

The condition that contrasts with hardness and heaviness we may call, following Milan Kundera, the unbearable lightness of being.[21] For Kundera lightheartedness would be the appropriate though unsustainable attitude toward the lightness of being. Kundera fails to see that lightness is all sparkle and pleasure for a very short time and tends to devolve into insubstantial flimsiness. The promise and liabilities of postmodern being have most clearly come to light in the realm of electronically mediated information William Gibson has taught us to call cyberspace.[22]

Cyberspace has no metric. It lacks the spatial extension that in ordinary space requires us to travail and travel from one thing to another, all the while paying tribute to the heaviness of our bodies and the hardness of the terrain. "Travel was a meat thing," says Case, the hero of William Gibson's *Neuromancer*.[23] Cyberspace, to be sure, is not the sole or first instance of the dissolution of distance and the disburdenment from gravity. In the 1950 lecture "The Thing," Heidegger himself had noted: "All distances in time and space are shrinking." He mentioned air travel, radio, film, and television – just then emerging – as the manifestation of the dissolving metric. More important, he stressed that technology fails to make near what is far: "Everything is being swept into the uniformly distanceless."[24]

In distanceless cyberspace one can move easily and instantly from one experience to the next and indulge one's desires in numerous ways and, if the promises of cyber enthusiasts can be trusted, in every conceivable way before long. To the ease and instantaneity of movement corresponds the movers' ability to escape from the inertia and imperfection of their bodies. They can now reverse the course of Case in *Neuromancer*, who had lost his ability to move in cyberspace:

> For Case, who'd lived for the bodiless exultation of cyberspace, it was the Fall. In the bars he'd frequented as a cowboy hotshot, the elite stance involved a certain relaxed contempt for the flesh. The body was meat. Case fell into the prison of his own flesh.[25]

In multiuser domains, in chatrooms, and even on e-mail, one is able to project oneself in whatever profile, however ethereal and glamorous.

As reality lite is coming up on the screens of cyberspace, the heaviness and hardness of the world withdraws. As Heidegger had already put it in 1929–30, "Every withholding has its edge in this: it indicates at the same time and with utmost duress what it is that is being withheld, i.e., being indicated and held before us in its necessity."[26] Later in the same lecture, Heidegger sketches the philosophical attitude that will be equal to the withdrawal of the hardness of being: "Philosophy as a creative and essential activity of human existence rests in the *fundamental attitude of melancholy*."[27] Melancholy in German is *Schwermut*, the mood that is heavy with the concealed burden of being.

Contemporary ethics, both as a theory and as a practice, has had a hard time with this concealment. The prevailing supposition in scholarly ethics assumes that, if only the obligatory requirements are met, the good life will flourish all by itself. But the actual ignorance and incompetence of so many people stand condemned by the possibilities of excellence that are open to all. The scholarly optimism is also belied by a widespread perplexity about the shape of the good life at the end of history.

We get a glimpse of this problem in an article about the predicament teenagers find themselves in when called upon to give an account of their lives. The occasion was the notorious essay that must accompany applications to prestigious universities and is meant to reveal the applicants' sense of themselves. But what moral contour can a seventeen-year-old hope to have at the end of history? As the reporter sympathetically put it:

> In her desperation, 17-year-old [Jane Doe] found herself wishing that somebody – anybody – in her family had died.

"Because then I could write about it," she said. "It's horrible and I hated myself for it. But I just wished I had something tragic happen to me."[28]

It makes one long for the ancient pain of sticks and stones, and some have been privileged to feel it, e.g.,

[Joe Smith], a white Newton North senior who grew up in Africa and "actually did have a big thing happen."

"I wrote about racism toward myself," he said. "When I was about 11 or so, a group of kids threw stones at me, and that stuck in my head. That was just a big, big experience for me, and I guess I'm really lucky to have that because I know kids that are writing about, like, concerts they went to and stuff like that."[29]

In a similar vein, Sven Birkerts, having chronicled "the average day of the average American businessman," asks his reader:

If you are a writer committed to the project of writing about your times, how do you write this life, this experience, into your fiction? How do you give Mr. Case's life a meaningful, never-mind dramatic contour?[30]

The evidence of these anecdotes is supported by broader social science research. John Robinson, who has undertaken some of the most painstaking investigations of the texture and flavor of ordinary life, has, with coauthor Geoffrey Godbey, summarized the confused state of contemporary society this way:

Cut the amount of work time in American society, and Americans may believe they are working longer hours. Give Americans more free time, and they devote most of that time to television, an undemanding, unresponsive activity that they now generally rate as lower in pleasure than many household chores. Give Americans the opportunity to purchase labor-saving technology, and they subvert its time-saving features, even though they say they are starved for time and presumably purchase such technology in order to save time.[31]

Similar observations have been made by Juliet Schor, Robert Wuthnow, David Glen Mick, and Susan Fournier.[32]

Heidegger saw this perplexity early and was ready to see it met by standard ethics to the extent possible. Yet he insisted that the deeper moral problem of what I have called the postmodern setting had to be faced all the same. In the 1947 letter "On Humanism" he said:

The desire for an ethics demands satisfaction all the more urgently as the evident no less than the concealed perplexity of people is growing immeasurably. All efforts must be devoted toward binding ethical norms, given that people, creatures of technology and surrendered to a mass culture, can achieve reliable solidity only through a coordination and an order of plans and actions that are commensurate with technology.

Who could overlook this distressing state of affairs? Should we not save and serve the existing bonds however poorly they hold humanity together in merely ephemeral conditions? Of course. But does this distress disburden thought of having to consider what at once remains, prior to all there is, our warrant and truth?[33]

A more pointed and particular case of misplaced moral and philosophical concern was for Heidegger the danger of nuclear armament. Members of the peace movement used to tell us that, if the nuclear threat was not met, nothing else really mattered. In 1946 Heidegger had disagreed and said: "It is not the widely discussed atom bomb, taken as this particular killing machine, that is deadly."[34] In 1955 he acknowledged that the atom bomb was the emblem of the rising era, "but," he continued, "this sign is a superficial one."[35] And more emphatically he noted in the same address that the global situation was perilous. "Why?" he asked. "Merely because a third world war may suddenly erupt and lead to the total destruction of humanity and the devastation of the earth? No. There is in the dawning nuclear age a far greater danger – precisely if the danger of a third world war is eliminated."[36]

For a decade now, the overt danger of another world war has been receding and, if Heidegger is right, the far greater danger has been upon us. Most philosophers and lay people in this country appear to be oblivious to this danger. One who is well aware of Heidegger's warning but finds it ungrounded is Richard Rorty. He admonishes us to be grateful for the blessings of "Postmodern Bourgeois Liberalism."[37] Though he respects the passionate discontent with our times as represented by someone like Christopher Lasch, behind whom he sees the great lamentationist Heidegger, he cannot agree with either, and in conclusion tells his reader this about the great plaint:

If you believe *that*, of course, you may well be content to offer, as Heidegger did, despair without counsel. But if, like Freud, you think nothing could be more illusory than the promise of supernatural redemption through the renunciation of happiness, you may persist in believing that a merely material and secular goal suffices: mortal life as it might be lived on the sunlit uplands of global democracy and abundance. You may see contemporary human beings not as enfolded in a fated spiritual darkness but as still trying to master fate, still bravely stumbling through the seemingly endless minefields that separate them from those glimpsed uplands.[38]

Rorty saves his outrage, as all of us should, for the cruelty we inflict on one another. Outrage goes well with the passions that principally moved morally sensitive people before history ended. But outrage is misplaced and fails to instruct us when it comes to the contemporary moral predicament. Despair for its part has a defeatist finality that is as unhelpful as outrage is misplaced.

Remarkably, Rorty himself points the way beyond outrage and despair. While Christopher Lasch reminded Rorty of one side of the later Heidegger's thought, Charles Taylor reminded him of the other. In his gracious and insightful comments on Taylor's *Sources of the Self*, Rorty honors Taylor's moral realism and says: "So the only thing that Taylor seems willing to count as a transaction between the world and ourselves is something the world initiates – a response to a call from something already there in the world. In short, he wants Heideggerian and Rilkean gratitude rather than simply Deweyan and Whitmanian social hope."[39] A little later, Rorty considers a reply to Taylor on behalf of Dewey, Rorty's protagonist. "Dewey thought," Rorty says, "that once the subject–object way of thinking faded out, so would the sense of awful and magnificent solitude which ensued upon the death of God, and so would any temptation to arrogant self-celebration. Taylor doubts this, and he may be right."[40]

"Heideggerian gratitude" is more than a broad gesture in the direction of the later Heidegger's thought. At about the time when Heidegger surmised the entrenchment of technology, he also proposed a way out of this confinement, a way that originates in the truth of being and requires on our part thankfulness as the appropriate response to being.[41] Thinking is a kind of thanking as Heidegger explains a decade later.[42] The other trait that Heidegger thinks will characterize the overcoming of technology is simplicity. In the letter "On Humanism" he says: "The strange thing about this thought of being is its simplicity."[43]

What we can gather from these reflections on Heidegger and postmodern ethics is the need for an ethics that in a spirit of gratitude and simplicity is able to reply to the unbearable lightness of being and to the slackness and smugness that correspond to that lightness. To find such an ethics, however, we must go beyond Heidegger's hints and suggestions toward a more tangible and detailed account of how and where "the saving power" is to be found.[44] We may be able to make some headway by departing from the postmodern ontology that is missing in Heidegger's discussions of technology.

Cyberspace is the purest instance of the lightness of being. Television is at present its most expansive if more rudimentary version. Whenever social scientists inquire into the ways Americans shape their leisure, television is the looming phenomenon, and a vague uneasiness looms above the television culture.[45] Moral misery today is no longer focused sharply on this commission and that omission. It surfaces in the vague apprehension that we are wasting our time and in time our lives, that we have become unfaithful to things out there, to people, and to our best talents. We watch on television what and where we would like to be, outside somewhere, bravely and skillfully facing real challenges; but we never get around to doing and being what we watch. That is the reason why the moral concern that the typical human condition inspires today is not outrage or indignation but the sort of searing regret one feels when something beautiful is being defaced by neglect.

Moral life under premodern conditions was simpler though no easier.[46] Presumably people found it as difficult to be good then as they find it now. But the call to goodness used to rise more clearly from the tangible circumstances of life. At a time when the family was the economic fundament of life, the basic welfare of children could not be assured outside of or prior to the establishment of a family, and since reliable contraception and safe abortions were not to be had, the reasons for sexual discipline were palpable. When leaving one's spouse meant grave economic jeopardy for the remaining spouse and children and servitude the only route to survival for the departing spouse, marital fidelity was strongly advised by material circumstances. At a time of scarce food and expensive liquor, lack of moderation in eating was the cause of someone else's starvation and intemperance of drinking meant abject poverty. Nor did it require resolve courageously to confront reality out there, to keep in touch with the neighbors, or to exercise one's body. Walking was then the primary means of traveling, not to work with one's hands the privilege of nobility, and interaction with one's neighbors the fabric of survival.

Much of premodern morality was the response to tangible demands, and the primary question was not whether but how well one would follow those requirements. Today technological devices have disburdened and distanced us from the material exigencies of chastity, fidelity, temperance, courage, charity, vigor, and community. These virtues have become supererogatory and remote; we no longer see them but only hear their faint voices. On those occasions, however, when someone has prevailed on us to answer those voices, the presence and power of those things was restored to us. When, e.g., someone begged us to turn off the television and go to a concert or for a walk in the park, the real presence of persons, of music, of lawns and trees flooded us with grace and restored our vigor. And similarly, when we submitted to the discipline of fasting, or at any rate, of abstinence between meals, the life-sustaining force of food came home to us.

There has been an inversion of the material and moral forces of things. In premodern times, the material presence and force of things issued in moral demands. In the postmodern era, the moral demands of things call us back to the material splendor or reality. It is then mere semblance to see postmodern reality as soft, yielding, and elusive, and it is a mistake to think that, there being no resistance, the normal postmodern condition is to be without shape and character.

The postmodern world has a hardness that can restore definition to our minds and discipline to our bodies. It is a hardness that first meets us as the duress of heeding the call of persons and things and of having to cross the threshold of comfort. Hyperactive overachievers, by the way, have to cross the same threshold albeit from a different angle. For them, the duress lies in letting go of the adrenalin rush, of the blandishments of competition and control, and of the seductions of unambiguous goals and successes. The reality of nature, urbanity, athletics, and art or religion seems as boring to the hyperactive as it seems forbidding to the sullen. In any case, once the threshold of duress has been crossed, the hardness of postmodern reality engages us as the firmness of those things that claim and test the fullness of our bodily, spiritual, and communal skills.

But why do we so regularly fail to answer those claims? Broadly put, it is the implicitness and individualism of our moral lives. The official discourse in this society that pertains to the ways we order our fundamental material and social relations carefully and inevitably stops short of the ultimate and actual ways we inhabit those relations. We have much to say about Sam Walton and Walmart, but we rarely discuss the issue of just how all of the stuff Walmart sells ends up in a home and informs the moral complexion of the household.

In practice, of course, we must somehow answer these questions. But the answers remain implicit and hence unexamined. We assume, moreover, that, however the answers are arrived at, they spring from the decision of the individual consumer. But this assumption overlooks the fact that it was not the individual consumer who invented television, refrigeration, automobiles, suburbs, the separation of work and home, etc. These devices and arrangements have been put in place cooperatively and so as to imply a default decision for the evening of a weekday – enter the house, turn on the TV, open the refrigerator. To regain character and definition, we need to put the final enactment of daily life on the public agenda, and we must collectively and cooperatively make sure that interaction with one another and the common devotion to the great things of the city and of the country are the normal response to the way we have laid out our world.

This is the reply to the supposed lightness of being. The good life in fact is so hard that most of us fail to rise to its call, and it is so heavy that most of the time it seems to overburden us. But the hardness and heaviness are moral, not material. It is crucial to recognize, however, that having taken up the burden and having crossed the hard threshold of the good life, reality itself is restored to material hardness and heaviness or, better, to substantial firmness. And as Heidegger has it, the characteristic response to urban and natural reality regained is not the vanity of conquest and triumph, but thankfulness to be graced by the splendor of reality. And in the penumbra of gratitude we can hope to discover the postmodern sense of such virtues as courage, self-discipline, fidelity, and community.

What about Heidegger's point regarding the simplicity of reform? He makes that point by recounting the episode that has come down to us from antiquity. It tells us that Heraclitus was sought out by tourists who were eager to meet the great man. They discovered him, however, by an oven where he was warming himself, and they seemed disappointed; but Heraclitus bade them come closer and said: "Here too gods reside."[47]

In this country philosophers do not draw tourists. Still, when philosophy somehow does draw attention, a definite expectation is voiced by other philosophers no less than by lay people. It is the demand for a program of reform. Lay people want to see their problems fixed. Philosophers want to have their liberal leanings indulged. God knows that the problem of pollution needs fixing and that the distance between the richest and the poorest needs to be reduced. But little philosophical acumen is needed to see that better technology or reduced consumption will cure pollution and that a more steeply progressive income tax plus a decent social minimum will alleviate social injustice.

Heidegger has it exactly right, however, when he stresses that we must "save and secure the existing bonds however poorly they hold humanity together in merely ephemeral conditions," and stresses the greater danger and the graver task, and warns us that the entrenchment of technology will make it a difficult and lengthy process to discuss and dislodge the culture of technology.[48]

What needs to be remembered finally, however, is the inconspicuous simplicity of the task. In the private and personal sphere it comes down to being grateful for the splendor of simplicity that still surrounds us. In the public and political sphere it is a matter of instigating a conversation like ours today.

NOTES

1 Martin Heidegger, *Being and Time*, trans. John Maquarrie and Edward Robinson (New York: Harper and Row, 1962).
2 Martin Heidegger, *Vom Wesen der Wahrheit*, ed. Hermann Mörchen, *Gesamtausgabe*, vol. 34 (Frankfurt a.M.: Klostermann, 1988), p. 100.
3 Martin Heidegger, "Brief über den Humanismus," *Gesamtausgabe*, vol. 9 (Frankfurt a.M.: Klostermann, 1976). I will cite the marginal page numbers of this *GA* text: 153, 154–5, 191.
4 Heidegger, "Humanismus," p. 183.
5 Gerold Prauss, "Heidegger und die Praktische Philosophie," in *Heidegger und die praktische Philosophie*, ed. Annemarie Gethmann-Siefert and Otto Pöggeler (Frankfurt a.M.: Suhrkamp, 1988), pp. 177–92.
6 Reinhart Maurer, "Von Heidegger zur praktischen Philosophie," in *Rehabilitierung der praktischen Philosophie*, ed. Manfred Riedel (Freiburg: Rombach), pp. 434–6.
7 On the history and state of the art of supererogatory ethics, see David Heyd, *Supererogation: Its Status in Ethical Theory* (Cambridge: Cambridge University Press, 1982). On the distinction between the morality of duty and the morality of aspiration, see Lon L. Fuller, *The Morality of Law*, 2nd edn. (New Haven, CT: Yale University Press, 1969), pp. 3–32.
8 William J. Bennet, *The Book of Virtues* (New York: Simon and Schuster, 1993).
9 Aristotle, *Nichomachean Ethics*, book 3.
10 Martin Heidegger, "The Question Concerning Technology," in *The Question Concerning Technology and Other Essays*, tr. William Lovitt (New York: Harper & Row, 1977), pp. 3–35.
11 Martin Heidegger, *Beiträge zur Philosophie*, ed. Friedrich-Wilhelm von Herrmann, *Gesamtausgabe*, vol. 65 (Frankfurt a.M.: Klostermann, 1989), pp. 157 and 408–9 (written 1936–8); "Überwindung der Metaphysik," in *Vorträge und Aufsätze* (Pfullingen: Neske, 1954), p. 83; "Die onto-theo-logische Verfassung der Metaphysik," in *Identität und Differenz* (Pfullingen: Neske, 1957), p. 71.
12 Heidegger, *Being and Time*, pp. 210–24.
13 Martin Heidegger, *Die Grundbegriffe der Metaphysik*, ed. Friedrich-Wilhelm von Herrmann, *Gesamtausgabe*, vol. 29/30 (Frankfurt a.M.: Klostermann, 1983), pp. 7, 32, 238, 241, 245, 426.
14 Jeffrey Herf, *Reactionary Modernism* (New York: Cambridge University Press, 1984); Michael E. Zimmerman, *Heidegger's Confrontation with Modernity* (Bloomington: Indiana University Press, 1990).
15 Heidegger, *Beiträge*, p. 124.
16 Ibid., pp. 61–2, 406–9.

17 Francis Fukuyama, "The End of History?" *The National Interest* 16 (1989), 3–18; *The End of History and the Last Man* (New York: Free Press, 1992).
18 Winfried Franzen, "Die Sehnsucht nach Härte und Schwere," in *Heidegger und die praktische Philosophie*, pp. 78–92.
19 In discussion at the Heidegger conference.
20 Martin Heidegger, "The Self-Assertion of the German University," in *Martin Heidegger and National Socialism*, ed. Günther Neske and Emil Kettering, trans. Lisa Harries and Joachim Neugroschel (New York: Paragon, 1990), pp. 5–13.
21 Milan Kundera, *The Unbearable Lightness of Being*, trans. Michael Henry Heim (New York: HarperCollins, 1991).
22 William Gibson, *Neuromancer* (New York: Ace Books, 1984), pp. 4–5.
23 Ibid., p. 77.
24 Martin Heidegger, "Das Ding," in *Vorträge*, pp. 163–4.
25 Gibson, *Neuromancer*, p. 6.
26 Heidegger, *Grundbegriffe*, p. 245.
27 Ibid., p. 270.
28 Cary Goldberg, "Admissions Essay Ordeal: The Young Examined Life," *New York Times*, 31 December 1997: A1.
29 Ibid.
30 Sven Birkerts, *The Gutenberg Elegies* (New York: Fawcett Columbine, 1995), p. 206.
31 John P. Robinson and Geoffrey Godbey, *Time for Life* (University Park: Pennsylvania State University Press, 1997), p. 299.
32 Juliet Schor, *The Overspent American* (New York: Basic Books, 1998); Robert Wuthnow, *Poor Richard's Principle* (Princeton, NJ: Princeton University Press, 1996); David Glen Mick and Susan Fournier, "Paradoxes of Technology," *Journal of Consumer Research* 25 (1998), 123–43.
33 Heidegger, "Humanismus," p. 183.
34 Martin Heidegger, "Wozu Dichter?" in *Holzwege* (Frankfurt a.M.: Klostermann, 1957), p. 271 (first presented in 1946).
35 Martin Heidegger, *Gelassenheit* (Pfullingen: Neske, 1959), p. 16 (first presented in 1955).
36 Ibid., pp. 24–5.
37 Richard Rorty, "Postmodern Bourgeois Liberalism," *Journal of Philosophy* 80 (1983), 583–9.
38 Richard Rorty, "Two Cheers for Elitism," *New Yorker*, 30 January 1995, p. 89.
39 Richard Rorty, "Taylor on Self-Celebration and Gratitude," *Philosophy and Phenomenological Research* 54 (1994), 200.
40 Ibid.
41 Martin Heidegger, *Was ist Metaphysik?* 8th edn. (Frankfurt a.M.: Klostermann, 1960), pp. 49–51. The reference is to the postscript written in 1943 and revised in 1949.
42 Martin Heidegger, *Was heisst Denken?* (Tübingen: Niemeyer, 1961), pp. 94–5,

157–9. The text was first presented as a series of lectures in 1951–2.
43 Heidegger, "Humanismus," p. 192.
44 Heidegger, "The Question Concerning Technology," pp. 33–4.
45 Robert Kubey and Mihaly Csikszentmihalyi, *Television and the Quality of Life* (Hillsdale, NJ: Erlbaum, 1990). Robinson and Godbey, *Time for Life*, pp. 123–53.
46 Peter Laslett, *The World We Have Lost*, 3rd edn. (New York: Scribner, 1984).
47 Heidegger, "Humanismus," pp. 185.
48 Ibid., p. 183.

PART 2

Heidegger in context

CHAPTER 6

People of God, people of being: the theological presuppositions of Heidegger's path of thought

John D. Caputo

Theology has found it a very agreeable business to appropriate Heidegger, not least because a great deal of what Heidegger has to say arises from a genuine proximity to theology, a certain appropriation of theology that Heidegger has all along been making. When theology looks deeply enough into Heidegger's well, it often finds its own face looking back. For his thought, both early and late, is marked throughout by a transparent theological analogy. These unmistakable theological presuppositions constitute what Heidegger himself would call *das im Sagen Ungesagte,* what is unsaid and unthought in what someone says and thinks, the exposition of which constitutes a genuine interpretation (*Auslegung*) of a thinker. As someone whose work has always been situated in the distance between theology and philosophy, my first interests lay in exploring the intersection of Heidegger with religious mysticism and Heidegger's own beginnings in medieval philosophy and mysticism. With time, I grew more suspicious of Heidegger and in 1993 I made my concerns public under the banner of what I called "demythologizing" Heidegger.[1] I continue that project of demythologizing here, with an eye to the mutual interaction of theology and Heidegger.

THE EARLY CHRISTIAN DAWN, THE EARLY GREEK DAWN

The much celebrated "path of thought" (*Denkweg*) was first set in motion in the first Freiburg period (1919–23) by the project of a "hermeneutics of factical life," which was an attempt to find a new conceptuality in which to "indicate," however "formally," the character of pretheoretical, prephilosophical, indeed even preconceptual life. This provocative and paradoxical task, to find a concept for the preconceptual, was undertaken in close dialogue, not only with Aristotle's ethics, but also with the earliest texts of the New Testament communities, which represented for Heidegger a particularly rich prephilosophical and experiential resource, one that he regarded as unspoiled by traditional and ultimately Greek philosophical concepts. Indeed, Heidegger was much impressed by the radical argument of the Christian theologian Franz Overbeck that, by the time of the New Testament theologies, this original stratum of Christian factical life had already been covered over and that "Christian theology" already represented a compromising of primitive Christian experience.[2] After all, Overbeck argued, the first Christians believed that the end of time was at hand and so they hardly thought it would be necessary, or that they would even have the time, to draw up a "theology." By the time Christian theologies began to coalesce at the end of the first century, when the texts which make up the New Testament were being assembled, the Christians were already beginning to make their peace with the "wisdom of this world," which means with Greek philosophy. The advent of theology meant they were unpacking their bags and beginning to prepare for a longer stay on earth than they originally envisaged.

So Heidegger's first project, in his 1920–1 winter semester lectures, was to return to the very *earliest* Christian documents, to Paul's two letters to the Thessalonians, in order to sketch the structure of a *radically Christian* experience, one that was uncorrupted and unspoiled by Greek philosophy. This he located in an experience of the *kairos*, an experience of time as the coming of something which is, in the language of *Being and Time*, "certain but indefinite," in which we are called upon not to count the days but to transform ourselves and be ready. He thus set out to explore a radical Christian "dawn" (*eine Frühe*) before it had vanished in the harsh light of Greek philosophical theology. The idea was not to *replace* philosophy with radical Christian faith but to *renew* philosophy by means of the shock of a whole new conceptuality that would get philosophy off dead center, by which he meant the inherited system of concepts and the tired debates of an exhausted history that characterized the academic setting of philosophy then (and now). The lectures on Paul were followed by a lecture course given in the next semester (Summer, 1921) entitled "Augustine and Neoplatonism," on the tenth book of the *Confessions* in which Heidegger identified a tension between the overlay of Greek metaphysics and Christian "factical experience" in Augustine's theology.[3]

In the later writings, after the National Socialist years, the hermeneutics of facticity is entirely displaced by what Heidegger called "essential thinking" (*wesentliches Denken*), or the thought of being (*Seinsdenken*). Here fact gives way to essence, the hermeneutics of the happening or coming to pass of concrete, factical life now steps aside in favor of the thought of the essencing or presencing (*Wesen* taken verbally) of being's coming to pass, of being's world-historicizing or epochal happening. In a parallel but inverse gesture to his study of the earliest texts of the *Christian* tradition, texts that were the least contaminated by Greek philosophy, Heidegger now ruminates on the earliest texts of *Greek* thinking before philosophy, texts that were uncorrupted and uncontaminated by Christianity. Now he searches for a radical Greek dawn, another *Frühe*, or beginning (*Anfang*) before it vanished under the harsh light of metaphysics and Christianity. Indeed, these later writings on being's shining glow and beauty, *die Schönheit des Seins*, look a great deal like the *theologia gloriae* to which the *theologia crucis* was mortally opposed in Luther.

The parallel structure of these projects which define the early and later Heidegger is unmistakable: (1) a common love or privileging of the early: either of a Christian dawn before it is corrupted by Greek philosophical theology (which is what is called in theology a project of "de-Hellenizing theology") or of a Greco-western dawn before it is corrupted by Christianity; (2) a common situating of the thinker as a *Spätlinger*, a latecomer always come too late: either as one who has missed the apostolic age, the first coming of Jesus, or as one who missed the first beginning of early Greek thinking; and (3) a common task of thought: to track down the almost vanished traces of the first dawn as a way to meditate on either the second coming ("Come, Lord Jesus"), or the "other beginning," the coming of a god to save us, the sending of Being to come, *zu kommen*, as the *Zukunft des Gewesens*.

The theological sources, analogy or presuppositions of *Being and Time* are unmistakable, but in the present study I want to explore the way in which Heidegger's later writings and readings of Greek philosophy continued to be inhabited or haunted by this theological analogy, continued to be guided by crucial theological presuppositions, but this time behind Heidegger's back, and not, as in the early writings, as an explicit program. The argument of *Being and Time* is derived in an important way from the commentaries on Paul and Augustine and was structured around a line that ran from Paul to Augustine to Luther to Kierkegaard. *Being and Time* turns on the intensely existential motif of the call to personal conversion, the call of Dasein to Dasein to become Dasein. The later writings retain the centrality of the call, but this time, taken as the call of being to come back to being. Now the task is to lend our ear to the stirring of being's – or the god's – sending and withdrawing. The task of thought is to answer and respond to being's address, to hear the call and be responsive and responsible, to let being be, to let it come to words in language. This language is not our own but being's own *Sprache*, even as history is not precisely human history, but being's own history, for being would be our own even as we would be being's own people.

Now the point I wish to press is that the discourse of call, address, and response in Heidegger's later writings, the discourse of hearing and responsibility, is structured like and in fact draws upon the discourse of biblical religion, despite the sharp distinction that Heidegger wants to enforce between thinking and faith. This discourse is borrowed from the biblical tradition of a salvation history, from the religions of the Book, which are set in motion by the Shema, the sacred command or call – "Hear, O Israel, the Lord Thy God is One" (Deut. 6:4) – a command that defines and identifies a sacred people: one God, one people, one place. Heidegger uses the structure of this call-and-response to frame his reading of the texts of Greek philosophers who have not the slightest idea of a history of salvation. In contrast to almost anyone else who has studied what Heidegger refuses to call the "presocratics" or Plato and Aristotle, Heidegger reads these texts *not* as discourses *about* (*peri*) *physis, logos* or *aletheia*, not as investigations of a subject matter, works of theory and thematization, of *episteme* or *Wissenschaft*, but as texts that *call* to us, that call upon us and ask for our response, that constitute "us" westerners as being's own, as being's people, people who "belong" (*gehören*) to being, who are "en-owned" (*er-eignet*) by being as being's own. That means that for Heidegger these texts constitute us not simply as readers or students but as actors in their drama, as followers of their invocation, assigned a vocation, constituted as a people of being – one call, one people, one place – as responsible for and to being, as players in being's own game.

In short, Heidegger does not read these texts scientifically or philosophically but religiously, on an analogy which tends to become a literal truth with *sacred* texts, as texts in which our very destiny is at stake. He treats our recalling of them not as a reproduction of the past but as something more like a religious devotion, an *Andenken*, by which we keep them in our heart (*Gedanc*), which enters us into the *Heilsgeschichte* that they themselves inaugurate. He does not read them as texts that offer us a theory or an interpretation of a subject matter, the way Euclid offers us mathematical theorems, but as texts that demand our self-transformation, texts constituting not assertions but commands, imperatives, calls, claims, solicitations. So while Heidegger does everything he can to put a distance between his meditations on early Greek thinking and Christian or biblical faith, while he insists that the rigor of thought is to abide strictly in the element of being,[4] as far removed from biblical faith as possible, the overarching framework and guiding presupposition of his reading of the Greeks is a religious and specifically a biblical one. These antique texts inaugurate a sacred history by being addressed to us and laying claim to us, and we are the people who we are, a new people, being's people, the people constituted by these texts, only by hearing and heeding their call.

This means that Heidegger continues to do in the later writings what he set out to do in the early ones, to think in dialogue with scriptural experience, but with this difference. What was an explicitly formulated program in the early writings goes on behind his back in the later writings. Heidegger has constructed a rival narrative of being – structurally analogous in all of its main points to the biblical model, that is to the narratives of the Jews and their God in the Tanach, but in Heidegger's narrative the Jews are *totally silenced*, one might even say *repressed.* The Jews, the Judeo-Christian tradition generally, indeed virtually *everybody* except a short list of Greco-Germans, figure not at all in this rival sacred history, this narrative of the history of being, except as distortions of the early Greek dawn. The Jews do not speak words of being, and being does not speak Hebrew. The two are separated by an abyss. But, as Marlène Zarader argues,[5] that is only half the truth, for the fact of the matter is that when Heidegger makes the leap of thought, beyond faith, on the one hand, and calculative thinking, on the other hand, when the words of being are laid out for us by Heidegger, when the primordial sense of *logos* is meditated for us, the whole thing takes on a suspiciously Jewish ring. The repressed returns. The biblical narrative of a history inaugurated by a call to a people who are called upon to respond to and ever recall that inaugural call is reconstituted, transcribed this time from Hebrew into Greco-German, even though Heidegger assured us that "thinking" and the Bible are worlds removed from each other. The Jews constitute what Zarader calls Heidegger's "unthought debt," providing the fundamental terms or presuppositions for his reading of the Greeks even while being systematically silenced by that reading. The Jews, the biblical narratives, belong to *das im Sagen Ungesagte*, what is unsaid and unthought in what Heidegger himself says.

PEOPLE OF GOD

Heidegger's *Heilsgeschichte*, his rival history of salvation, was cast in terms not of God but of being or *Ereignis*, not in terms of the holiness of *hagios*, of moral purity, but of a more poetic *Heilige.* He called his sacred history the *Seinsgeschichte*, the history of being. Like its biblical exemplar, this is a history of calling and answering, which turns on a rival originary call, "Hear O Israel," which he called the originary call or claim of being (*Seinsanspruch*). As with its biblical counterpart, hearing had the sense of heeding, of remaining loyal to a call that claimed our loyalty, keeping it in our hearts. The call was issued in a rival sacred language, not Hebrew but Greek, which left behind its sacred texts whose depths can be endlessly plumbed. The call was addressed to a rival chosen people, not the Jews but the Greeks and their spiritual heirs, the Germans, in a rival new Jerusalem, not Israel but the Third Reich, with a rival prophet, not Hosea but – if truth be told and with all due modesty! – Heidegger. One call, one people, one place. It even has its rival chief priests and faithful, who regularly rend their garments whenever Heidegger's worst side is put on display for all the world to see. Heidegger was pitting a rival *Seinsvolk*, being's people, against the *Gottesvolk*, the people of God.[6] The Germans were being's elect, the people summoned by being, the *Volk* and the *Sprache* which was alone fitted to respond to being's call from the Origin. They alone were uniquely chosen to answer, to say *hineni*, *me voici*, when Being called, but this time everything was *auf Deutsch.* That is why, as deeply as their work is opposed, there are important *structural* similarities between Heidegger and Levinas, for both of whom everything turns on a discourse organized around call and response.

The distinctive Greek thematic of *a-letheia*, of concealment and un-concealment that Heidegger so brilliantly articulated, is complicated by and interwoven with another and distinctively Hebrew component of calling and responding that he has grafted on to his reading of the texts of the Greeks, thus complicating the more visual or ocular thematics with an aural and auditory motif. All the while that he is thinking and thanking, singing and poetizing being's sendings and withdrawals from its chosen *Sprache* and people, Heidegger is relentlessly, perhaps unconsciously, reproducing – repeating with a difference – a rival to the story of the people of God, who thus far, not in their own right and not in their own name, continually speak in his work in the mode of the unthought and the unsaid. Zarader argues that, under Heidegger's hand, the Hebraic component in western culture has been suppressed and excluded, not by a simple omission or oversight, but by a gesture arising from the deep logic of his thought. This "oblivion" or denial of the Hebraic in Heidegger, she argues, is accompanied by a curious, paradoxical "memory" or "repetition" of the Hebraic, but not under the proper name of the Hebraic. In short, the Hebraic *re*surfaces in Heidegger's work, despite the interdiction, "*en contrabande*,"[7] as contraband, "bootlegged" we would say in American English.

It is well known that Heidegger's thought turns on a logic of "derivative and original," a schema that is employed from the first Freiburg lectures to the very latest essays and seminars, constituting one of his most fundamental presuppositions. Heidegger's usual procedure is to begin with a familiar, traditional and hence (for him) derivative sense – of thought or language, to take two most important examples – and to proceed from there to the "originary" or founding sense of these structures which, he claims, has been covered over by the "history of metaphysics," an expression that he tends to use interchangeably with the West or western history. The derivative sense is always "metaphysical," but as derivative it bears within itself the traces of the more originary experience, in the "early Greek dawn," now long forgotten and unthought, from which it falls/derives. Indeed, there is some reason to think that in his *last* writings Heidegger explores a radical suggestion, that the originary is *nowhere* to be found in any historical document, *not even in the early Greek dawn*, where the originary has at best left its trace, but has instead some sort of ante-historical status. But then how does Heidegger, or indeed how would anyone *know* what this originary sense is? At that very critical point Heidegger forgets the Greeks and turns for help to the meaning of old high German words.

As Zarader rightly argues, the primordial or ante-historical sense of thinking and language has not fallen from the sky, is not really some sort of ante- or supra-historical sense at all, but one with a well-known historical name and geographical location, viz., the biblical and more broadly Hebraic tradition. The contributions of this tradition are well known to cultural historians, to everyone, it seems, except Heidegger who has taken it into his head to erase every trace of the Hebraic. The ugly truth is – although Zarader herself tends to steer clear of this sort of polemic – that Heidegger is of a mind to make the West *Judenrein*, which is to reproduce on the level of "thinking" what the Nazis were doing in the streets.

Let us, following Zarader,[8] look more closely at these two crucial examples: language and thought. (1) *Language*: in the "traditional" and hence "derivative" sense, language is taken to be formed by propositions whose function is to express thought on the one hand and intend or represent reality on the other. In its more "originary" sense, which we are supposed to learn by meditating on the originary sense of the Greek word *logos*, to hear it *griechisch*, Heidegger claims that language means a saying (*Sage, Spruch*), address or call (*Anspruch*) that comes to and over us from beyond us and lays claim to us. This saying does not signify or represent things but brings them into appearance for us. Our human speaking is a responding and corresponding, an answer and response (*Antwort*) to this prior and more primordial address. In fact, that originary essence – and let us, for the sake of argument, agree this is a more originary essence and not merely a *different* sense, a different language game, as Lyotard or Rorty would think – is, as Zarader shows, borrowed directly from the Hebrew scriptures. In the Tanach, language is not an instrument of representation but something in which existing things are held or contained. The Hebrew "*Davar*" means both word and thing, Hebrew words tolerating a surprising multivocity. The world is what God has said, the saying that God has said. The word accompanies all coming into being. Furthermore, in the Bible, the word is not principally a word "about," a thematizing and objectifying discourse, but a word "from," an address to an interlocutor, which is why the Shema is the central saying in the Tanach. That is what the Covenant and Revelation testify to above all. The language of revelation is not an "expression" of what God is thinking but the very encounter with God, of the mouth which offers and the ear which hears. As Zarader points out, if God simply wished to "show himself," phenomenologically, he could have done so in a hurricane or fire, but that is paganism. Instead of showing himself, God *speaks* which demands a hearing and a response. Revelation, as the word *of* God is at the same time a word *to* humankind. Language is experienced as a call and hearing, a call which lays claim to us. If a person would write, she or he must learn to incline or lean over, to incline one's ear, listen and keep silent, make ready and prepare a welcome. That is the very structure of prophetic speech.[9] Now it is perfectly true, as Levinas objects, that Heidegger has emptied this structure of its ethical content – Yahweh and the prophets were, after all, concerned with justice – but the formal structure of the two senses of language in Heidegger and the biblical tradition is the same; for both, language is a mode of openness to an "other," a radical heteronomy.

(2) *Thinking*: in the traditional sense thinking refers to some sort of adequational or representational relationship of the mind to reality. Rejecting this as derivative and superficial, Heidegger goes back to the Greeks and ponders over a certain number of key words, offering us a reflection upon them that is both familiar and strange: it is strange to philosophy but very familiar to the biblical mind. Heidegger thinks about thinking by casting it in the discourse of memory and fidelity

(*Gedank*), grace and recognition (*Danken, Gunst, Gabe*), which, Zarader argues, summons up the "essential dimensions" of the biblical world.[10] Heidegger installs himself in the space of notions that are traced out for him in advance in the Bible, but then he applies them where they were *not* applied in the Bible, viz., to the question of "thinking" (*Denken*). The "non-metaphysical" determination of thinking is taken from a biblical history organized around the "Hear, O Israel," the call which calls Israel to be faithful to the covenant, so that the very being of Israel is to be called, to be faithful, not to forget, to re-call the call by which it is constituted, to keep this call in its heart. As Derrida points out,[11] the attitude of *Zusage*, abandoning oneself to what gives itself in the promise, even precedes questioning itself, which Heidegger had earlier taken to be the privileged mark of thinking, so that thinking is ultimately not determined as questioning but as the hearing of that which is "accorded" to us, entrusted to our heart. In the Bible, humankind is defined by hearing, as opposed to the Greek paradigm of the being who by nature loves to see. That means that thinking in the biblical sense means receiving or welcoming, "conceiving" not as grasping but as being impregnated. *Ya'da* can also describe sexual intimacy: that is because the Jews regard both love and knowledge as fidelity, fidelity to that which *gives*. Thus the knowledge of God is not a cognitive grasping but a receptive sympathy. Because God reveals himself in history, he needs to be "remembered." Remember, *zakor*, appears 169 times in the Tanach. But at this crucial point in his work, Heidegger does not meditate on the Greek *mnemosyne*, which is turned to the past, but the German *Gedanc* as a gathering of the whole mind and heart to that which lays claim to it. In the Bible, the call to remember has to do not with reconstituting the past but with transforming ourselves now, in the present, and with making ourselves new in the future. The whole of wisdom lies in recognizing that everything has been received. So "thinking" does not exist as a separate category in the Bible but is situated within the call and the promise. One can at least find the "site" for thought in the Bible. It belongs within language, as a listening to language, which is why the Book produces such an extensive exegetical tradition. The tracc of the Other who withdraws is found only in the text.

HEIDEGGER'S SMALL WORLD

Under Heidegger's hand, religion undergoes a *double reduction*: it is first of all reduced to Christianity, to the Greek New Testament, and then Christianity itself is reduced to and identified with "faith." Faith, like science, does not "think," which it does not want or need to do, because it is exclusively preoccupied with imitating the crucified Christ, while thinking is something thoroughly Greek and akin to poetizing, but quite otherwise than faith. When faith does think, the result is "ontotheologic," which distorts thinking. So, if one is willing to live in Heidegger's small world and to abide by Heidegger's rules, then, if one wants to "think," one must (1) "overcome" ontotheological thinking and (2) "suspend" faith, put it out of play. One can thereby be admitted (*eingelassen*) to the sphere of thought, enabled to make the leap into poetic and meditative thinking, which is quite otherwise than faith or calculation. The spheres are rigorously separated and do not over overlap or communicate: if one wants to "think," one must both renounce calculation and purge or purify thinking of biblical religion, suspend ratiocinating and make a phenomenological epoché of the scriptures, where nobody is thinking. Then one should try to be as Greek as possible, try indeed, if one could even imagine such a thing, to be more Greek than the Greeks, try to reach over and leap beyond the Greeks to something proto-Greek.

The irony is, when Heidegger executes this leap he seems to land, alas (for him), back in the holy land, back on Hebrew soil, maybe somewhere on the West Bank, reproducing the dynamics of the Shema, of calling and responding, around which the Jewish history of salvation is structured. Thus, this *ursprüngliches Denken*, this originary hitherto-unthought-and-long-forgotten "essence of thinking" (*Wesen des Denkens*), turns out to have a familiar ring to anyone outside this little world, to anyone who reads something other than philosophy, especially something other than Heidegger's philosophy. There is a deeply *poetic thinking* at play in the narratives of the Hebrew scriptures – their poetry is thoughtful and their thinking is poetic – that does not reduce either to *calculative rationality* or to *faith.*

Heidegger's reduction of religion to faith is a peculiarly *Protestant* presupposition on his part. For the Jews, as Johannes Climacus pointed out, lacking the idea of the Absurd, the God-Man, were not called upon either to appease their intelligence by inventing onto-theo-logic, which answers the question *cur deus homo?* (Catholicism), or to crucify their intelligence in a leap of faith in a God-made-man (Protestantism). Their major idea was of a transcendent and holy God who expected us to behave ourselves on ten explicitly stated and, by now, well-known points. Now, as Johannes Climacus points out, all this makes a certain amount of *sense*, which is unfortunate for *faith.* What the Jews believe does not demand of us that most intensive passion of subjective truth required by the belief that the Almighty and Eternal Creator of Heaven and Earth, the Most High, the Ancient of Days, was a carpenter from Nazareth who got himself crucified in a remote corner of the Roman empire. The best the Jews could do in the way of faith was Abraham, whom Johannes de Silentio says lives in the suburbs, residing on the "outskirts" of faith (like Job). Even at that, Abraham's story is told by Johannes Climacus from Paul's point of view as a story about faith, whereas many rabbis thought it was a story about the end of human sacrifice. What Heidegger knew about the scriptures was this faith-centered line that went from Paul through Augustine to Luther and Kierkegaard. He knew next to nothing in a direct way about the Hebrew scriptures. Now if Hegel took the notion of "Hebrew poetry" to be a *contradictio in adjecto*, the Jews being too wooden and alienated from the sensuous to be capable of anything like poetry, the idea of Hebrew poetry never so much as crosses Heidegger's mind. He did not read Hebrew, and when he studied theology, he confined himself to the Greek New Testament, and the indications are that, as a purely personal matter, he did not like Jews a great deal, and when he thought of poetry, he thought of Hölderlin.

In the small world in which Heidegger traveled, one is either a calculating technocrat (probably an American) who is out to blacktop the Black Forest, or a (Christian) believer blindly imitating the crucified Christ in a mad leap of faith; in neither case does one "think." Or else one does "think," which means thinks poetically, *dichtendes Denken*, and that is exclusively and primordially a matter for early Greeks and Hölderlinian Germans. At the very least, if thinking is also permitted to French or Americans or Russians, they must switch to German to do so, as indeed it seems must the Most High Himself, the Ancient of Days, if He too would like to think Himself, as Aristotle thought he did all the time. It never entered Heidegger's Greco-German head that in the Hebrew Bible we encounter something that is neither calculative rationality (onto-theo-logic) nor simply faith, but *poetry*, by which I mean *Dichtung*, very great poetry not just verse, not Ogden Nash, but indeed a certain *poetic thinking*. It was, however, a poem to justice, hospitality, to the widow and the orphan, not to being's shining glow, which is part of the reason Heidegger did not notice it. Nor – and this is ironic and still more interesting – did it ever enter his Greco-German head that the line he was selling is *found already* in the Hebrew narrative of the history of salvation, and specifically in the discourse they devised of the need for the people of God to be loyal to and welcome a claim that lays claim to them and constitutes them as a people. It never entered his Greco-German head that the Hebrews have a narrative they tell and retell in ancient texts and ancient rituals in order to remember, to think upon this narrative and keep it safe in their heart, in order to recall the call that called them into being as the people that they are called to be. It never hit him that the line he was trying to sell us about "our" relation to the "early Greeks" – did he include Jews in this "our"? – was already laid out in advance in the stories in the Tanach, the "formal indication" of which supplies him with the basic structure of what he calls thinking and *Seinsgeschichte*.

So the irony is that when the later Heidegger rows his way back up the great Greco-German river Ister, making his way all the way back to its *Ursprung*, what he finds (without knowing it) is a slightly Jewish *Urquell*! What is repressed, returns, readmitted *en contrebande*, as smuggled goods, bootlegged into Heidegger's *Seinsgeschichte*. The whole history of *das Heilige*, including the very idea that it is a *history*, all sound a little Jewish to anyone whose travels carry them beyond the tiny triangle traced by Freiburg, Todtnauberg, and Messkirch. The structure of a history of salvation borrowed from the Hebrew and Christian scriptures, and utterly unknown to the Greeks, became the overarching framework for his reading of Greek texts. The meditation on thinking and language in terms of welcoming a call and keeping it in our hearts, that Heidegger told us he found by ruminating upon Parmenides and Heraclitus, clearly reproduces the "essential dimensions" of the Hebrew world.

Heidegger continued to do in his later writings what he was doing in his early work, viz., draw upon the prephilosophical resources of the scriptures and to make use of the formal indications they provide, but the difference is that in the early writings this is a stated program, while in the later writings it happens behind Heidegger's back. The early Heidegger thought that the New Testament (he might have added the Tanach to his list) was rich with ideas that the mainstream philosophical tradition either ignored or were ignorant of, ideas which, if injected into the deliberations of philosophy, would renew and reinvigorate philosophy and get it off dead center. Something was needed, the young philosopher thought, to break the logjam of moribund philosophical debates between realism and idealism, or psychologism and logicism, or any of the other well-worn paths trod by tired neokantian feet. From Heidegger's point of view, these sterile academic debates – and this is a point he shared with the young Jaspers, the two of them together plotting an academic revolution – amounted to little more than rearranging the furniture on the deck of a sinking ship. Heidegger rightly thought there was something to be learned from these non-philosophical texts, something from which these weary academic philosophers stood to profit.

He could not have been more right about that. What he came up with when he went back to Paul's *Letters to the Thessalonians* and to the tenth Book of the *Confessions* – with a little help from Luther, Kierkegaard, and Franz Overbeck – was nothing short of revolutionary conception of time, thought in terms of *kairos* rather than the steady beat of Aristotelian now-time whose phenomenological chronology Husserl had spelled out, and the revolutionary conception of human "existence" as "being-in-the-world" and "care," rather than the familiar philosophical figure of a disinterested *Anschauer* looking on at chunks of *Vorhandensein*, that had dominated the imaginations of philosophers from Plato to Husserl. What he came up with was indeed revolutionary and it jolted philosophy off its neo-Kantian moorings. It got things going in a new and interesting way. True to his intentions, in *Being and Time* he has given twentieth-century philosophy, which now draws to a close, a great boost and has given weary academics something new to argue about at their endless conferences and in their unreadable journals.

The reason Heidegger was able to do what he did in the 1920s is that he did not then think in terms of what he later called the "rigor of thought" (*die Strenge des Denkens*), which rigorously restrained itself to remain in the purity of what he called the "element of thought," that is, which *enforced the deep divide* among separate regions called "thinking," "calculating," and "faith." Rather, he employed a "genealogical" schema borrowed from phenomenology which distinguished between the *conceptual* and the *preconceptual*, the founded and the founding, and the whole idea was to *establish communication* between the two domains. The phenomenological–genealogical idea was to lead back (*reducere*) the system of philosophical concepts currently in place – the tired, inherited, sedimented ideas of the philosophers, which flattened things out into *Anschauung* and *Vorhandensein* – to their *preconceptual or pre-philosophical sources*, the wellspring from which all concepts are originally drawn, of which the experience of *kairos* in the New Testament was a salient example. His idea was not to enforce a divide between them but to establish a genealogical communication between them such that by returning to the wellspring one would *renew the conceptual system* of which it was the source. In the early writings "religious life" (the New Testament) means an important preconceptual source of conceptual renewal; in the later writings "religion" (still the New Testament) meant thought-less faith, a region separated by an abyss from thought.

If in the later writings he lost his grip on the idea that the New Testament could feed "thinking" with any new lines, that was because of the war he waged on Christianity during his National Socialist years. It should never be forgotten that the privileging of the Greeks and the antagonism to Christianity is an innovation of the National Socialist period and a perfidious nationalism. Neither can be found in *Being and Time.* In the 1930s it is perfectly clear that "Greek" is a code for "German," that Greek is what gives the German – language and people – its spiritual authority and the spiritual right to wage war on the rest of Europe.

Far be it from me to deny that the later writings are also truly interesting – I have written two books trying to document what is so interesting about them – or that they have many lovely things to say about language and poetry, the thinging of the thing and *Gelassenheit,* by which I myself have been much nourished. But they would be a much greater joy to read if they were stripped of their absurd fetishizing of the early Greeks (who were certainly the West's proto-scientists, effecting the transition from mythic and oracular thinking to scientific thinking). Everyone except the most fanatical Heideggerian acolytes understands that this fetish is a thinly disguised nationalism, that it amounts to little more than a jingoistic celebration of Heidegger's small world, the tiny triangle traced by Freiburg, Todtnauberg, and Messkirch, within which Heidegger passed his days. Heidegger's little golden triangle was populated only by Greek thinkers and German farmers without electricity or typewriters. The Greeks however were dead, and no English Members of Parliament or American scientists, no Irish or French poets, no African, Asians or South Americans, and no Jews, above all, no Jews, are anywhere to be found there.

Except *en contrebande.*

CONCLUSION: DEMYTHOLOGIZING HEIDEGGER

I remain as convinced today as I was ten years ago when I made an argument – in my *third* book about Heidegger (talk about the repressed returning!) – about the need to "demythologize" Heidegger. Given that, on Heidegger's telling, what comes to words in the language of the early Greeks renders the Hebrew language silent, indeed every modern language except German, we would do well to restore the complexity of the West. We would do well to reestablish open lines of communication between philosophy and the religious, something which Heidegger early on set out to do and continued to do later on without knowing it or acknowledging it. What is perhaps most ominous about Heidegger's repression of the biblical provenance of his thought, is that he has stripped this call of its character as a call for *hospitality* and *justice.* Heidegger's mono-Greco-genealogy is mono-manically preoccupied with a discourse on clearing and unconcealment, manifestation and shining beauty. It is a call to let things flicker in the play of concealment and unconcealment. It is a philosophy of *Sein, Scheinen,* and *Schönheit,* of the shining glow of *Sein,* what I called in *Demythologizing Heidegger* a "phainaesthetics." It leaves no room for an unrepresentable ethical idea which commands our respect and bows our head in humility before the holiness (*hagios*) of its demand that we serve the neighbor, upon whose face is inscribed the trace of God. Heidegger's alethiology leaves no room for a hagiology.

We need to break with the deeply hierarchical logic of original and derivative, with the myth of the originary language, the originary people, the original land, by means of which Heidegger reproduces the myth of God's chosen people, of God's promised land, which is no less a problem for religion and the root of its violence. We need to break the logic that allows the myth to flourish that certain human beings speak the language that being or God would speak, had they vocal chords and lungs and writing instruments, the murderous twin myths of the people of God and of the people of being, myths which license murder in the name of God or in the name of the question of being.

We need to let justice flow like water over the land.

NOTES

1 See John D. Caputo, *Demythologizing Heidegger*, Indiana Series in the Philosophy of Religion (Bloomington: Indiana University Press, 1993); *Radical Hermeneutics: Repetition, Deconstruction and the Hermeneutic Project*, Studies in Phenomenology and Existential Philosophy (Bloomington: Indiana University Press, 1987); *Heidegger and Aquinas: An Essay On Overcoming Metaphysics* (New York: Fordham University Press, 1982); *The Mystical Element in Heidegger's Thought* (Athens: Ohio University Press, 1978; revised, paperback edition with a new "Introduction," New York: Fordham University Press, 1986).

2 Franz Overbeck, *Über die Christlichkeit unserer heutigen Theologie* (Leipzig, 1903; photographically reproduced: Darmstadt: Wissenschaftliche Buchgesel-

lschaft, 1989). For a comment by Heidegger on Overbeck, see "Phenomenology and Theology," trans. James G. Hart and John C. Maraldo, in Martin Heidegger, *Pathmarks*, ed. William McNeill (Cambridge: Cambridge University Press, 1998), pp. 39–40; for a commentary on Heidegger and Overbeck, see Istvan Feher, "Heidegger's Understanding of the Atheism of Philosophy," *American Catholic Philosophical Quarterly* 69 (1995), 202–6.

3 See Martin Heidegger, *Phänomenologie des religiösen Lebens*, ed. Claudius Strube, *Gesamtausgabe*, vol. 60 (Frankfurt a.M.: Klostermann, 1995).

4 Heidegger, *Pathmarks*, ed. Mcneill, p. 271.

5 *La dette impensée: Heidegger et l'héritage hébraïque* (Paris: Editions du Seuil, 1990). For a good discussion of Heidegger's "omission" of the biblical source, see Robert Bernasconi, "On Heidegger's Other Sins of Omission," *American Catholic Philosophical Quarterly* 69 (1995), 333–50.

6 For a good critique of Heidegger's use of the concept of *Volk*, see Berel Lang, *Heidegger's Silence* (Ithaca: Cornell University Press, 1996).

7 Zarader, *La dette impensée*, p. 213.

8 In the following analyses of language and thought, I am summarizing Zarader, *La dette impensée*, pp. 50–100.

9 In *Erläuterungen zu Hölderlins Dichtung*, ed. F.-W. von Herrmann, *Gesamtausgabe*, vol. 4 (Frankfurt a.M.: Klostermann, 1981), p. 114 Heidegger says the Greek poets are "prophetic" not in the Judeo-Christian sense of a seer or a divine but in the sense of opening up a world. See Derrida, "Faith and Knowledge," in *Religion*, ed. Jacques Derrida and Gianni Vattimo (Stanford: Stanford University Press, 1998), pp. 67–8, n9. The biblical idea of a prophet, exemplified in our own times in the "prophetic voice" of Martin Luther King, implies a ringing call to make justice flow like water over the land, not, as Heidegger claims, predicting the future. Heidegger has adapted the structure of the Jewish prophet, denuded it of its ethical content, and grafted it upon Greek "physiologists."

10 Zarader, *La dette impensée*, p. 85.

11 Jacques Derrida, *Of Spirit*, trans. G. Bennington and R. Bowlby (Chicago: University of Chicago Press, 1989), pp. 129–31 n5.

CHAPTER 7

Heidegger for beginners

Simon Critchley

It's not always easy being Heideggerian

Deleuze and Guattari, *What Is Philosophy?*

I have two questions in this essay. Where should one begin with Heidegger? And why should one begin philosophizing with Heidegger rather than elsewhere? I will turn to the second of these questions in detail presently, but let me begin by giving the most formal of indications as to how I answer the first question.[1]

The beginning of Heidegger's philosophy is phenomenological. That is, Heidegger's thought begins as a radicalization of Husserlian phenomenological method. To make good on this claim, I give a reading of the Preliminary Part of Heidegger's important 1925 lecture course, *Prolegomena zur Geschichte des Zeitbegriffs*, a text that I see as the buried phenomenological preface to *Sein und Zeit*.[2] Rejoining Heidegger's magnum opus to its phenomenological preface permits one, in my view, to clarify the philosophical presuppositions that are required in order for *Sein und Zeit* to begin. That is, in order for the question of the meaning or truth of being to be raised as a matter of compelling philosophical interest, and not as some magical and numinous vapour.

My basic premise, to echo one of Heidegger's reported remarks from the 1962 *Protokoll* to the seminar on *Zeit und Sein*, is that "In der Tat, wäre ohne die phänomenologische Grundhaltung die Seinsfrage nicht möglich gewesen" (Actually, without the basic phenomenological attitude, the question of being would not have been possible).[3] If this is true, then it means that the interpretation of the *Prolegomena* assumes great importance, for it is there that Heidegger's radicalization of phenomenology is *systematically* presented as part of a critical confrontation with Husserl and not gnomically intimated, as the novice to *Sein und Zeit* often feels in reading the crucial methodological paragraph 7 for the first time.

The reading of Husserl is dominated by a double gesture which permits Heidegger both to inherit a certain understanding of Husserl, whilst at the same time committing an act of critical parricide against him, what von Herrmann sees as the ambiguity of speaking against Husserl in Husserlian language.[4] Let me quickly sketch the first moment of this double gesture. For Heidegger, there are three essential discoveries of Husserlian phenomenology: intentionality, categorial intuition, and the original sense of the *a priori*. These discoveries are linked together in what we might call a "nesting effect," where intentionality finds what Heidegger calls its "concretion" in categorial intuition, whose concretion is the *a priori*, which provides, in turn, the basis for a new definition of the preliminary concept (*Vor-Begriff*) of phenomenology itself, a definition that is only accidentally modified in paragraph 7 of *Sein und Zeit*. I believe that this definition of phenomenology remains at least formally determinative for the rest of Heidegger's philosophical itinerary.

To put this into a schema: *intentionality* + *categorial intuition* + *the a priori* = *the preliminary concept of phenomenology*. It should be noted that the condition of possibility for Heidegger's concept of phenomenology is a certain understanding of the intentionality thesis. That is, for Heidegger – like Husserl – intentionality is the essential structure of mental experience, insofar as it has the character of "directing itself towards" (*Sich-richten-auf*) objects, things or matters. However – unlike Husserl – the fundamental quality of intentionality is not located in the contemplative immanence of consciousness, but is rather *Da*, it is had there, outside, alongside things and not divorced from them in some mental capsule full of representations (*SZ* 62). Heidegger's handling of the intentionality thesis therefore permits him to make the passage from *Bewußtsein* to *Dasein*, from theoretical consciousness to practical being-there, in a reading of Husserl which, beneath the apparent generosity, ultimately works against the latter's intentions. That is, under the surface of the exposition in the *Prolegomena*, Heidegger has already insinuated an anti-Husserlian, pretheoretical model of intentionality, what one might call a *phronetic* intentionality.[5] However, although intentionality is the essential structure of mental experience, it is not the original or *a priori* structure, which is given in the analysis of categorial intuition. That is, the doctrine of categorial intuition provides Heidegger with a method that allows the philosopher to pick out the *a priori* features of intentional experience, what Kant in the transcendental analytic saw as the deduction of the categories. In *Sein und Zeit*, however, insofar as they are predicated of a practically embedded being defined by a "who" rather than decontextualized consciousness defined by a "what," these *a priori* features of intentionality are not called categories but "existentials" (*SZ* 44–5). The phenomenologist is meant to describe these "existentials." This is why Heidegger can, with complete consistency, define phenomenology in the *Prolegomena* as the "analytic description of intentionality in its *a priori*" (*PGZ* 108/*HCT* 79).

As we all know, Heidegger's thinking is preoccupied – and perhaps a little too preoccupied, but that is another story for a separate occasion – with the *Seinsfrage*, the question of being. Now, for Heidegger, phenomenology opens a space where the question of being can be raised, releasing being from the subjectivistic determination to which it had been submitted in philosophical modernity, most obviously in Descartes, but more closely in the neo-Kantianism of Heidegger's peers and superiors in Marburg. Heidegger's leading, but hardly self-evident, philosophical claim is that being is an aspect of phenomenological seeing, in some sense a matter for phenomenological intuition.[6] We might say that being is the "seeing" of what is seen, or the "appearing" of what appears, although this should not be misunderstood as announcing some sort of metaphysical dualism (Heidegger's philosophical instincts are always holistic). Thus, for Heidegger, against the modern philosophical self-understanding, phenomenology grants to being a new sense of *non-* or, better, *trans*-subjective givenness. As Klaus Held insightfully remarks, Husserl's discovery for Heidegger is "die Vorgegebenheit einer transsubjectiven Offenbarkeitsdimension" (the pre-givenness of a trans-subjective dimension of manifestation).[7]

As the work of Jacques Taminiaux has shown in detail, the pregivenness of this trans-subjective dimension of manifestation is the work of categorial intuition.[8] When Heidegger famously remarks at the end of paragraph 7 of *Sein und Zeit* that the latter book only became possible on the ground or basis (*auf dem Boden*) laid down by Husserl, then this *Boden*, this ground or basis, alludes to categorial intuition (*SZ* 38). The central position that Heidegger gives to categorial intuition in the interpretation of Husserl and to Heidegger's self-understanding as a phenomenologist remains unaltered from *Sein und Zeit* to the final seminar in Zähringen in 1973. In my view, Heidegger's contribution to philosophy is his radicalization of the basic idea of phenomenology, a radicalization that paradoxically shows the extent of his debt to Husserl, and, by extension, the radicality of Husserlian phenomenology. As Heidegger points out in 1963, with an explicit look back over his shoulder to the very same lines from paragraph 7 of *Sein und Zeit* that were cited above, phenomenology must not be understood as a movement or school, but as the possibility of thinking as such. That is, phenomenology is the possibility of corresponding to the claim of that which is to be thought (*"dem Anspruch des zu Denkenden zu entsprechen"*).[9] For the early Heidegger, what is to be thought is the meaning of being, and for the later Heidegger, the truth of being.

However (putting the Heideggerese to one side), in order to conceive of the task of thinking as a correspondence between thought and that which is to be thought, what has to be presupposed is the idea of phenomenological correlation that Heidegger finds in Husserl's intentionality thesis and pursues in his analysis of categorial intuition. The difference with Husserl is that the thought of phenomenological correlation is deepened by the claim, ultimately inherited from Dilthey, into the primacy of factical life that requires a corresponding mode of practical or hermeneutic insight.[10] But it is this idea of a phenomenological correlation irreducible to either subjectivism or objectivism that is the basis, in my view, for the early claim that Dasein and World must be viewed as a unitary phenomenon, and for the later claim that *das Ereignis*, the appropriative event, is to be understood as the belonging together of the human being and being (*die Zusammengehörigkeit von Mensch und Sein*). The thought of phenomenological correlation thus bridges "Heidegger 1" and "Heidegger 2" and problematizes the whole idea of the *Kehre*.[11] The unity of Heidegger's work is phenomenological.

However, my claim that the beginning of Heidegger's thought is phenomenological opens itself to the objection, raised by John Sallis and Robert Bernasconi at the Utah Heidegger conference, that such an approach plays down the *destructive* or *deconstructive* side to Heidegger's project.[12] That is, as Heidegger puts it at the end of paragraph 6 of *Sein und Zeit*, "The question of being does not achieve its true concreteness until we have carried through the destruction of the history of ontology" (*SZ* 26). On this understanding, the beginning of Heidegger's philosophy is found in his repetition or retrieval (*Wiederholung*) of the question of being as it was first articulated by the Greeks in the ontology of Plato and Aristotle. This is why the text of *Sein und Zeit* begins on the untitled first page with a quotation from Plato's *Sophist*.

This is an important objection, but let me clarify what I am trying to do in the project of which this essay is a part. I am seeking to analyze and, if possible, justify, the formal-methodological concept of phenomenology at work in Heidegger. Now, such an approach undoubtedly needs to be de-formalized, to use Heidegger's word "*entformalisiert*" (*SZ* 35), through both the specific phenomenological analyses of *Sein und Zeit* and the destruction of the ontological tradition, if the concreteness of which

Heidegger speaks above is to be achieved. Therefore the phenomenological approach I am recommending has to be *complemented* by a destructive or deconstructive approach in terms of Heidegger's engagement with the philosophical tradition. For example, Heidegger's strategy with regard to the three discoveries of phenomenology in the *Prolegomena* is to locate the point where each of these concepts crosses the path of the ancient ontology of Plato and Aristotle. Ultimately, the trans-subjective givenness of being expressed by the doctrine of categorial intuition allows Heidegger to reactivate the Greek determination of being as presencing (*Anwesenheit, ousia*) (*SZ* 26), and hence to reawaken the link between being and time. This is what Taminiaux calls, in a nice formulation, "the Aristotelianization of Husserl."[13] The deformalization of the phenomenological approach is achieved, for Heidegger, by way of a repetition of the Greek beginning of philosophy, what he calls in the *Prolegomena*, the "assumption of the tradition as a genuine repetition" (*PGZ* 187/*HCT* 138). However, my ambition is simply to analyze the formal-methodological tools that permit this deformalizing assumption of tradition. By itself – I would insist – tradition can and should assume no authority in philosophical matters.

In this highly abridged version, this is all I want to say in response to my first question as to where one should begin with Heidegger. I now want to turn, more slowly and in greater detail, to my second question as to why one should begin philosophizing with Heidegger rather than elsewhere. This will take us in a rather different direction.

TRANSFORMING THE NATURAL ATTITUDE

As I said above, Heidegger's reading of Husserl is governed by a double gesture. For the remainder of this essay, I would like to turn to the other side of this double gesture, Heidegger's critique of Husserl's later phenomenology, the tenor of which also remains unchanged in his later work. The general claim here is that if Husserl's notion of categorial intuition is the *Boden* upon which the question of the meaning of being can be raised as a substantive philosophical issue, then after the publication of the *Logical Investigations* in 1900, Husserl failed to pursue the *Seinsfrage* with sufficient radicality. The publication of the first volume of Husserl's *Ideas* in 1913 constitutes, for Heidegger, a philosophical *decision* to sacrifice radicality for traditionality.

This pairing of terms in Heidegger's work of this period should be noted, where what is continually valorized in philosophy (and in much else, it would appear) is an absolute *radicality* whose antonym is *tradition*. Heidegger's work – and this is hardly a neutral matter, particularly when one thinks of the somewhat overdetermined philosophical and political thematics governing the language of the decision (*Entscheidung*) in the Germany of the 1920s – is motivated by a passion for absolute philosophical radicality. As is common in Heidegger, tradition is always understood in terms of the Cartesian legacy of the modern determination of being as subjectivity. Husserl's traditionality is therefore synonymous with his alleged Cartesianism, where the phenomenological field in *Ideas I* is constituted as a realm of pure consciousness, and where the latter is determined as what is called "absolute being," whose investigation is the subject matter of a rigorous science: transcendental phenomenology.

Heidegger takes a rather malicious delight in referring extensively to paragraphs 46–50 of *Ideas I*, where consciousness is determined as indubitable, pure, absolute and immanent being in opposition to the dubitability, relativity, and contingency of reality, and where Husserl famously claims that consciousness would be *modified* (indeed!) by the nullification of the world, but not affected in its own existence.[14] But the core of Heidegger's critique of the later Husserl is that in determining the phenomenological field as that of pure consciousness, he fails to pose the question of what consciousness is; in Heidegger's parlance, the question of "the being of the intentional" (*das Sein des Intentionalen*). As a consequence, Husserl loses sight of the *Seinsfrage*. In other words, in determining pure consciousness as "absolute being," Husserl takes over a conception of consciousness from the tradition without interrogating its meaning.

If this claim is justified – and I am not saying that it is, as Heidegger's reading of Husserl's work after the *Logical Investigations* is extremely myopic – then this explains why Heidegger goes on to claim that the Husserlian notion of consciousness is *unphenomenological* insofar as it is not drawn from the matters themselves, i.e. from the lived experiences of a concrete human being, but is inherited from the tradition, specifically the Cartesian tradition (*PGZ* 147/*HCT* 107).

Now, if this is the fate of Husserlian phenomenology, then the Heideggerian question becomes: how should one begin phenomenology such that philosophizing can maintain itself in absolute radicality? For Heidegger, this means returning to the beginning point of phenomenological reflection in the natural attitude and attempting to give a redescription of how human existence is first given. This is what

Heidegger attempts to do in paragraphs 12 and 13 of the *Prolegomena*, which in many ways are the most intriguing pages of the Preliminary Part of the lecture course, where, despite giving a rather limited and unfair reading of the development of the personalistic attitude in *Ideas II*, he makes some more penetrating remarks on Dilthey's and Scheler's attempts to produce a personalistic psychology.

How is human Dasein given in specifically personal experience? (*PGZ* 162/*HCT* 117) It is with the response to this question that Heidegger begins the existential analytic of Dasein in paragraph 9 of *Sein und Zeit* (*SZ* 41–2). In this sense, the beginning of Heidegger's philosophical project is not only methodologically dependent upon Husserlian phenomenology, but can be seen specifically as a radicalized extension of the phenomenology of the person in Dilthey, Scheler, and the later Husserl. As Heidegger rather gnomically remarks at the beginning of the Main Part of the *Prolegomena*, "There is an *intrinsic material connection* [*innerlicher sachlicher Zusammenhang*] between what we treated in the Introduction (i.e. the Preliminary Part) and what we now take as our theme" (*PGZ* 192/*HCT* 141–2). To put this in terms that Heidegger would doubtless have refused, the First Division of *Sein und Zeit* attempts to transform the natural attitude with which phenomenology begins. Access to the beginning point of Heidegger's existential analytic is achieved by a transformation in our understanding of the natural attitude, what we might call a hermeneutic redescription of this moment of facticity.[15]

Let me pause and try to clarify this important point. Phenomenology begins in the natural attitude, as a description of our pretheoretical immersion in the familiar, everyday, environing world, as the reality of our intentional lives.[16] This leads Heidegger to raise the question: "To what extent is the being of the intentional experienced and determined in the starting position?" (*PGZ* 152/*HCT* 111). That is, is there a moment when the question of the being of intentional is raised by phenomenology if only to be subsequently discarded?

This moment is described by Husserl as the general thesis of the natural attitude. But, how is the natural attitude experienced in Husserlian phenomenology? As Heidegger puts it, "what being is attributed to it?" (*PGZ* 153/*HCT* 111). Heidegger claims that the reality of the natural attitude is experienced as "objectively on hand" (*objektiv vorhanden*) (*PGZ* 153/*HCT* 111). That is, in the Husserlian natural attitude, things are experienced in the mode of *Vorhandenheit*, as objects (*Gegenstände*) available to a theoretical inspection by consciousness, as things standing over against (*gegen*) a subject. But that is not all. Not only are things experienced in the mode of *Vorhandenheit* as objects, but this is also the determination of the being of the person intentionally relating to things. Thus, the being for whom the world appears in its reality as something on hand to a theoretical regard is also fixed as something real and on hand, as an entity objectified into an ego. Such is the *Boden* upon which the impoverished world of naturalism erects its structures.

Thus, Heidegger's claim is that the Husserlian understanding of the natural attitude presupposes an understanding of both things and persons that is part of an ontology of *Vorhandenheit*, the present-at-hand, to which Heidegger will oppose, in the opening chapters of *Sein und Zeit*, an ontology of things based in the category of *Zuhandenheit* or handiness, and a fundamental ontology of persons rooted in the analysis of *Existenz*.

But is the natural attitude natural? Is it even an attitude? Heidegger seems to respond with a double negative. Let me take up the first question: is the natural attitude natural? The natural attitude is unnatural because it presupposes a particular theoretical orientation borrowed from tradition and not taken from the things themselves. That is, the natural attitude is a theoretical attitude, and insofar as it is theoretical the philosophical obligation of the phenomenologist is to work against it in order to be true to the maxim "to the things themselves." If our access to things were not blocked by the theoreticist prejudice of the tradition, then the maxim "to the things themselves" would have no meaning, for we would already be with those things.

This is a point fascinatingly amplified by Levinas in the Conclusion to his 1930 Doctoral Thesis, *The Theory of Intuition in Husserl's Phenomenology*, a work utterly pervaded by the climate of the early Heidegger, where Levinas completely accepts the necessity for an ontological critique of phenomenology and claims that the natural attitude is fatally framed by the presuppositions of a representationalist epistemology.[17] Levinas argues that Husserlian phenomenology is theoreticist and intellectualist and thereby overlooks the historical situatedness of the human being, which is a claim that Levinas obviously made in ignorance of the *Krisis* manuscripts. He writes, "Consequently, despite the revolutionary character of the phenomenological reduction, the revolution that it accomplishes is, in Husserl's philosophy, possible because of the nature of the natural attitude, to the extent that the natural attitude is theoretical."[18] Of course, the dramatic irony of Levinas's remarks in relation to his later critique of the fundamentality of ontology must be noted, and I have explored this elsewhere.[19] But, crucially, Levinas's later claim that ethics and not ontology is first philosophy continually presupposes the Heideggerian critique of Husserl. This is why, in the Introduction to *De l'existence à l'existant* in 1947, he claims that not only are his reflections commanded by the need to leave the climate of Heidegger's philosophy, but – more importantly – that one cannot leave that climate for a philosophy that would be pre-Heideggerian, "we cannot leave it for a philosophy that one could qualify as pre-Heideggerian."[20] The Heideggerian paradigm shift in twentieth-century philosophy is as important a turning point as Hegel's for the nineteenth century, which is a point that even Habermas begrudgingly concedes.[21] Everything turns here on Levinas's word "climate," which I would choose to view as a translation of *ethos*, and, of course, it is with that word that all the problems with Heidegger begin.

Turning to the second question, if the natural attitude is not natural, then, secondly, it is also not an attitude. The human being's "natural" manner of experiencing the world is not an *Einstellung*, something I put myself into (*einstellen*) in the same way as I might put a car in the garage, a book on the shelf, or my pet hamster in the refrigerator. Why? Because, for Heidegger, I always already find myself (*ich befinde mich*) in the world. I am always already practically disposed in a world that is familiar and handy, a world in which we are immersed and with which we are fascinated. Thus, adopting an attitude towards experience is already to look at things from the standpoint of reflection, in an act by which we consider life, but no longer live it.

Thus, the Heideggerian beginning point for the question of the being of the intentional is already distorted by the Husserlian description of that beginning point with the thesis of the natural attitude. That is, it is the wrong description of the right beginning point. The natural attitude, with its theoreticist, intellectualist, *vorhanden* understanding of reality and consciousness is an unphenomenological distortion of the human being's primary practical and personal access to the world. In this regard, Heidegger's *Sein und Zeit* can – minimally but compellingly, I think – be seen as attempting to provide clarification of what is first given in personal experience, as a hermeneutic redescription of the natural attitude.

Of course, the meta-question that should be raised here is whether Heidegger is justified in his critique of the natural attitude in Husserl. Even if it is granted that he gives a plausible interpretation of the natural attitude in *Ideas I*, is this valid for Husserl's later work? In this regard, simply as a counter-balance to Heidegger's claims, one might consider Merleau-Ponty's remarks about the natural attitude in his stunning late essay, "The Philosopher and his Shadow" (Le philosophe et son ombre).[22] Although the avowed hermeneutic strategy employed by Merleau- Ponty in this essay is Heideggerian, attempting to locate the unthought in Husserl's texts, the whole essay can be read as a problematization of Heidegger's portrayal of transcendental phenomenology, based on a reading of *Ideas II*.[23] Of course, the unpublished manuscript of the latter text was lying on Heidegger's desk in 1925 (*PGZ* 167–71/*HCT* 121–3) and he even refers obliquely to it in an early footnote to *Sein und Zeit* (*SZ* 47). For Merleau-Ponty, "It is the natural attitude that seesaws [*bascule*] in phenomenology." Or again, "When Husserl says that the reduction goes beyond the natural attitude, he immediately adds that this going beyond preserves 'the whole world of the natural attitude' ".[24] That is to say, from *Ideas II* onwards Husserl recognizes that the natural attitude contains a higher phenomenological truth that must be regained. To capture this truth, Husserl makes the distinction between the *naturalistic attitude*, the theoretical or *vorhanden* relation to things that defines the methodology of the natural sciences, and the *personalistic attitude*, which tries to capture the sense of life as it is lived in terms of what is first given in personal experience, what Merleau-Ponty calls "notre proto-histoire" (our proto-history).[25] So, the natural attitude only becomes the theoretical understanding of things and persons when it is transformed into the naturalistic attitude. The task of a personalistic phenomenology, then, is one of trying to "unveil the pre-theoretical layer" (*dévoiler la couche pré-théorétique*) of human experience upon which the various idealizations of naturalism are based.[26] It is this obdurate yet almost intangible dimension of pretheoretical experience that phenomenology has the job of elucidating, the mystery of the familiar that Merleau-Ponty tried to express with the notion of the perceptual faith (*la foi perceptive*).

DOING PHENOMENOLOGY – NEITHER SCIENTISM NOR OBSCURANTISM

Now, although such a run of thought needs to be wrested from the Black Sea of a mystical neo-Schellingianism into which, like other trends in contemporary thinking, it risks sinking, it is something like this conception of personalistic phenomenology that I want to defend.[27] In a nutshell, I think this is why one should begin philosophizing with Heidegger rather than elsewhere. On my understanding, it is a question of *doing* phenomenology in order to try and uncover the pre-theoretical layer of the experience of persons and things and to find a mode of felicitous description for this layer of experience with its own standards of validity. For me, such a conception of phenomenology can be employed to avoid two pernicious tendencies in our current thinking: *scientism* and *obscurantism*.

Let me begin with scientism. Scientism rests on the fallacious claim that the theoretical or natural scientific way of viewing things, what Heidegger calls *Vorhandenheit*, provides the primary and most significant access to ourselves and our world, and that the methodology of the natural sciences provides the best form of explanation for all phenomena *überhaupt*. Heidegger shows that the scientific conception of the world, what Carnap and Neurath called the *wissenschaftliche Weltauffassung*, is derivative or parasitic upon a prior practical view of the world as *zuhanden*, that is, the environing world that is closest, most familiar, and most meaningful to us, the world that is always already colored by our cognitive, ethical and aesthetic values. That is to say, scientism, or what Husserl calls objectivism, overlooks the phenomenon of the *life-world* as the enabling condition for scientific practice. The critique of scientism, at least within phenomenology, does not seek to refute or negate the results of scientific research in the name of some mystical apprehension of the unity of man and nature, which is a risk in some of the ecstatical pronouncements of the later Merleau-Ponty; rather, it simply insists that science does not provide the primary or most significant access to a sense of ourselves and the world. Antiscientism does not at all entail an antiscientific attitude, and nor does it mean that "science does not think," which is a remark of Heidegger's that has caused more problems than it has solved. What is required here is what Heidegger called, in a much-overlooked late remark in *Sein und Zeit*, "an *existential conception of science*" [*einen existenzialen Begriff der Wissenschaft*] (*SZ* 357) that would show how the practices of the natural sciences arise out of life-world practices, and that the latter are not simply reducible to the former.[28]

Moving to more contemporary philosophical concerns, it is at least arguable that such a position is approached by John McDowell in his highly influential *Mind and World*.[29] McDowell borrows Aristotle's notion of second nature and Hegel's notion of *Bildung* in order to try and escape the traditional predicament of philosophy, namely the epistemological subject–object construal of how to relate thought to things and mind to world and, in particular, the naturalistic version of that construal in someone like Quine. McDowell seeks to avoid the Scylla of "bald naturalism" (the reduction of reason to nature) (p. 69) without falling into the Charybdis of "rampant Platonism" (the idealist separation of reason from nature) (p. 77). What is so interesting about McDowell for my purposes is that the view he advances, what he calls "naturalised Platonism," implicitly borrows at least four Heideggerian themes (via Gadamer's account of them in *Truth and Method* – a choice which is itself revealing): (a) the unintelligibility of skepticism, which recalls the argument of paragraph 44 of *Sein und Zeit* (p. 113); (b) the attempt to construe experience as "openness to the world" which recalls Heidegger's notions of disclosure and the clearing (*die Lichtung des Seins*); (c) the idea that human life in the world is structured environmentally, which recalls Heidegger's idea that *Welt* is first and foremost an *Umwelt* (p. 115); and (d) the claim that language is the repository of tradition, which recalls Heidegger's ideas about historicity and heritage (p. 126). Thus, the attempt to avoid the traditional predicament of philosophy, and the baldly naturalistic construal of that predicament, leads someone like McDowell to the adoption of a number of leading Heideggerian motifs.

Also interesting in this regard is Robert Brandom's rather Hegelian reconstruction of the argument of *Sein und Zeit.* Brandom tries to show how the Heideggerian claim that the present-at-hand arises out of the ready-to-hand – that is, how knowing is a founded mode of being-in-the-world – implies a social ontology where the condition of possibility for the scientific, criterial identification of entities (Quinean ontology) arises out of a shared communicative praxis based on a mutual recognition of shared norms (fundamental ontology). Such is the position that Brandom describes as Heidegger's "ontological pragmatism"; that is, it is a question of acknowledging and describing the social genesis of the categories and criteria with which the world is described, "fundamental ontology . . . is the study of the nature of social being – social practices and practioners."[30]

Let me develop this point a little further with reference to Heidegger's notion of phenomenology as a pre-science (*Vor-wissenschaft*). Although one can find this idea in Heidegger as early as his 1919 lecture course *The Idea of Philosophy and the Problem of Worldviews* (*Die Idee der Philosophie und das Weltanschauungsproblem*),[31] it is also prominently discussed in his 1924 lecture *The Concept of Time* (*Der Begriff der Zeit*), which Gadamer famously and rightly described as the *Ur-form* of *Sein und Zeit.*[32] In the latter lecture, Heidegger describes his reflections as belonging neither to theology nor to philosophy, but rather to a pre-science (*Vor-Wissenschaft*), that would be a hermeneutics of the factical conditions of possibility for scientific research, i.e. their social genesis in life-world practices. In what I shall generously assume is an attempt at humor on Heidegger's part, he describes this pre-science as the police force (*Polizeidienst*) at the procession of the sciences, conducting an occasional house search of the ancients and checking whether scientific research is indeed close to its matter (*bei ihrer Sache*), and hence phenomenological, or whether science is working with a traditional or handed down (*überlieferten*) knowledge of its *Sache* (One imagines the mass arrest and detention of whole crowds of naturalists by such a phenomenological police force, with summary beatings, torture, and execution for the worst scientistic offenders). In the *Prolegomena,* this phenomenological policing is called – and it is a phrase retained in paragraph 3 of *Sein und Zeit* – a *productive logic* (*SZ* 10; *PGZ* 2/*HCT* 2). That is, it is a prescientific disclosure of the life-world that leaps ahead (*vorausspringt*) and lays the ground for the sciences.[33] What Heidegger would seem to mean here is that unlike the empiricist or Lockeian conception of the philosopher as an underlaborer to science, a productive phenomenological logic – which for Heidegger corresponds to the original logic of Plato and Aristotle – leaps ahead of the sciences by showing their basis in a fundamental ontology of persons, things and world, the pretheoretical layer of experience spoken of above. What I have called "a phenomenological pre-science" or "an existential conception of science" does not dispute or refute the work of the sciences. On my understanding, it shows three things:

1. that the theoretical attitude of the sciences finds its condition of possibility in our various life-world practices;
2. that such practices require hermeneutical clarification and not causal hypotheses or causal-sounding explanations;
3. that the formal *a priori* structure of persons, things, and world can be deduced from that hermeneutic clarification, which is what Heidegger attempts to do with his various "existentials." The latter are what Heidegger calls "formal indications," a key term in Heidegger's early work.[34]

Allow me a final word on obscurantism. It is important to point out that such a phenomenological antiscientism *can* lead to an antiscientific obscurantism, which in many ways is the inverted or perverted counter-concept to scientism, but it *need* not do so if we are careful enough to engage in a little intellectual policing. Obscurantism might here be defined as the rejection of the causal explanations offered by natural science by referring them to an alternative causal story, that is somehow of a higher order, but essentially occult. That is, obscurantism is the replacement of a scientific form of explanation, which is believed to be scientistic, with a counter-scientific, mysterious, but still causal explanation (the earthquake was not caused by plate tectonics but by God's anger at our sinfulness). As a cultural phenomenon, this is something that can be observed in every episode of *The X-Files*, where two causal hypotheses are offered, one scientific, the other occult, and where the former is always proved wrong and the latter right, but in some way that still leaves us perplexed. Now, as a cultural distraction, arguably this does little harm, but elsewhere its effects can be more pernicious. Familiar candidates for obscurantist explanation are the will of God, the ubiquity of alien intelligence, the action of the stars on human behavior, or whatever. Less obvious, but arguably equally pernicious, candidates are the Jungian archetypes, the Lacanian real, Foucauldian power, the self-occlusion of the trace in Derrida, the trace of God in Levinas, or – indeed – the epochal withdrawal of being in and as history in the later Heidegger. This list might be extended.[35]

In my view, what we can still learn from phenomenology is that when it comes to our primary and most significant access to persons and things, what we might call our entire stock of tacit, background know-how about the social world, we do not require causal scientific explanations, or pseudo-scientific hypotheses in relation to obscure causes, but what I am tempted to call, in a Wittgensteinian spirit, *clarificatory remarks*. For example, "The aspects of things that are most important for us are hidden because of their simplicity and familiarity. (One is unable to notice something – because it is always before one's eyes.)"[36] Clarificatory remarks make familiar phenomena more perspicuous, change the aspect under which they are seen, and give to matters a new and surprising overview. Of course, viewing Heidegger's work in this way does not sound as exciting as talking about the epochal donation of being in its withdrawing movement or whatever, but perhaps that sort of excitement is something we are best off without.[37]

NOTES

1 A word of clarification is necessary here. The full version of this essay runs to about 20,000 words, and therefore somewhat exceeds the word limit for essays in this volume. It contains detailed discussions of the key concepts that Heidegger takes from Husserl: intentionality, categorial intuition, and the *a priori*. The discussion of categorial intuition is of particular importance, and I attempt to give a rational reconstruction of this doctrine in order both to minimize certain of Heidegger's rather grandiloquent claims about it, and

to defend categorial intuition against certain objections and misunderstandings. My discussion of these concepts is then built into an extensive account of the formal concept of phenomenology in paragraph 7 of *Sein und Zeit* that provides Heidegger with the methodological tool of his early and (so I contend) later work. It is hoped to publish this text in its entirety, together with an interpretation of *Being and Time,* at a later date.

2 Martin Heidegger, *Prolegomena zur Geschichte des Zeitbegriffs* (Frankfurt a.M.: Klostermann, 1979). Hereafter *PGZ. History of the Concept of Time*, trans. T. Kisiel (Bloomington: Indiana University Press, 1985). Hereafter *HCT.* Martin Heidegger, *Sein und Zeit,* 15th edn. (Tübingen: Niemeyer, 1984). Hereafter *SZ.* All references are to the German pagination, which can be found in the margins of the English translations of the text.

3 Martin Heidegger, *Zur Sache des Denkens,* 3rd edn. (Tübingen: Niemeyer, 1988), p. 48.

4 F. W. von Herrmann, *Der Begriff der Phänomenologie bei Heidegger und Husserl* (Frankfurt a.M.: Klostermann, 1981), p. 8.

5 In this connection, see Mark Okrent's argument for intentionality in terms of the priority of action over self-consciousness or self-attribution in his essay in this volume, "Intentionality, Teleology, and Normativity," pp. 191–206.

6 Although intuition is always categorially structured and perception is always already shot through with concepts. That is, for Heidegger, language is the condition of possibility for the meaningful visibility of perceptual items – seeing is always already a saying. Heidegger writes, "we do not say what we see, but rather the reverse, we see what one says about the matter" (*PGZ* 75/*HCT* 56). I deal with the question of the relation of perception to conception in the full-length version of this text.

7 Klaus Held, "Heidegger und das Prinzip der Phänomenologie," in *Heidegger und die praktische Philosophie*, ed. A. Gethman-Siefert and O. Pöggeler (Frankfurt a.M.: Suhrkamp, 1988), p.113. See also Held's "On the Way to a Phenomenology of World," *Journal of the British Society for Phenomenology* 30.1 (1999), 3–17.

8 See, Jacques Taminiaux, "Heidegger and Husserl's *Logical Investigations*: in Remembrance of Heidegger's Last Seminar (Zähringen, 1973)," in *Dialectic and Difference*, trans. Robert Crease and James T. Decker (New Jersey: Humanities Press, 1985), pp. 91–114. See also "D'une idée de la phénoménologie à l'autre," in *Lectures de l'ontologie fondamentale* (Grenoble: Millon, 1989), pp. 19–88.

9 *Zur Sache des Denkens*, p. 90.

10 The extent of Heidegger's debt to Dilthey has become increasingly apparent with the discovery in 1989 of the so-called "Aristoteles-Einleitung" written by Heidegger in just three weeks and sent to Paul Natorp in connection with Heidegger's candidature for a position in Marburg in 1922. It is published in the *Dilthey-Jahrbuch für Philosophie und Geschichte der Geisteswissenschaften*, vol. 6 (Göttingen: Vandenhoeck und Ruprecht, 1989), pp. 228–74. For a helpful overview of the significance of this text, see Rudolf Makkreel's "The Genesis

of Heidegger's Phenomenological Hermeneutics and the Rediscovered 'Aristotle Introduction' of 1922", *Man and World* 23 (1990), 305–20. For a thorough account of the influence of Dilthey on Heidegger in his critique of Husserl, see John van Buren, *The Young Heidegger* (Bloomington: Indiana University Press, 1994), see esp. the discussion of Husserl, pp. 203–19. Van Buren usefully analyses Heidegger's 1925 lectures on Dilthey, held in Kassel in April 16–21, under the title "Wilhelm Dilthey's Forschungsarbeit und der Kampf um eine historische Weltanschauung."

11 I refer here to William Richardson's *Heidegger: Through Phenomenology to Thought* (The Hague: Nijhoff, 1963).

12 For good examples of such an approach, see John Sallis "Where Does *Being and Time* Begin?" in *Heidegger's Existential Analytic* (New York: Mouton, 1978), pp. 21–43; Robert Bernasconi, *The Question of Language in Heidegger's History of Being* (Atlantic Highlands, NJ: Humanities Press, 1985).

13 Taminiaux, *Lectures de l'ontologie fondamentale*, p. 59.

14 Edmund Husserl, *Ideas*, trans. W. R. Boyce Gibson (New York: Humanities Press, 1976), p. 151.

15 This is a point well discussed by Barbara Merker in her interesting book, *Selbsttäuschung und Selbsterkenntnis. Zu Heideggers Transformation der Phänomenologie Husserls* (Frankfurt a.M.: Suhrkamp, 1988), see esp. pp. 7–9, 78–80. Merker, reading *Sein und Zeit* as a quasi-Christian *Konversionsgeschichte*, shows how Heidegger replaces the natural attitude with the realm of inauthenticity,

> Die "narzißtischen" Projektionen des phänomenologischen Theoretikers verhindern demnach eine adäquate Analyse des alltäglichen Besorgens, der Gegenstände, mit denen es umgeht, wie der Welt, in der es sich bewegt. Nur wenn es gelingt, dieses theoretisches Vorurteil zu vermeiden, wird eine adäquate Beschreibung der alltäglichen Existenzweise möglich, die Heidegger an die Stelle der "natürlichen Einstellung" Husserls setzt. (p. 79)

16 Husserl, *Ideas*, pp. 105–6.

17 Emmanuel Levinas, *La théorie de l'intuition dans la phénoménologie de Husserl*, 6th edn. (Paris: Vrin, 1989), pp. 219–23.

18 Ibid., p. 222.

19 Simon Critchley, "Post-Deconstructive Subjectivity?," in *Ethics–Politics–Subjectivity* (London and New York: Verso, 1999), pp. 51–81.

20 *De l'existence à l'existant*, 2nd edn. (Paris: Vrin, 1986), p. 19. Interestingly, given the hysteria that broke out in France because of "the Heidegger affair," one finds a similarly measured tone with regard to Heidegger in a paper given some forty years after *De l'existence à l'existant*, at the height of the affair in 1987. See, "Mourir pour," in *Heidegger. Questions ouvertes* (Paris: Osiris, 1988), pp. 255–64.

21 "From today's standpoint, Heidegger's new beginning still presents probably the most profound turning point in German philosophy since Hegel." Jürgen Habermas, "Work and *Weltanschuung*: The Heidegger Controversy from a German Perspective," in *Heidegger: A Critical Reader*, eds. H. Dreyfus and H. Hall (Oxford: Blackwell, 1992), p. 188.

22 In *Eloge de la philosophie et autres essais* (Paris: Gallimard, 1960), pp. 241–87. Translated in *Signs*, trans. R. McCleary (Evanston: Northwestern University Press, 1964), pp. 159–81.

23 *Ideas*, Book 2, *Studies in the Phenomenology of Constitution*, trans. R. Rojcewicz and A. Schuwer (Dordrecht: Kluwer, 1989). For the reference to Heidegger's notion of *das Ungedachte*, see "Le philosophe et son ombre," p. 243.

24 'Le philosophe et son ombre," pp. 252, 248.

25 Ibid., p. 286.

26 Ibid., p. 253.

27 For an example of such neo-Schellingianism, see Slavoj Zizek, *The Indivisible Remainder. An Essay on Schelling and Related Matters* (London and New York: Verso, 1996).

28 For a Heideggerian approach to science that argues for a "robust realism" where science gives us access to things independently of our everyday practices, see Hubert Dreyfus and Charles Spinosa, "Coping with Things-in-themselves: A Practice-Based Phenomenological Argument for Realism," *Inquiry* 42.1 (1999), 49–78. See also the five responses to this paper in the same issue of the journal, and Dreyfus's and Spinosa's response to their critics in *Inquiry* 42.2 (1999), 177–94, For a more "deflationary realist" account of Heidegger and science, see Joseph Rouse, *Knowledge and Power* (Ithaca, NY: Cornell University Press, 1987). See also Rouse's very helpful article, "Heideggerian Philosophy of Science," in the *Routledge Encyclopedia of Philosophy*, vol. 4, ed. E. Craig (London and New York: Routledge, 1998), pp. 323–7.

29 *Mind and World* (Cambridge, MA: Harvard University Press, 1994), pp. 77, 67, 91.

30 See Robert Brandom's "Heidegger's Categories in *Being and Time*," in *Heidegger: A Critical Reader*, pp. 45–64, see esp. 53–5, 62. See also in this regard, Mark Okrent's *Heidegger's Pragmatism* (Ithaca, NY: Cornell University Press, 1988).

31 In *Zur Bestimmung der Philosophie, Gesamtausgabe*, vol. 56–7 (Frankfurt a.M.: Klostermann, 1987).

32 *Der Begriff der Zeit* (Tübingen: Niemeyer, 1989); *The Concept of Time*, trans. W. McNeill (Oxford: Blackwell, 1992).

33 Heidegger also speaks of *Vorausspringen* as stepping in for the other as the positive mode of solicitude (*Fürsorge*) in *Sein und Zeit* (*SZ* 122).

34 For the importance of formal indication, see Kisiel's *The Genesis of Heidegger's Being and Time* (Berkeley: University of California Press, 1993).

35 For good or ill, my talk of scientism and obscurantism gave rise to lots of interesting questions at the Utah Heidegger conference, in particular from John Caputo and Albert Borgmann. All of which added up to making the distinction much more fluid than I allowed in my paper. First, obscurantism might not be one thing, as I seemed to suggest. Namely, there is indeed the obscurantism based on faith in some numinous enigma. We might call this "obscure obscurantism." But there are other obscurantisms that do not

believe themselves to be obscure, but perfectly self-evident or even scientifically provable: "Doctor, can't you see that my sleeplessness and aggression is caused by the fact that I was abducted by aliens when I was camping last summer?"; or "Just one more year of research and I will finally have proved that matter is the product of divine effusions." And of course there are scientisms which are taken on faith and are thus the equivalent of obscurantism. For example, I might believe that all mental states can be reduced to evolutionary dispositions without knowing how or why. We might call this an "obscure scientism" or whatever. Let's just say that there is a need for a more detailed taxonomy of the scientism/obscurantism distinction.

36 Ludwig Wittgenstein, *Philosophical Investigations*, trans. G. E. M. Anscombe (Oxford: Blackwell, 1958), paragraph 129.

37 I explore these rather sketchy thoughts on scientism versus obscurantism in more detail in relation to the conflict between Heidegger and Carnap in my *Continental Philosophy* (Oxford: Oxford University Press, forthcoming). But it might be clear from what I have said in this essay that I am attempting a mini-pathology of the contemporary philosophical scene, which is meant to comment on and maybe curb the worst excesses of both continental and analytic philosophy. On the one hand, there is a risk of obscurantism in some continental philosophy, where social phenomena are explicated with reference to forces, entities, and categories so vast and vague as to explain everything and nothing at all. For example, a phenomenon like the internet, mobile phones, or even mobile homes, might be seen as further evidence of the Heideggerian *Gestell* and thereby tributary to the forgetfulness of being. And any aspect of personal and public life might be seen as evidence of the disciplinary matrices of power, the disintegration of the "Big Other" and the trauma of the real, or whatever. Where such obscurantism exists, then the therapy has to be what Caputo calls "demythologization," that is, a critique of this kind of talk and perhaps also some suggestions as to why we engage in it in the first place. But on the other hand, there is the risk of a chronic scientism in some areas of analytic philosophy. As Frank Cioffi wittily remarks, if we can imagine a philosophical paper with the title "Qualia and Materialism: Closing the Explanatory Gap," then why not papers with titles like, "The Big Bang and Me: Closing the Explanatory Gap" or "Natural Selection and Me: Closing the Explanatory Gap?" (*Wittgenstein on Freud and Frazer* [Cambridge: Cambridge University Press, 1998], p. 302). My question is whether this is a gap that can and should be closed, i.e. is the question of the meaning of life reducible to empirical inquiry? In philosophy, in my view, we need to clip the wings of both scientism and obscurantism and thereby avoid what is worst in both continental and analytic philosophy. That is, we need to avoid the error of believing that we can resolve through causal or causal-sounding explanation what demands phenomenological clarification. But, of course, this is much easier said than done.

CHAPTER 8

The critique of anthropologism in Heidegger's thought

Françoise Dastur

Instead of seeing a new and extreme form of the modern subject in Heidegger's Dasein, as has been the case in some recent commentaries, I would like to show that his new approach to human being is made necessary by the attempt to rediscover the most original idea of philosophy, namely to take care of the All. This requires not only putting an emphasis on the ontological dimension of the existential analytic in *Being and Time,* but also showing the importance of Heidegger's debate with the Kantian "question of man" and with the Nietzschean ideal of the "superman." Finally, from this perspective, we must also understand the necessity of the "reversal" that occurred in Heidegger's thinking in the thirties – a reversal that led to a new conception of the divine in the figure of the "extreme God" and of the world in the form of the fourfold of earth and sky, mortals and divinities.

In Germany, the end of the eighteenth century was marked by the development of the problematic of subjectivity on the basis of Kant's Copernican turn. It was a time when the young Schelling became the upholder of Fichtean egology and the propagator of the new principle of philosophy, the absolute I. Two hundred years later, at the end of the twentieth century, philosophy is no longer identified with egology, but with ethics, and its new principle (whose propagators are no longer German, but French) is the absolute Other. But it does not seem that by proceeding from the absolute I to the absolute Other, modern philosophy has really been able to get out of the anthropological framework that has been its framework since the Cartesian discovery of the *cogito.* The human being remains the insurmountable horizon of his own thinking. However, with the word *phenomenology*, which appeared at the beginning of this century as the new name for philosophy in Husserl's *Logical Investigations,* a breach was made, a clearing appeared. Although Husserlian phenomenology was later understood as a new form of Cartesianism and as a new theory of transcendental idealism, its first objective was the struggle against psychologism and anthropologism. Even in his late writings, Husserl maintained that phenomenology was the restitution of the most ancient idea of philosophy, in other words, of a universal science, the science of All. I intend to show that this task of rediscovering the full scope of the idea of philosophy against his modern reduction to anthropologism is also the leading motive of Heidegger's thought.

The maxim of phenomenology, the return to the "things themselves," to the phenomena, to what shows itself, was first understood by Husserl as a return to lived experience, to the *Erlebnisse*. This explains the idealistic turn of Husserlian phenomenology, which, less than ten years after the breakthrough of the *Logical Investigations,* became the theory of the reduction of world to the constitutive operations of the transcendental ego.[1] In his *Cartesian Meditations* of 1929, Husserl finally rejoins the Fichtean idealistic position by proclaiming the identity of ontology and egology.[2] But the introduction of the transcendental standpoint does not mean that man is reintroduced at the center of the constitutive structures of the experience. For Husserl did not only reject all forms of empirical anthropologism, but also what he later named "transcendental anthropologism."[3] Under this title, he refers to Heidegger's existential analytic in which he only sees, as it becomes clear from his annotations in the margins of *Sein und Zeit,* a "philosophical anthropology."[4] For Husserl, man and the empirical ego are mundane realities and relative beings, whereas the transcendental ego, who is not born and who never dies, is an absolute being. This question of the difference between the empirical ego and the transcendental ego was the center of the debate between Husserl and Heidegger in 1927 when, together, they were preparing the article "Phenomenology" for the *Encyclopaedia Britannica.* Heidegger could not accept the duality of the two egos and saw in Husserl's theory of the transcendental subject a new form of the metaphysics of the absolute subjectivity, whereas Husserl considered the Heideggerian analysis of Dasein as a betrayal of the phenomenological standpoint and a downfall of philosophy into anthropologism.[5]

This misunderstanding concerning the status of the analysis of Dasein in *Sein und Zeit* was shared by many readers of Heidegger's first work who saw in it the insufficient attempt at a philosophical anthropology. This misunderstanding, which was made easier due to the fact that the "ontological" third section of the first part of *Sein und Zeit* was never published, was the origin of the "philosophy of existence" whose manifesto is Sartre's essay, "Existentialism is a Humanism," against which Heidegger took a position in 1947 in his "Letter on Humanism." In his response to Sartre, who maintains that in existentialism, "we are precisely on a level where there are only human beings," Heidegger explains that, from the perspective of *Being and Time*, this should say instead: "we are precisely on a level where principally there is being."[6] Therefore, in this period immediately following the *Kehre,* in other words, the reversal of the being-question into the thinking of the *Ereignis*, Heidegger stressed the necessity of an ontological and not only anthropological reading of *Being and Time*. But Heidegger did not first discover the necessity of an ontological reading of *Being and Time* in this period, the period of his first attempt at a self-interpretation. The question of anthropology had already been raised much earlier, namely in 1929, in *Kant and the Problem of Metaphysics*.

In the same year, 1929, in his winter semester course dedicated to *The Fundamental Concepts of Metaphysics*, Heidegger defended the thesis that man is "world forming" (*weltbildend*), a thesis that constitutes the elaboration of the problem of world that has not been fully developed in *Sein und Zeit*, where the analysis of world starts with the analysis of equipment and where we find only an analysis of the surrounding world (*Umwelt*), in other words, of the daily world which consists in nothing other than in the ontological structure of meaningfulness (*Bedeutsamkeit*). In *Sein und Zeit* there is no possibility of experiencing the world in itself on the basis of daily existence because the world only announces itself when equipment is not working properly, is missing or is adapted. The world can only be discovered in the fundamental mood of anxiety ((*Angst*) in the form of nothingness, in other words, as a being that is not ready-to-hand. For in anxiety, Dasein discovers himself not as a separate being, but precisely as a being-in-the-world. This is the sense of the often misunderstood expression, "existential solipsism," that Heidegger uses in this context.[7]

In *Sein und Zeit*, we find only an analysis of the human world; nothing or almost nothing is said about nature as such. Heidegger himself acknowledges this in 1929 in a note from *Vom Wesen des Grundes*, where he stresses that the analysis of the *Umwelt* in *Sein und Zeit* is only a first determination of the phenomenon world and has only a preparatory value.[8] The conception of world that is exposed in the 1929–30 lecture course is the result of the temporal and transcendental ontology developed by Heidegger in the years immediately following the publication of *Sein und Zeit*. But the thesis of the *Weltbildung*, the formation of world by man, can be viewed as the most extreme subjectivistic thesis in the sense that it seems to imply that world is only the product of man's ontological activity. For example, this was the opinion of Eugen Fink, who was present during the 1929–30 lecture course and to whose memory Heidegger, on the day of his death (26 June 1975), dedicated the volume of the *Gesamtausgabe* into which it was planned to publish the text of the course. Fink takes up again, but in an original manner, the same task of the exposition of the problem of world in a lecture course on *World and Finitude* (*Welt und Endlichkeit*) that he gave in 1949 and 1966, but which was published only in 1990. In that lecture course, Fink, recalling that in *Vom Wesen des Grundes* Heidegger tries to elucidate the transcendental projection of world by showing that it originates in the finite freedom of the human being, declares that "for the problem of world, this essay of Heidegger means *the summit of a subjectivistic conception of world.*"[9] Jacques Taminiaux shares the same view in his *Readings on the Fundamental Ontology* (1989), where he defends the general thesis that fundamental ontology constitutes the culmination of the metaphysics of subjectivity.

There is obviously some truth in these judgments, but they nevertheless presuppose that there is a deep split between fundamental ontology and what follows. They imply what Heidegger himself always denied, that the *Kehre,* the reversal, from which the "Letter on Humanism" speaks, is an operation of thought, "a consequence of altering the standpoint, much less of abandoning the fundamental issue, of *Being and Time.*"[10] Such a conception of the *Kehre* is in fact itself the result of a still subjectivistic perspective that sees in thought the mere product of the activity of a subject. Heidegger himself considers the *Kehre* not as an *act* of thinking, but as an *event* of thinking. He says in his famous letter of 1962 to Richardson that the reversal is "play[ing] within the matter itself" designated by the heading "Being and Time" and cannot be considered as his own invention.[11] But the matter in *Being and Time* is no longer the subject–object relation; the starting point of the whole questioning is found outside the sphere of subjectivity and the being into which it inquires cannot, therefore, be considered to be something that the human subject posits. This means that already in its initial steps the thought of *Being and Time* is called upon to undergo a change.

If we want to accept the interpretation that Heidegger gives here from his own way of thinking, we must try to show that the 1929 thesis, a formation of world by man, is not a subjectivistic thesis. It must first be stressed that there already has been a change in the conception of world from 1927 to 1929. In *Sein und Zeit,* the world structure is indirectly analyzed through the phenomenon of *Umwelt,* which means that world remains limited to the totality of instruments (*Zeugganzheit*), whereas in *Vom Wesen des Grundes* world is related to the totality of beings (*das Seiende im Ganzen*) as such, which also involves the realm of "nature." But world is still defined, as was already the case in 1927, as "the totality of whereunto of a Dasein" (*die Ganzheit des Umwillens eines Daseins*), it is still related to the project of Dasein, in that case, *der Überwurf der entworfenen Welt über das Seiende*, the projection of the projected world beyond the being.[12] Such a transcendental projection, which is the possibility condition for the manifestation of beings, constitutes by itself *die Weltbildung*, the formation of world. This formation of world is not a pure production, but because world is always already open with Dasein, *ein Geschehenlassen der Welt*, a letting happen of world. Already in *Sein und Zeit* Heidegger had made clear that we primarily have access to world through our dispositions (*Stimmungen*) and not through a pure intuitive or perceptive act, so that our being-in-the world is not our accomplishment, but is always already passively disclosed with the existential of *Befindlichkeit*. The projection of world is connected to the factical disclosedness that is always involved in the projection of world through Dasein. We therefore have no voluntary command on the horizonal projection that we spontaneously give ourselves in order to make possible our action and our relation to the beings.

This is why we cannot consider the projection of world as the act of a transcendental subject, but rather as identical with the very happening of human existence. Because Heidegger insists on the fact that all projection is always thrown, in other words that existentiality and facticity are intimately connected to each other, we cannot consider his position to be identical with what is traditionally called transcendentality. However, is it not possible to consider the Heideggerian conception of the transcendental to be the culmination of the Kantian or Husserlian transcendentality? This was the position of Fink, who declared that in his existential concept of world Heidegger thinks the Kantian concept of world to its end and brings the subjectivistic conception to its culmination, to the point where it can only overturn into a truly cosmological conception where world no longer depends on Dasein but, on the contrary, Dasein depends on the happening of world.[13] But Heidegger himself does not aim at such an inversion of priority between world and Dasein. The question is not for him, as it is for Fink, to develop a cosmological phenomenology and to inverse the transcendental way of thinking by giving the active role to the world and a mere passive role to Dasein, but to think in a more intimate manner the identity of Dasein and world, so that there will no longer be two different instances linked to each other in a relation of causality, but a single happening. This thinking of the simultaneous happening of Dasein and being, which is nothing other than the thinking of *Ereignis*, can only take place if transcendentality or finite freedom is itself thought of not as a property of Dasein but as the dimension that makes Dasein itself possible. It could be shown in detail that the Heideggerian reading of Kant's philosophy between 1929 and 1930 aimed at such an overcoming of the Kantian determination of the transcendental. In other words, the overcoming of the transcendental position is only possible if transcendentality is understood in terms of existence and facticity, and not in terms of subjectivity.

For the overcoming of the Kantian determination of the transcendental implies the debate that Heidegger undertakes at the end of *Kant and the Problem of Metaphysics* with Kant's foundation of metaphysics in anthropology. Heidegger refers here to the famous question of man that in the introduction to his lecture course on *Logic* Kant adds to the three metaphysical questions commanding the elaboration of the three disciplines of rational cosmology, psychology, and theology that constitute *metaphysica specialis*. Kant not only adds a fourth question to the three traditional ones, but also explains that the first three questions refer to the fourth one and belong to anthropology.[14] Thus, it seems that only a philosophical anthropology can provide the foundation of metaphysics. But the idea of a philosophical anthropology, understood as a regional ontology of man or as constituting the goal of philosophy as such, remains quite indeterminate as long as the question of the relation of the philosophical questions to the being of man is not raised. Heidegger shows that the three questions of *metaphysica specialis*, What can I know? What should I do? What may I hope?, only have meaning when we understand them as testimonies of the finitude of human being, which explains why they can be brought back to the fourth question: What is man? For only a finite being can raise questions about his capacity, his moral obligation, and about what he is legitimately allowed to hope for. In the questions of the *metaphysica specialis*, the finitude of man does not only appear, but is assumed and cared for. The foundation of metaphysics is therefore itself grounded on the question of finitude in man.

But the problem is not only of demonstrating the facticity of finitude, but of determining its essence. Therefore, what has to be shown is the *internal* relation between the foundation of metaphysics and the question of finitude in man. Finitude, if it is understood only in the sense of a dependency on the pregivenness of beings, a sense which corresponds to the Kantian concept of finitude, is not what is most radically finite in man. Kant elaborated this concept of finitude by externally determining it, in opposition to an *intuitus originarius*, a productive intuition, as the *intuitus derivatus* of the human being and by still understanding him as an *ens creatum*.[15] But if human being is understood in itself as internally characterized by the tendency to raise metaphysical questions, by what Kant himself called *metaphysica naturalis*, an internal relation can be established between the question of *metaphysica generalis*, the question of being, and the prephilosophical behavior of man, who already possesses a preconceptual understanding of being. A human being has to be primarily understood on the basis of his preconceptual understanding of being, his specific mode of being which Heidegger names existence. But existence has to be understood not only as the privilege of being open to being, but also as the necessity of assuming the dependency on the pregivenness of beings. For it is only through the transcendental projection of the horizon of being that the human being can behave towards the beings that he encounters. A pure and immediate intuition of his factual situation is denied him, as Heidegger showed before *Being and Time* when he explained in his early lectures that the only access that human life can have to itself is a "hermeutic intuition," in other words, a look that makes explicit what is looked at.[16] This explains why in *Being and Time* he defines facticity not as a *factum brutum* but as a facticity which must be assumed (*Faktizität der Überantwortung*).[17] It is therefore the understanding of being, which Heidegger names Dasein, that constitutes the most internal ground of the finitude of man: the "internal" finitude that defines the human being is the need to understand being in which Dasein shows itself as Dasein. It is this transcendental neediness that fundamentally ensures the possibility that there is Da-sein, which constitutes the fundamental being of man, and this explains Heidegger's famous statement in *Kant and the Problem of Metaphysics*: "More original than man is the finitude of Dasein in him."[18]

From there, it becomes clear that the question of man, as far as it constitutes the ground of metaphysics, cannot be an anthropological question, since anthropology already presupposes a concept of man and does not inquire into the being of man. Instead of considering that all metaphysics has an anthropological and factual ground, it is necessary to understand that metaphysics can be grounded only on an ontological basis, on the analysis of the being of man, in other words, on an existential, and not only existentiell analysis. But such an ontological analysis is already a metaphysical inquiry in the sense of *metaphysica generalis*. Metaphysics can therefore only be grounded on the metaphysics of Dasein, which means, as Kant himself acknowledges in a letter to Marcus Herz quoted by Heidegger, that the problem of the foundation of metaphysics is in fact the problem of metaphysics of metaphysics, in other words, a meta-metaphysical problem.[19]

For Heidegger himself, as far as the question of the being of man constitutes the grounds of the question of being, it has nothing to do with anthropology, but is part of the ontological questioning. This was already said in *Being and Time*: "The analytic of Dasein is not aimed at laying an ontological basis for anthropology; its purpose is one of fundamental ontology." [20] The analytic of Dasein is named *fundamental ontology* insofar as it constitutes the grounds of metaphysics, which is for Heidegger, the finitude of Dasein. A privilege is thereby attributed to Dasein, but this privilege has nothing to do with anthropocentrism. In the already quoted essay from 1929, *Vom Wesen des Grundes*, Heidegger himself refers to the misunderstanding leading to the assumption that *Being and Time* works from an anthropocentric standpoint. There, he says this interpretation makes sense only if one fails to understand the ecstatic and therefore eccentric essence of Dasein, in other words, if one still identifies man and Dasein, whereas the whole problematic of *Being and Time* already aimed at showing that the traditional conception of man as a separate being cannot allow the being-question to be raised. Therefore, what must first be understood is the "eccentricity" of Dasein, which cannot be considered as a separate entity, but only as the locus, the *Da*, of being.[21]

It was never possible to see Dasein in an independent instance, but Heidegger later realizes that the perspective of fundamental ontology still presupposes the priority of the self and the centrifugal movement of the self toward being, whereas what has to be thought is, on the contrary, the response of Dasein to the gift of being. The reversal in Heidegger's thought consists in understanding the ecstatic movement of Dasein no longer as a centrifugal one, but as the neither active nor passive openness to being which allows Dasein to stand in being, existence being now interpreted as instancy (*Inständigkeit*), as he explains in the 1949 Preface to *What is Metaphysics?*.[22] It means the rejection of the interpretation of the existential analysis in terms of a fundamental ontology, but not of the existential analysis itself, which can be reinterpreted in a new perspective. The new perspective, the perspective of the *Ereignis*, is where the thrownness of Dasein no longer appears as a mere fact, but has to be understood as thrown by being itself, as Heidegger says in his *Letter on Humanism*.[23]

In this new perspective, the critique of anthropologism and anthropomorphism receives a deeper meaning, as it becomes clear in the writings, recently published from the years 1936–40, where Heidegger constantly writes "Da-sein" with a hyphen to show clearly the correlation between Dasein and being, or their belonging together – *die Zugehörigkeit von Dasein zum Sein*.[24] Now anthropology means oblivion of being (*Seinsvergessenheit*), the desertion of being (*Seinsverlassenheit*), says Heidegger in *Die Geschichte des Seins*,[25] since man is no longer able to understand his own being on the basis of the relationship with beings that he has achieved through reason and language. And in 1938, in *Besinnung*, following his course on Schelling, Heidegger undertakes the analysis of the concept of anthropomorphism. Anthropomorphism, the conviction that the whole of being depends on human representation and which, in modernity, takes the form of subjectivism, can be understood only on the basis of the oblivion of being, which means, for Heidegger, on the basis of metaphysics. For the humanization of the whole of being presupposes the humanization of man himself, which remains unnoticed. Metaphysical man is for himself also a being among others and depends in his being on representation: this forgetting of himself as the representative instance allows him to consider human being to belong to the domain of life and to the animal realm. This primary humanization of man, which is the ground of the conception of man as a given being belonging to the animal realm, explains why being itself can be understood as a specific creation of the animal rationale. But such a deconstruction of anthropomorphism can be undertaken only if man becomes aware of his participation in the event of being, which means nothing else than his transformation into Da-sein.[26]

Heidegger's critique of anthropologism and of anthropomorphism cannot therefore be understood as an antihumanism, as has often been the case, but as a critique of all previous humanism, in other words, of metaphysical humanism, which was only able to think the *homo animalis* and not the *homo humanus*, in other words which could not really understand what constitutes the specificity of humanity. For Heidegger, the essence of man consists of being more than a rational creature, which means that it is less than being a subject, it consists in existing as the counter-throw, the *Gegenwurf*, of Being. As he explains in his "Letter on Humanism," "To think the truth of being at the same time means to think the humanity of *homo humanus*. What counts is *humanitas* in the service of the truth of being, but without humanism in the metaphysical sense."[27]

Because Nietzsche sees, in a clearer way than any other thinker, the necessity of transforming the "human, all-too-human" being, Heidegger cannot avoid the debate with the Nietzschean ideal of the superman, which constitutes for Heidegger a very important moment of thought. In spite of his powerful critique of anthropocentrism, Nietzsche remains inside the metaphysical framework when he defines man as *das noch nicht festgestellte Tier*, as the animal that is not yet determined. The two opposed figures of "the last man," who does not want his self-overcoming and his decline, and of the "superman," who wants to bring the human being to its truth, are still two forms of the metaphysical man who, because he understands himself as the ground of being, cannot see in being something other than himself and consequently defines being, as is the case with modern metaphysics, as will. For Heidegger, Nietzsche's superman does not mean the authentic decline of the metaphysical man and the overcoming of anthropocentrism, because instead of freeing himself from will, he wants the eternity of will in the shape of the eternal return of the identical. By wanting the eternity of will, man remains attached to a selfhood that is not his proper self, but a self which results from his representation of himself as a living being among others.[28] In contrast, Heidegger does not understand the authentic selfhood of man on the basis of his belonging to the realm of will and life. This brings us back to the "Letter on Humanism," where Heidegger declares that metaphysics does not think of the *humanitas* of the human being, but only his *animalitas*, even when it sees in reason or spirit the specific difference of man compared to animals.[29] Metaphysics defines man as a living being amongst others and thus considers him as a thing, a separate entity, and is therefore not able to see him as part of the unveiling process, as participating in the coming into being of the world, as the collaborator to the *koinos kosmos* that is man for Heraclitus.[30] To be able to think man as being part of the event of being, as *Da-sein*, one must think man in his relation not to life, but to death, as was clear already in *Being and Time*, where the assumption of Dasein's own mortality is the only possibility offered to Dasein to become what it is, a singular existent. The assumption of one's mortality, being-unto-death, is what constitutes the real difference between man and animal, and not reason or spirit.

But is the thinking of man in the light of death really different from the metaphysical thinking of man as belonging to life's realm and to the animal realm, and are not life and death two phenomena so intimately connected that they cannot really be opposed? At first this seems to be quite a legitimate objection. But metaphysics, which is always metaphysics of life, and therefore biologism, sees in man only an already given being, whereas the existential analysis considers man not as a reality, but as a possibility, as a being which is not, but has to be. Now death is the only possibility that Dasein cannot realize, so that it constitutes for it a kind of absolute future. Considered from the standpoint of this absolute future, death, Dasein can no longer be understood as a being among others, but as essentially deprived of all substantiality, as the *Platzhalter des Nichts*, "the lieutenant of the nothing," as Heidegger says in *What is Metaphysics?*[31] But in 1929 it is Dasein itself, defined as "being held out into the nothing," who accomplishes the transcendental movement that lets beings appear as a whole and that thereby forms the world. After the turn, the nothing appears as belonging to being itself, as far as being refuses itself or withdraws itself in an essential manner. However, this does not mean that the event of world has become independent from Dasein. On the contrary, it means that Dasein is in fact wanted and employed, "handled" (*gebraucht*) by it, since Heidegger considers that the word *Brauch*, which means "enjoyment" rather than "need," is the proper name of being, as he explains in his essay on Anaximander written in the same year as the "Letter on Humanism."[32] Nevertheless, this implies a transformation of the meaning of man as being-in-the-world, as Heidegger points out in the "Letter on Humanism": the openness of world is no longer formed by man, but, on the contrary, world opens from itself in such a manner that, at the same time, it opens the being-in-the world of man, who therefore cannot ever be considered as a subject resting in itself before having a relation to the world. Dasein's being-employed by being is the mark of its deprivation of any "interiority" that could make of it a separate being.

From this new perspective, the transformation of the metaphysical man into Da-sein means *becoming* mortal, in other words, "to become capable of death as death," as Heidegger explains in *The Thing*, a lecture from 1950. In fact, in this period, Heidegger no longer speaks of the being of man in terms of Dasein, but refers to human being only by the collective name of "the mortals," insofar as they are part of the worlding of world, which has now to be understood as the unity of a fourfold event that has no ground and cannot be explained by something else. This means that the four "regions" of the world – sky and earth, divinities and mortals – cannot be considered to be separate realities that could be explained by another reality or founded on one another. Heidegger insists on the fact that each of the four is the mirror of the others, in the sense of a mutual belonging to one another: "None of the four insists on its own separate particularity. Rather, each is expropriated, within their mutual appropriation, into its own being."[33] To think the non-substantiality and the mutual belonging of the four, Heidegger uses the concept of play, so that the worlding of world can be understood as the "appropriating mirror-play of the simple onefold of earth and sky, divinities and mortals."[34]

In this new conception of world, it has to be stressed that human beings still play an important role: they are part of the worlding of world and as such they are inseparable from the other elements. But they are part of the worlding event only as *mortals*, as beings capable of death *as* death, and not as mere living beings. But what does it mean to be "capable" of death? Heidegger explains in his lecture from 1951 on *Building, Dwelling, Thinking*: "The mortals are the human beings. They are called mortals because they can die. To die means to be capable of death as death. Only man dies, and indeed continually, as long as he remains on earth, under the sky, before the divinities."[35] Human existence, as far as it is part of the worlding of world, is considered as a continuous death, and not as a life. But again, what does it mean, to die continually as long as we exist? It can only mean to let death have power on us, and death is here again, as in *Sein und Zeit*, the only possibility that we can never realize, our utmost passivity. To let death have power over us means, therefore, to become aware that we are deprived of the initiative of our own being, that we are not the masters of being – that we are by no means "subjects" in the sense given to this word by modern idealism which considers being as posited by the human subject. This only constitutes the *humanitas* of the *homo humanus* and at the same time makes the worlding of world possible.

However, just as, far from being really human (in the sense of the *homo humanus*), rational living beings, metaphysical men, still must *become* mortal, the world as the fourfold is still to come, it still refuses itself in the same manner as being itself. Therefore, it is not surprising to find in *Zur Seinsfrage*, a small text published in 1956, a connection between this new meaning of *world* and the new meaning of being as *Ereignis*. After having crossed out the word *being*, so that it becomes impossible to represent it as a being in itself facing us and coming to us only occasionally, Heidegger explains that this crosswise crossing out of being has not only a negative meaning, but must also be referred to the unity of the fourfold.[36] The withdrawal of being, its abyssal character, could not be understood by metaphysics which reduces being to an immense objective thing or being, to the *ens realissimum*, and sees in God the ground of all that exists, the *causa sui*. But it becomes clear here, with the crossing out of being, that Heidegger's intention is not to destroy metaphysics, but to bring it back to its truth. However, this truth, which is still concealed and remains still to come, can show itself only if mortals, in their still-to-come abode on earth and under the sky, can also remain before the divinities. The divine dimension of world, which can as such reappear only after the death of the metaphysical God, is also one of the dimensions of the non-anthropological being of man. This is the meaning of the often quoted phrase of the *Spiegel* interview "*Nur ein Gott kann uns retten*," only a god can save us,[37] where the word *save* should not be taken in a soteriological sense, but as Heidegger himself indicates in "The Question Concerning Technology" (in connection with the Hölderlin verse that says "But where danger is, grows/the saving power also"), in the old sense of "to bring the essence for the first time into its proper appearing."[38] Only a god can let us appear as the mortals that we are. The indefinite article here, as the plural in *divinities*, implies a non-monotheistic approach to God, but this does not mean a return to polytheism, to the mythical gods, and a downfall of the rational and philosophical discourse into poetry and mythology. Such an interpretation, which is, for example Levinas's interpretation, is based on presuppositions and prejudices that should first be brought to light.[39] Heidegger's approach to the divine does not imply any presupposed idea of religion and wishes to remain opposed to all anterior conceptions of God, especially the Christian one, as he explains in *Beiträge*, in the famous section dealing with the last or extreme god.

For this god is not the last of a long series of gods, but the extreme figure of the divine, which cannot take the form of a definite entity, because it appears only in a transitory manner. Such a temporal and finite god is beyond all opposition between plurality and unicity, but it must nevertheless divide itself in order to be able to pass into time. For the extreme god is a "passing god," not a god that remains in itself and can be understood as the infinite and absolute Other, but a god that gives to the mortals a sign (*Wink*) that reveals to them the most intimate finitude of being, this finitude of being which implies that being cannot be without man.[40] This does not mean a reduction of divine transcendence to the level of human history. On the contrary, it means a more authentic understanding of the divine that is approached in an inadequate manner through the notion of transcendence, which still implies a reference to man and to the ego as its ground. Neither immanent nor transcendent, the extreme god can manifest itself only by withdrawing, and by giving a sign to mortals, to human beings who have become able to overcome egoism and anthropocentrism. Such a god needs the *Ereignis*, the appropriation of man and being, because it can give a sign in passing only in this meeting place which is being thought as event of the clearing.

Appropriation is one translation of the word *Ereignis*, in one of the senses that Heidegger gives to this word. Its usual sense is "event." To appropriate something does not mean to claim ownership of it, but to bring it to its proper, to let it happen. But to let being happen, a human being has to become what he is, he has to assume his finitude and mortality, and this means also to become able to experience this particular *Stimmung* or mood that in *Beiträge* Heidegger calls "*Verhaltenheit*," restraint, and in which he sees at the same time the fundamental disposition of man and of the thinking of *Ereignis*.[41]

It is in this light that I understand what it means to appropriate Heidegger.

NOTES

1 In his lecture course from 1907, *Die Idee der Phänomenologie*, Husserliana vol. II (The Hague: Nijhoff, 1973), which was published much later and where we find the first account of the phenomenological reduction.

2 See Edmund Husserl, *Cartesianische Meditationen*, Husserliana vol. I (The Hague: Nijhoff, 1950), paragraph 41.

3 In his 1930 preface for the English edition of the first book of his *Ideas*. See *Ideen III*, Husserliana vol. V (The Hague: Nijhoff, 1952), p. 140.

4 See Edmund Husserl, *Notes sur Heidegger* (Paris: Editions de Minuit, 1993), p. 13.

5 See Walter Biemel, "Husserls Encyclopaedia-Britannica Artikel und Heideggers Anmerkungen dazu," *Tijdschrift voor Philosophie* 12 (Leuven: The Institute of Philosophy, 1950), pp. 246–80.

6 Martin Heidegger, *Basic Writings*, ed. D. Krell (San Francisco: Harper, 1993), p. 237 (translation slightly modified).

7 Martin Heidegger, *Sein und Zeit* (Tübingen: Niemeyer, 1963), p. 188.

8 Martin Heidegger, *Vom Wesen des Grundes* (Frankfurt a.M.: Klostermann, 1955), note 55, p. 36.

9 Eugen Fink, *Welt und Endlichkeit* (Würzburg: Königshausen & Neumann, 1990), p. 171.

10 William. J. Richardson, *Heidegger: Through Phenomenology to Thought* (The Hague: Nijhoff, 1963), Preface, p. xvi.

11 Ibid., p. xvii.

12 Heidegger, *Vom Wesen des Grundes*, p. 39.
13 Fink, *Welt und Endlichkeit,* p. 154.
14 Martin Heidegger, *Kant und das Problem der Metaphysik* (Frankfurt a.M.: Klostermann, 1973), p. 201.
15 See Martin Heidegger, *Phänomenologische Interpretation von Kants Kritik der reinen Vernunft, Gesamtausgabe,* vol. 25 (Frankfurt a.M.: Klostermann, 1977), p. 410.
16 Martin Heidegger, *Zur Bestimmung der Philosophie, Gesamtausgabe,* vol. 56/57 (Frankfurt a.M.: Klostermann, 1987), pp. 116–17.
17 Heidegger, *Sein und Zeit,* p. 135.
18 Heidegger, *Kant und das Problem der Metaphysik,* p. 222.
19 Ibid., p. 223.
20 Heidegger, *Sein und Zeit,* p. 200.
21 Heidegger, *Vom Wesen des Grundes,* note 59, p. 42.
22 Martin Heidegger, *Was ist Metaphysik?* (Frankfurt a.M.: Klostermann, 1969), p. 15.
23 Heidegger, *Basic Writings,* p. 245.
24 See *Beiträge zur Philosophie, Gesamtausgabe,* vol. 65 (Frankfurt a.M.: Klostermann, 1989), pp. 317–18.
25 Heidegger, *Die Geschichte des Seins, Gesamtausgabe,* vol. 69 (Frankfurt a.M.: Klostermann, 1998), p. 160.
26 See Martin Heidegger, *Besinnung, Gesamtausgabe,* vol. 66 (Frankfurt a.M.: Klostermann, 1997), pp. 159–63.
27 Heidegger, *Basic Writings,* p. 254.
28 See Martin Heidegger, *Was heisst Denken?* (Tübingen: Niemeyer, 1954), pp. 24–47.
29 Heidegger, *Basic Writings,* p. 227.
30 See Heraclitus, Fragment 75 (Diels-Kranz).
31 *Was ist Metaphysik?*, p. 106.
32 See Martin Heidegger, *Holzwege* (Frankfurt a.M.: Klostermann, 1963), pp. 338–9.
33 Martin Heidegger, *Poetry, Language, Thought,* trans. Albert Hofstadter (New York: Harper & Row, 1975), p. 179.
34 Ibid.
35 Ibid., p. 150.
36 Martin Heidegger, *Zur Seinsfrage* (Frankfurt a.M.: Klostermann, 1959), pp. 30–1.
37 "Spiegel-Gespräch mit Martin Heidegger am 23. September 1966," in *Spiegel,* no. 23 (1976), p. 209.
38 Heidegger, *Basic Writings,* p. 333.
39 From what Levinas says in *Totality and Infinity* (Pittsburgh: Duquesne University Press, 1969), p. 79, Levinas's strictly monotheistic conception of religion, which he openly considers to be superior to all other religious conceptions, can be understood only as a humanistic, and in fact a "too humanistic" understanding of the divine: "It is our relations with men . . . that give to theological concepts the sole signification they admit of . . .

Everything that cannot be reduced to an interhuman relation represents not the superior form but the forever primitive form of religion."

40 Heidegger, *Beiträge zur Philosophie,* p. 410.

41 Ibid., p. 69.

PART 3

Reading Being and Time

CHAPTER 9

In respectful contempt: Heidegger, appropriation, facticity

Rudi Visker

The respectful contempt to which I refer in my title is not my own. Nor does it concern Heidegger. At least not directly. It is Hilary Putnam who in *Reason, Truth and History*[1] in the course of a discussion on relativism, just after showing that it is self-refuting, suddenly reminds himself and his readers of the ambivalent attitude which he has to one of his colleagues with whom he has been engaged in a political discussion over many years without them coming any nearer to one another. Putnam refuses to draw relativist conclusions from this. Neither he, nor his co-disputant, Bob Nozick, he assures us, would agree that what divides them is "just a matter of taste" (*RTH* 165). Such a "false relativism" is "dishonest" (*RTH* 166), it lacks the courage to admit that in such a fundamental disagreement each of the disputants feels "something akin to contempt, not for the other's *mind* . . . nor for the other as a *person* . . . but for a certain complex of emotions and judgments in the other" (*RTH* 165). There is "respect for the intellectual virtues in the other," but it goes together with "contempt for the intellectual and emotional weaknesses" (*RTH* 166). Each of the parties in such a discussion may find the other to be excelling in open-mindedness, willingness to consider reason and arguments, honesty, integrity, kindness etc., but nonetheless "regards the other as lacking" with respect to the issue they disagree on "a certain kind of sensitivity and perception" (*RTH* 165). In such a situation, Putnam suggests, "respectful contempt" is clearly the "more honest attitude." It is to be preferred to the relativist "pretense that there is no giving reasons, or such a thing as better or worse reasons on a subject, when one really does feel that one view is reasonable and the other is irrational" (*RTH* 166).

I am not particularly impressed by the sort of conclusions that Putnam would like to draw from this example, nor by his way of handling it. Suffice it to say that a "certain complex of feelings and judgments in the other" is a rather hazy notion which does not, to my mind, become more precise by Putnam's repeated assurance that the mixed feelings with which he reacts to that complex do not bear on the other as a person. In fact, it is quite striking to observe with what apparent ease Putnam can introduce what he himself calls an "interestingly mixed" (*RTH* 165) and "ambivalent" (*RTH* 166) attitude like respectful contempt, only to take it apart on the next page into the two components of respect and contempt, that apparently owe their independence to a reference to different parts or "complexes" in the other. There is a whole ontology of the person involved here, and although Putnam has, of course, no doubt thought deeply about that too, my reason for mentioning his anecdote has not to do with the views he himself takes on it, but with the anecdote as such. For I think that Putnam, whatever his other merits may be, has certainly a point about the analogy which he would like to build between a political discussion of the kind he had with Nozick, and (at least some) philosophical discussions, for example those between different schools of thought, like those that each of the essays in this volume is supposed to represent. I would not go so far as to suggest that what the contributors feel for each other is – or should be, if we are "honest" – a mixture of respect and contempt – not only because that would be both presumptuous and presumptive, but also because I am inclined to believe that if one transposes the sort of situation that Putnam describes to philosophical conferences like that which gave rise to this volume, what one feels is not first and foremost a mixture of respect and contempt, but something more akin to what Heidegger has called in paragraph 29 of *Being and Time*[2] a *fahle Ungestimmtheit*, a pallid lack of mood which is "not nothing" (*BT* 173/134), but a mood (a *Stimmung*) in its own right, and, as Heidegger suggests, not the least current one in everyday life.

Everydayness is, of course, not just a condition of those who are outside of philosophy. It affects philosophers too. Not just outside their professional life, but in its very heart, although philosophers have found all sorts of tricks to prevent it from contaminating the kind of mood (wonderment etc.) which they deem worthy of philosophy. The most common of these tricks consists in recognizing the presence of everydayness and its accompanying lack of mood,[3] while locating it in the margins of philosophy. Heidegger is no exception here: one only needs to open some of the volumes of the *Gesamtausgabe* to enjoy the delicate sarcasm with which he treats philosophical conferences, that aim to "generate an understanding" through "the cumulation of lack of understanding" (*GA* 20: 376/273).[4] But even if one would be inclined to think that he is exaggerating when in the *History of the Concept of Time* he scolds those "people who travel from one conference to another" – people like the other contributors and me – "and are convinced in doing so that something is really happening" (ibid.), the fact remains that those of us who think that the sort of conferences that Heidegger is critizing here are the ones *they* do not attend, nonetheless introduce their own margins into the sort of conferences which they do attend. There is, for example, the official conference time, the lectures and the discussions, and then there is that marginal time, for example between two lectures when one exchanges views or impressions which basically come down to expressing one's interest in what one has just heard, or one's "pallid" (*BT* 173/134) lack of interest or enthusiasm. Something has been said there, some discussion took place, but it failed to catch our attention. We do not know really what to think of it, whether it is true or not, we have no particular problem with it, and cannot think of a good counter-argument, it was just not our sort of thing. Or if it was, we profit from the break to state to our companion what we did not allow ourselves to say in public. It is true that the speaker had our attention, we even did him the honor of raising what we honestly thought to be a serious objection, but between you and me, although I could not tell you what was missing in his lecture, something was. I would not like my students to write like that; that is not the way it should be done; or was that not typical of X or Y, I do not know what they see in him; and no, no, I am not saying that he did not have a point, it is just that . . .

I have been eavesdropping at the margins of philosophy, and what I heard would be according to the author of *Being and Time* just the noisy hubbub of idle talk with its typical ambiguity, distantiality (*Abständigkeit*) and uprootedness. But my reason for doing so was a bit more complicated than such an orthodox application of Heidegger's insights seems to suggest. As I mentioned before, and I am certainly not the first one to underline it, it is not so evident that one can label the murmur in the margins of thought in the strict sense, with tags like "everydayness" or "the 'they'," "*doxa*" or "sophistry." When Heidegger says that "there is a sophist in every philosopher" because "philosophy is essentially a human, that is: a finite possibility" (*GA* 27: 24), or when, making fun of philosophical conferences in the passage I quoted from the *Prolegomena*, he adds that "ancient sophistry" displayed the same "essential structure, although it was perhaps shrewder in certain ways" (*GA* 20: 377/273), he is not exactly original in this attempt to separate philosophy or thought from its inessential margins. It is true that Heidegger, in speaking of an essentially human, finite possibility and in explicitly recognizing therein "a possibility which is constitutive of the structure of Dasein" (ibid.), seems already to be engaged in a rather complicated attempt to keep philosophy uncontaminated, on the one hand, whilst on the other hand outdoing himself in trying to understand the structure of that tendency that makes philosophy – and not just philosophy, but *Dasein* as such – prone to a contamination in which he sees a covering up and an untruth. I will come back to this later, when discussing thrownness, falling, and facticity. But for now, let me just stress that Heidegger is in no way taking the fashionable line of deconstructing the strict demarcation between philosophy and sophistry or between thought and doxa. And this is an observation which should concern us all, given the theme of this volume and its chosen motto from *What Is Called Thinking?*: "Every confrontation of two different interpretations of a work . . . is in reality a mutual reflection [*Besinnung*] on the guiding presuppositions: it is the discussion [*Erörterung*] of these presuppositions – a task which, strangely, is always tolerated only marginally [*am Rande*] and *covered up* with empty generalities."[5]

Perhaps the shortest possible way of summarizing what I am up to here would be to state that, as you may already have suspected, I want to contest Heidegger's perception of these margins. Or rather, I would like to take another look at what exactly is happening in these margins, which Heidegger divides into two: the margins filled with empty generalities, which tend to usurp the text they are supposed only to accompany; and, as a result of that usurpation, the margins into which the true task of thinking, which should really be at the center of our attention, gets marginalized. What should be uncovered is covered up, forced to move into the margin, and into a solitude in which it humbly continues its task: "No thinker ever has entered into another thinker's solitude. Yet it is only from its solitude that all thinking, in a hidden mode, speaks to the thinking that comes after or that went before."[6]

If we would put this quote from *What Is Called Thinking?* next to the one which the editors of this volume have offered us as a motto, the standard Heideggerian explanation for the marginality of the task of thinking immediately jumps into view: given that thinking is a solitary business, it is, on second thought, not so strange that a mutual *Besinnung* on the guiding presuppositions is something that is, more often than not, covered up with empty generalities – or as the German says more precisely: with *allgemeine Redensarten*, with *common ways of speaking*. What such commonality does is precisely to cover up a solitude that, in the last instance, would be what *Being and Time* has been trying to unearth as *the* solitude of solitudes: the solitude of every *Dasein* which it cannot share with others, since it comes from the heart of its being as an obligation to exist. It is, as we shall see in more detail later, this "naked that" of existence (*das nackte Daß*) which forms the core of Heidegger's analytics of *Dasein* and which explains how he can both come to distrust sophistry and see in its twin brothers, skepticism or relativism, at once "a fruitful rebellion" (*fruchtbare Rebellion*) against what he calls the "exteriorization of philosophy" ("Veräußerlichung der Philosophie") and "eine Halbheit," something that stops mid-way (*GA* 17: 99).

Heidegger's qualified sympathy for these rebel movements is not so difficult to understand: he shares their enemies. As he says in his 1924 lecture for the Marburg Theological Society: "anxiety in the face of (*vor*) relativism is anxiety in the face of (*vor*) Dasein."[7] The context is the contemporary "moaning about historicism" and the belief that one needs, again, the "supra-historical." It is precisely this craving for a firm grip, above or outside of time, which betrays, according to Heidegger, an anxiety in the face of Dasein, an attempt "to steal away from time," i.e. from what makes up the "Da" of such Dasein. But the sort of easy embrace of time (one need only think of Ranke's famous "gleich unmittelbar zu Gott" – although Heidegger does not mention him) implied in historicism is not, of course, what Heidegger would advocate instead. Historicism is but the flipside of the craving for the supra-historical, just as relativism and skepticism are merely absolutism reversed (cf. *GA* 61: 162 ff.). It is remarkable with what tenacity Heidegger keeps raising the same critical question in the lecture courses leading up to *Being and Time* (see, for example, *GA* 60: 31ff.): what exactly is it that one wants to secure oneself against by seeking refuge in either side of these oppositions? And whether he is analyzing Husserl's *Philosophy as a Rigorous Science* or Troeltsch or Spengler (there is almost no lecture course which does not bring up Spengler at some point or other), Heidegger's answer is always the same: "wir müssen also das Bekümmerungsphänomen im *faktischen* Dasein *unverdeckt* zu Gesicht zu bekommen versuchen" (*GA* 60: 52) (roughly: we have to try to get a direct look at this phenomenon of worrying in factical Dasein without anything covering it up). This means that instead of joining the public chorus that cries out "the universal validity" (*Allgemeingültigkeit*) of knowledge is in danger, skepticism!" (*GA* 61: 88), we have to turn our attention toward the being that is addressed here, the being that is supposed to sense this danger and sensibly react to it, and we have to wonder whether what is implicitly presented as that being's *only* sensible response is not precisely the kind of response which "alienates"[8] that being from its being. In other words, we have to undertake an analytics of Dasein, and in the course of that analysis, we have to understand against what kind of "unrest" (*Unruhe*) Dasein is, first and foremost, trying to protect itself. Heidegger is going to raise what Deleuze once called the Nietzschean question par excellence: "Who is speaking?". In Heidegger's terms: what sort of care (*Sorge*) is behind the care for a firm, absolutely valid knowledge, for a *strenge Wissenschaft*? Who is the "subject" of that care? And what or who is it trying to subject? Foucault should perhaps have thought twice before letting Nietzsche get the upper hand over Heidegger, who to my mind did not influence him enough.

This last reference, tongue in cheek, to Foucault's famous last interview,[9] which shocked his readers with its unexpected revelation of his earlier obsession with Heidegger (from which Nietzsche relieved him), will not have surprised those readers who are somewhat familiar with my interests.[10] The reason why I bring it up is that my own "appropriation of Heidegger" was triggered by my disappointment with Foucault's turn to Nietzsche.

It seemed to me that Foucault's "genealogical" writings (*Discipline and Punish*, *Power/Knowledge*, etc.), that marked the breakthrough of his popularity in the US, represented some sort of decadence in comparison with the earlier "archaeological" phase (*The Order of Things*, etc.), which earned him his chair at the Collège de France. The sort of Nietzscheanism that inspired him in his genealogies seems to have been won at the cost of a complete obliteration of what comes closest, in contemporary continental philosophy's jargon, to what Heidegger called "ontological difference," i.e. the idea of a "symbolic order."[11] In the roughest of strokes: when Foucault reverses Clausewitz and sees in politics a war continued with other means, then links Truth to power, and thus to politics, and goes on suggesting that the Truth is always the Truth *of someone*, and that like the code of law, it is written with the blood of the besieged, and is constantly trying to muffle the clamor of the war continuing underneath it, he is in fact naturalizing what Lacan, Lévi-Strauss or Lefort would call the symbolic.[12] As these authors have stressed in various ways, the symbolic is not what mirrors or reflects something prior to it, but what gives it form and structure. Foucault is, of course, right in asking "*whose* form?," but he is so charmed by the possibilities of this new "genealogical" question that he forgets a point he made with great clarity in his archaeological writings: that every imprinting of a form or a structure or an "order" (like in *The Order of Discourse*) brings with it its own limitation, exclusion, and rarefaction. The voids that are necessary to tell any meaningful story are not by themselves political. Politics contests the sort of voids and the sort of meaning it generates. It would be wrong to contest there being voids as such. And this is exactly what genealogy implies when it blames the law for not being as "founded" as it should be, i.e. for not being a law at all, but a war-machine. By uncovering *all* law as martial law, Foucault misses what is written in Lacanian psychoanalysis as Law. He reduces that dimension, without which no law could ever be a law, to its *present* (*vorhanden*) representative, and thus falls short of what again, in psychoanalytic terms, one would call *symbolic* castration (which has nothing to do with male domination, or with the penis and its envy, but with that void which there is, of necessity, between an arbitrary symbolic system [e.g., the linguistic chain of signifiers] and what it is "about"; in Heideggerian terms: language is a world-disclosive power, which cannot be grounded exclusively in what it discloses, for "world" is not a being, but an ontological function). In other words, Foucault, notwithstanding his fervent denials, is re-entering with his turn to genealogy the naturalism which he has always sought to escape (and which he in fact escaped in his archaeology). In accusing the law of not being a good law, he implicitly stipulates what he *would accept* as a good law: a law which would be entirely founded, and thus a law which would miss what one could call with Lyotard or Levinas, the moment of "obligation". With the idea of an entirely legitimate law where the one for whom it holds would be perfectly interchangeable for the one who issues it, genealogy, again psychoanalytically spoken, has not only discovered perversion (*The History of Sexuality I*) as a new object of study, it has raised it to the dignity of a method.

Hence my own turn away from genealogy and from the Foucault of archaeology to the later Heidegger, who thought that there was a *lèthè* which no *alètheia* could ever do away with; an untruth not equiprimordial to truth, as *Being and Time* still held (paragraph 44), but an untruth that, as Heidegger tells us in *Vom Wesen der Wahrheit*, would be older than truth.[13] It is a phrase which led me to speculate about what for us was still at stake in that mysterious *Kehre* which everyone evoked, but which I failed to understand until I "appropriated" it in my own way. I do not know whether that was a happy decision, it is one that I cannot undo. But since

I want to "repeat" it, in the Heideggerian sense of *Wiederholung*, allow me to draw just a few more lines on the map on which I am trying to find my co-ordinates.

If Foucault's genealogy turned to a "politics of truth," his archaeology seemed to call instead for something like an "ethics of truth." Not a set of moral rules, but an *èthos* in the sense that Heidegger had invoked in his "Letter on Humanism": "The word names the open region in which the human being dwells . . . The abode of the human being contains and preserves the advent of what belongs to the human being in his essence."[14] Or again: "More essential than instituting rules is that human beings find the way to their abode in the truth of being."[15] Abode, *èthos*, is rendered by Heidegger as *Aufenthalt*, which can both mean "residence" (hence: abode), but also something like "delay." One could say that the *Halt* in *Aufenthalt* is both what holds you and what holds you up. Heidegger is usually understood, and perhaps understood himself, as pointing to the first of these meanings (the abode contains and preserves), but if one reads him with Foucault's archaeology in the back of one's mind, there seems in principle room for the second meaning too. Discourse, as Foucault understood it, seems to be both an open region in which we dwell and which holds us, but by thus being held we are also invested with a finitude the weight of which we feel when we don't manage to get (for example) our thoughts across. Like Putnam in his conversations with Nozick, we do not manage to drive home our point. Something seems to hold us up, but it is the same something that allows us to make our point in the way we make it. This something is not, of course, an ontic something. It is not a being, but that in the light of which beings can appear. It is of the same order as what Heidegger mysteriously calls Being. But there is nothing mysterious about it. It is not, as Putnam himself seems to suspect, his "point," his "argument" *as such* which lacks the refinement it would need in order to become acceptable to Nozick, it is, as Putnam rather helplessly tries to explain their endless moving in circles, a "certain kind of sensitivity and perception" which, however, he immediately hypostatizes into an ontic "complex of emotions and judgments *in* the other."

It is against this combination of such a hypostatization and the causalization which it allows (my reasons are sound, it's Nozick's sensitivity which I find lacking!) that Heidegger and Foucault, if read through each others' spectacles, seem to warn us. As Ian Hacking has superbly shown in his translation of Foucault's insight into the language of analytic philosophy,[16] with notions such as "discourse" we have what one can regard as a framework relativism of the non-Quinean type and hence as resistant to the Davidsonian attack: it is not the truth but the possible truth-value of a statement which is dependent on the framework, which simply means that one must be able to "hear" a proposition, in the sense of "taking it seriously," in order for it to be accepted as a candidate for either truth or falsity (for correspondence-truth). It is this "ability" or "sensitivity" which we owe not to ourselves, but to what Foucault calls "discourse" or Heidegger calls "clearing" (a parallel which I have argued for at length elsewhere, cf. note 10), which supports our speech, enables us to formulate what (and as) we do, and which can give it that strange gravity which hinders it to land on that planet that we call "the other" – not always, of course, but in those cases where the other sees (or formulates) things, as one says, in a different light than we do. Although one can never be certain, when one is trapped in the kind of disagreement that Putnam describes, the uncanniness that like mist seems to dim the light between us and our co-disputant may be due to him and us bathing in a different light. As *Being and Time* said, the other is not a subject. He is, like me, *Dasein*, being-in-the-world. But *Being and Time* never said that his world and my own need to be the same – neither ontically, nor, of course, ontologically. One is, Heidegger told us, always-already-in-a-specific-world. One always already "bathes" or "dwells" in a specific light through which certain phenomena can come to appear. And when Heidegger in paragraph 29 decided to move not beyond but before "all psychology of moods" by relating what one ontically knows as "moods" to what he ontologically termed "Befindlichkeit" (probably to be translated as "finding-oneself-in-a-situation"),[17] he was not just forestalling the flattening effects of analyses like that of Putnam (who, in his own way, misses the point of ontological difference), but in principle at least opening the door to the sort of "ethics" that we seem more than ever in need of. Instead of *locating* that which holds us up *in* the other (and thus potentially blaming him, or at least a part of him: Nozick's "complex"), Heidegger wanted to turn our attention to the fact that when "finding-ourselves-in-a-situation" we do not *find* ourselves in the ordinary sense of "find": "A mood assails us. It comes neither from 'outside' nor from 'inside', but arises out of Being-in-the-world, as a way of such Being" (*BT* 176/136). The "complex of emotions and judgments" to which we respond with "respectful contempt" is not hidden somewhere "outside" of us "inside" the other, nor is that affect which assails us somewhere "in" us or "between" us and the other. Like any other affect, Heidegger tells us, it "can be understood only in conjunction with the basic movement [*Grundbewegung*] of Dasein itself" (*GA* 20: 354/256). And as is well known, there are three "moments" in that movement which together constitute the structure of care as the "movement principle" (*Bewegungsprinzip*) of human being: existentiality (ahead-of-oneself), facticity (being-already-in), and falling (being-alongside-with). These moments are co-original, but the first is, as it were, *primus inter pares*. Indeed, it must be, not just for *Being and Time* to be the book it is, but also, I suspect, for it to be the project that failed, according to Heidegger's own admission, in the way it did: *Being and Time*, Heidegger says somewhere, had its defects (*Mängel*), but one did not notice them, "since its pagination continued" (cf. *GA* 49:27).

One of the first, if not *the* first, and still one of the very few not to be fooled by Heidegger's continuing pagination (including the pagination of those texts in which Heidegger after his "turn" tried to retrieve what went astray in *Being and Time*), was certainly Emmanuel Levinas, one of Heidegger's readers of the first hour who was going to introduce his work in France. Unfortunately Levinas's resistance to Heidegger – perhaps the only significant one in this century – was left largely unexplored, precisely because of the success and renown which the books which grew out of that resistance had brought him. *Totality and Infinity* and *Otherwise than Being* were (and still are) considered to be exercises in the grey zone between ethics, metaphysics, and religion, with the result that, for Heideggerians at least, Levinas's work became at best some sort of supplement to Heidegger, which could perhaps be inspiring (after all, Heidegger's answer to the young student in the *Letter on Humanism*, concerning the place of ethics in his work, did not fully satisfy all of his readers), but only after one had purged it of its clear misunderstandings of what had really been at stake in the "thought of Being." The countless remarks in which Levinas shows, from 1932 onwards, not only that he understood these stakes, but also understood why they were so high, were (and still are, with *very* few exceptions) simply ignored: "It is important," he writes after brilliantly summarizing Heidegger's project in *Being and Time*, "to stress this reduction to time of everything that one would be tempted to call 'supratemporal', the reduction to existence of everything one would like to call 'relation.'"[18] This was 1932, a remark in passing in his first text on Heidegger. Here are two random passages from some of his last works which underline the same tendency to what he was already calling "ontologism" (ibid.): "There is reduction of everything human to ontology. The privilege of Dasein resides in that it exists ontologically. Everything that man is, all his modalities are adverbs: not properties, but ways of being."[19] Or again: "Heidegger's being-in-the-world is a comprehension: technological activity itself is openness, discovery of Being, even if in the mode of a forgetting of Being" – an obvious statement to anyone familiar with Heidegger, to which Levinas adds the following, slightly less obvious remark: "The ontic, which at least involves an opaqueness, everywhere yields before the ontological, before a covered-over luminosity to be disengaged. The *existentiell* reveals its meaning in the existential, which is an articulation of onto-logy. An entity counts only on the basis of knowing, of appearing, of phenomenality."[20] And this included that very special entity that Heidegger no longer wanted to call a "subject":

> Being's *esse*, through which an entity is an entity, is a matter of thought, gives something to thought, stands from the first in the open. In that there is indeed a kind of indigence in being, constrained to an other than itself, to a subject called upon to welcome the manifestation . . . [It] follows that, outside of the part subjectivity plays in the disclosure of being, every game that consciousness would play for its own account would be but a veiling or an obscuring of being's *esse*.[21]

A last quote which will allow us to understand what is at stake in the previous one: "*Being and Time* has argued perhaps but one sole thesis: Being is inseparable from the comprehension of Being (which unfolds as time); Being is already an appeal to subjectivity."[22]

For someone familiar with Heidegger, the striking thing about these quotes is probably that, except for a few relics of a vocabulary that Heidegger has rendered obsolete ("subject," "consciousness"), they seem to add nothing new, underscoring the obvious as they do, whereas someone familiar with Levinas is likely already to have heard, in some of the terms that he uses here (such as "reduction" or "relation"), the echo of that "Otherwise than Being" which in his mature works Levinas tried to salvage from the *Seinsfrage*. But is there not a third way of listening to these quotes? Let me try to summarize what I hear in them in my own words.

Although we are all familiar with Heidegger's famous "the essence of Dasein lies in its existence" (*BT* 67/42), we are perhaps too familiar with it. For what is implied in this thesis is not only that the privilege of Dasein is to exist ontologically; it also means that if Dasein in its factical existence "covers up" this privilege, this covering up should be understood out of the very structure of that existence itself. Understood, but not justified. For "hermeneutics has the task of making Dasein, which is in each case our own, accessible to this Dasein itself . . . [and] to trace the self-alienation that has struck Dasein to its sources."[23] And the source of this self- alienation, which makes Dasein opaque to itself, lies not outside of Dasein, but in its very heart. Dasein's existence is by itself "burdensome" (*BT* 173/134) because it is a being without essence: a being that has to be its being. Not only does it have to be its being, it cannot but be its being. Whatever it does, whatever way it is, this will be a way of being its being, of filling it out, so to speak. This filling out has always already happened. Dasein exists factically. It is always already thrown into a given world, engaged in certain relations with beings, including others and itself. And as it is thrown, it tends to focus, without even noticing it, on what it is thrown into. It chooses, without noticing, the path of least resistance: falling along with the movement of its thrownness, Dasein has a "tendency to take it easy and make it easy" (*BT* 165/128 translation revised). This "it" is its own being, the "naked 'that' " of its existence: that it has to be its being, that it has to answer for it.[24] But before Dasein can reply to this responsibility, it always already has received a reply through its thrownness: it finds this reply in the world into which it has been thrown and in which it always already has taken up certain possibilities which that world made available to it. If it were asked to think of itself, Dasein would think of these activities, the relations they involve, the problems it faces in each of these, and the sort of future it can reasonably expect to build starting from these perspectives. But, says Heidegger, the problem is that these perspectives are "twisted" (e.g. *GA* 17: 287), not because they are wrong, but because the light in them comes from the wrong side. Although this light is in principle ontological, it reflects back on Dasein only after having touched its activities and the beings they engage with. Dasein's "own self is reflected back on it out of the things" that occupy it, with which it is busy (*GA* 24: 227). Its own possibility to be (*Seinkönnen*) is taken over by the things with which it is engaged: it tends to become determined by the success or failures of such engagement, by what it leaves to be done and shows as impossible (*GA* 24: 410). Through this "Reluzenz"-structure which belongs to the very structure of its being (for Dasein ex-ists), Dasein is, as it were, *blinded.* It is oblivious of itself (*GA* 24: 411), and what's more, it seems to like it. For the answer that the world has given it, still gives it some leeway, some possibility to prove itself. If Dasein exists factically as a philosopher, and if it is on a tenure-track, it can keep track of that track; if it has an endowed chair, it has a reputation to defend, conferences to go to, prizes to win. Some hold is given to it and it grabs for it (cf. *GA* 61: 117 ff., esp. 121–2) and will also defend it. If it happens to have a certain expertise in a field of philosophy because it has familiarized itself with the books of a certain philosopher, it may not feel inclined to engage with other such philosophers in a mutual *Erörterung* of the guiding presuppositions of their different interpretations of those books. It may rather think of them as belonging to different schools. It may even feel for such schools what Putnam called respectful contempt.

As is well known, all of what I have just described would be considered by *Being and Time* as a covering-up of Dasein's basic nothingness, of its being without a hold, a pure possibility to be. It would thus have to side with the untruth, with semblance, and irresponsibility. It would be a flight from a threat that comes out of Dasein itself: the threat that it has to be its being, and that there is no "what," no "content" to this being which is not *the "what" of such "that."* It is this thesis of every "what" being the "what" of a "that" which I am inclined to link to what Levinas called a reduction to the ontological, and which he linked himself, correctly I think, to *Being and Time*'s explicit attempt to show that all ontic opaqueness is a covered-over luminosity to be disengaged. This attempt in its turn issued in the further attempt, central to *Being and Time*, to show that the subject's own "game" is precisely the game of being: all parts that it tries to play outside the part it plays in the disclosure of being, its every attempt to turn away from that disclosure, is still a move within its script, testifying to Dasein's pre-ontological familiarity with being even where it may be ontically forgetful of it. Being, Heidegger says in paragraph 39, " 'is' only in the understanding of those entities to whose Being something like an understanding of Being belongs. Hence Being can be *unbegriffen* [not grasped], but not *unverstanden* [it never completely fails to be understood]" (*BT* 228/183). There will always remain a trace that betrays Dasein's having tried to turn away from (its) being. The cover up betrays itself. Without that premiss *Being and Time* could not be a *hermeneutics* of facticity, just as *Being and Time* could not be a hermeneutics *of suspicion* without the analyses of death and anxiety which show that it is a possibility for Dasein not to turn away from its being. Nothing can completely cover up the naked "that" of existence, since this nakedness is not that of a thing, but of the "No Thing" that Heidegger calls being. Man's true roots come from being, even if being in a certain sense uproots him. But only in a certain sense, for this "Unzuhause" brings man home into his own being; it allows him to give the response to that being for which he has to answer. "I am, that means I can," says the text of the *Prolegomena* and it explains: "Dasein itself, insofar as it is, is nothing but being-possible" (*GA* 20: 412/298) – which will lead *Being and Time* to that strange reasoning that since "facticity is not the factuality of the factum brutum . . . but a characteristic of Dasein's Being," this must mean that it "has been *taken up* [*aufgenommen*] into existence" (*BT* 174/135).

The question that bothers me and that should bother all of us, given the theme of this volume, is whether thereby "facticity" *as we know it* has not been *dissolved* into existence. As we know it, e.g. in light of the "fact" that this volume seems to have convinced most of us that our readings of Heidegger, indeed, depend on what the quote from *What Is Called Thinking?* referred to as "guiding presuppositions," and thus seem to display a certain "style" of thinking.[25] But if that is the case, one may wonder whether the true reason for our reluctance to engage in the task that the editors of this volume, like Heidegger, are urging us to engage in, could not be that we suspect that the "naked that" of existence may not be as naked as Heidegger would have liked it to be. In other words, the ontical alternative rooted/uprooted, which, turned around, still determines *Being and Time*'s fundamental ontology,[26] may not be the correct one. Man could be a being who is neither with nor without roots, and whose true unrest comes from the facticity of having both too many roots for the "that" of his existence to be naked, and too few roots for it to become absorbable into a "what."[27] Something does not stand out in man's existence, but it insists in it without, however, turning into one of those "properties" which Heidegger rightly denied that man has. Perhaps he would have glimpsed that something which is not a thing, neither ontic nor ontological, had he turned not to death but to the Other to let man be confronted with his finitude. Whereas death dissolves all "what" into a "that,"[28] the Other, like Nozick for Putnam, confronts the subject with its "that" always being the "that" of a "what" which both holds him and holds him up.

Perhaps what one calls style is the dust that covers the nakedness of existence. And as we all know, there is a dust through which things shine and get a glow. *Le style c'est l'homme*, but man *is* not his style. In the midst of its transition, being is interrupted by something that makes it less than a transitive verb.[29] It is also, I think, that something that had interrupted the pagination of *Being and Time*, somewhere between paragraphs 41 and 50. On p. 235/191, Heidegger writes: "That in the face of which we have anxiety is *thrown* Being-in-the-world;" on p. 295/251 he writes "That in the face of which one has anxiety is Being-in-the-world itself" (translation revised). In between these two quotes the facticity of thrownness (our always being in a *specific* world) has been dissolved into a facticity that could be taken up into existence which could then play the role of first among its equals. As a consequence, anxiety for relativism can come to be interpreted by Heidegger as an anxiety for Dasein, i.e. for its ex-istence, for its every "what" being the "what" of a "that." But if one insists upon the "that" being the "that" of a "what," which is neither "Nothing" nor an "object," a different unrest seems to creep into the heart of man's being. Anxiety for relativism could then perhaps be seen as an anxiety for what is not "Da" to Dasein, for what, in its facticity, cannot be taken up in its existence.[30] Instead of a primacy of the future, one would have to reckon, through such facticity, with the competing primacy of a past which has never been present. And these competing claims would not, as they have until now, point to the difference between ontology (Heidegger) and ethics (Levinas). They would, on the contrary, testify to "something" disrupting ontology *from within*, indicating perhaps that man's being is the being of a being *that has to care for "something"* (neither an object, nor Heidegger's "No Thing") *that does not care for it.* Being, that is, may not be a transitive verb after all. Something escapes that transition, hiding perhaps in the hyphen which Heidegger after his "turn" tried to introduce into Dasein's existence. But then the *ek-sistence* on which the *Letter on Humanism* insisted would stand, contrary to what Heidegger is claiming there, for something left unaddressed by the author of *Being and Time.*

NOTES

1 Cambridge: Cambridge University Press, 1981. Parenthetically quoted as *RTH.*

2 I will quote from *Being and Time*, trans. J. Macquarrie and E. Robinson (Oxford: Blackwell, 1962) with the pagination of *Sein und Zeit*, 15th edn. (Tübingen: Niemeyer, 1979) after the solidus. Parenthetically quoted as *BT.*

3 I am not suggesting that everydayness is necessarily *ungestimmt.* It knows other moods too. But the lack of mood is typical for the *Durchschnittlichkeit* characteristic of everydayness.

4 Martin Heidegger, *Gesamtausgabe* (Frankfurt a.M.: Klostermann). Parenthetically quoted as *GA* followed by volume and page number.

5 Martin Heidegger, *What Is Called Thinking?*, trans. anon. (New York: Harper & Row, n.d.), p. 177 (my italics)/*Was heißt Denken?*, 4th edn. (Tübingen: Niemeyer, 1984), pp. 109–10. These sentences had been printed on the poster announcing the "Appropriating Heidegger" conference.

6 Ibid., 169/164.

7 Martin Heidegger, *The Concept of Time*, trans. W. H. McNeill (Oxford: Blackwell, 1992), p. 20/20E.

8 A word that is used a lot by Heidegger in this period. The central passage in *Being and Time* is paragraph 38 where "Entfremdung" and "entfremdend" occur seven times.

9 Michel Foucault, "Le Retour de la morale," *Les Nouvelles Littéraires* (June 28–July 5 1984), pp. 36–41; trans. "The Return of Morality," in *Politics, Philosophy, Culture: Interviews and Other Writings, 1977–84*, ed. L. D. Kritzman (New York/London: Routledge, 1988), pp. 242–54, esp. p. 250 (on Nietzsche/Heidegger).

10 *Michel Foucault: Genealogy as Critique*, trans. C. Turner (London/New York: Verso, 1995) (original Dutch: 1990). Some of my later essays on Foucault and Heidegger are reprinted in my *Truth and Singularity. Taking Foucault into Phenomenology*, Phaenomenologica no. 155 (Dordrecht: Kluwer, 1999).

11 Admirers of Foucault's genealogy will, of course, object to the sort of caricature that I am going to give of it in the long sentence that follows (its length and its syntax being an indication of a certain loss of interest that often sets in after one has struggled with an author for years). In my defense I could point them to the meticulous analysis of the internal tensions in his genealogical writings which I have tried to make in my *Genealogy as Critique*, chs. 2 and 3, esp. pp. 54–73. My comments in the following lines refer to Foucault's recently published 1975–6 lecture course: *"Il faut défendre la société." Cours au collège de France (1975–6)* (Paris: Seuil/Gallimard, 1997). Foucault's summary of that course appeared significantly titled as "War in the Filigree of Peace: Course Summary," *The Oxford Literary Review* 4 (1980), 15–19. Fragments of it were published previously: "Two Lectures," in *Power/Knowledge: Selected Interviews and Other Writings 1972–1977*, ed. C. Gordon (New York: Pantheon Books, 1980), pp. 78–108 (esp. pp. 90–2 on Clausewitz) and the German bootleg publication of the two following lectures which caused quite a shock: *Vom Licht des Krieges zur Geburt der Geschichte*, ed. W. Seitter (Berlin: Merve Verlag, 1986); see e.g. p. 43 in "Il faut défendre la société", where Foucault seems to comment without any reservations on the "counter-history" that goes back to Edward Coke and John Lilburne in England and to Boulainvilliers in France, according to which "the laws are born in the blood and the dirt of battles" (my trans.).

12 For an extremely revealing comparison of Foucault's and Lefort's readings of Kantorowicz's *The King's Two Bodies: A Study in Medieval Political Theology* (Princeton, NJ: Princeton University Press, 1957), see Bernard Flynn, "Foucault and the Body Politic," *Man and World* 20 (1987), 65–84.

13 Cf. the essays reprinted in my *Truth and Singularity*, chs. 1 and 2.

14 Martin Heidegger, *Pathmarks*, ed. W. McNeill (Cambridge: Cambridge University Press, 1998), p. 269.

15 Ibid., p. 274.

16 E.g. in his "Language, Truth and Reason," in *Rationality and Relativism*, ed. Steven Lukes and Martin Hollis (Oxford: Blackwell, 1982), pp. 48–66.

17 I follow here Bruce Baugh's excellent "Heidegger on *Befindlichkeit*," *Journal of the British Society for Phenomenology* 20.2 (1989), 124–35.

18 "Martin Heidegger et l'ontologie" (1932), repr. in a modified and abridged form in Emmanuel Levinas, *En découvrant l'existence avec Husserl et Heidegger* (Paris: Vrin, 1988), p. 71, from which I am quoting here in my own translation.

19 *Dieu, la Mort et le Temps* (Paris: Bernard Grasset: 1993), p. 69 (my trans.).

20 *Otherwise than Being or Beyond Essence*, trans. A. Lingis (Dordrecht: Kluwer, 1997), p. 80: I have corrected the translation (*onto-logy* instead of ontology; *phenomenality* instead of *phenomenology*).

21 Ibid., p. 132.

22 *Totality and Infinity: An Essay on Exteriority*, trans. A. Lingis (Dordrecht: Kluwer, 1991), p. 45.

23 Martin Heidegger, *Ontology – The Hermeneutics of Facticity*, trans. John van Buren (Bloomington: Indiana University Press, 1999) p. 11, translation revised.

24 Cf. *BT* 173/134: "nacktes 'Daß es ist und zu sein hat' "; 321/276: "das nackte 'Daß' im Nichts der Welt"; 394/343: "das nackte Dasein"; 394/344: "seine nackte Unheimlichkeit." The English translation has not always rendered *nackte* as "naked."

25 I am thinking of an exchange between Robert Bernasconi and Mark Okrent, where the former, after a very long question which did not seem to get across, exclaimed: "I guess what I am asking is whether you can see why we are not so interested in what you are doing." But as I am sure Bernasconi would agree, it may not have been so much the content of Okrent's (to my mind interesting) argument which stood between them, but rather the "style" of that argument (it being understood that one cannot simply separate "content" and "style," as if the latter were just an outer wrapping. On this last point, see my remarks above on Foucault and Hacking).

26 Throughout *Being and Time* Heidegger opposes an everydayness characterized by "Entwurzelung" (uprootedness) and "Bodenlosigkeit" to a proper existence that is "verwurzelt" (rooted) and "bodenständig" (see the entries in Rainer A. Bast and Heinrich P. Delfosse, *Handbuch zum Textstudium von Martin Heideggers "Sein und Zeit,"* vol. 1 (Stuttgart: Frommann-Holzboog, 1979). These characterizations are *ontological*: *ontically*, everydayness may not feel "uprooted" at all, whereas, from Heidegger's ontological point of view, such "feeling at home" is just the tranquillizing suppression of Dasein's basic "uprootedness" (its "naked 'that it is and has to be' ") which in turn is Dasein's true "Boden." And conversely, what is ontically experienced as uprootedness could be seen ontologically as Dasein hitting "rock bottom" (as in anxiety). All of which seems to allow for the statement that I have just made. To put it more fashionably: one should "deconstruct" the influence the ontical alternative rooted/uprooted may have had on *Being and Time*'s fundamental ontology.

27 I should perhaps stress that in *Truth and Singularity* I have turned this same

idea about man's facticity *against* Levinas. So the point I shall be making in the next lines should not be confused with Levinas's.

28 I am alluding to the beautiful passage in *The Concept of Time*, p. 21/21E in which Heidegger sings the praise of the democracy of death: "In being together with death everyone is brought into the 'how' that each can be in equal measure; into a possibility with respect to which no one is distinguished; into the 'how' in which all 'what' dissolves into dust" (I take this "how" to be an early expression of what *Being and Time* will call Dasein's naked "that").

29 Being is called "transitive" when it has the sense that Levinas indicates in the quote corresponding with note 1: "I am *my being*."

30 This is the thesis that I defend in *Truth and Singularity*, though not in confrontation with Heidegger. The present essay has only been doing some reconnaissance-work on what, in the light of that book, seems to have turned out, quite unexpectedly, to be "enemy territory" – but this is where philosophy gets interesting.

CHAPTER 10

Could anything be more intelligible than everyday intelligibility? Reinterpreting division I of Being and Time *in the light of division II*[1]

Hubert L. Dreyfus

INTRODUCTION

It has always seemed to me that the text of a thinker is only worth studying if reading it makes a significant difference in how we see the world and ourselves. Our job as commentators, is to clarify the text and bring out its relevance. But how does one go about clarifying and applying a thinker like Heidegger? Since Heidegger, unlike contemporary analytic philosophers who attempt to give a logical analysis of concepts, always attempts to anchor his discussion in the phenomena, I try to use his text to draw attention to pervasive phenomena that are often overlooked, and then use an elaboration of these phenomena to cast exegetical light on the text. Finally, I test the significance of the result by seeking to show the relevance of Heidegger's insights to issues of current concern. The following remarks are meant to demonstrate this approach.

AVERAGE VERSUS PRIMORDIAL UNDERSTANDING

Heidegger says that division I of *Being and Time*[2] provides a phenomenology of average everydayness and so will have to be revised in the light of the authentic way of being he describes in division II. My attempt to write a commentary exclusively on division I[3] was, therefore, criticized on the ground that I presented as Heidegger's view theses that were taken back in division II. None of the critical reviewers, however, said what my exclusive concentration on division I led me to get wrong. And, as far as I could tell, none of the claims made in division I were taken back in division II.

I now see, however, that focusing exclusively on division I did, indeed, lead me to make at least one serious mistake. I overlooked warnings, scattered about in division I, that the average intelligibility described there would later be shown to be an inferior form of understanding, in contrast to a richer more primordial kind of understanding described in division II.

In my Commentary,[4] I spelled out Heidegger's basic theses that (1) people have skills for coping with equipment, other people, and themselves; (2) their shared everyday coping practices conform to norms; (3) the interrelated totality of equipment, norms, and social roles form a whole which Heidegger calls "significance"; (4) significance is the basis of average intelligibility; (5) this average intelligibility can be further articulated in language. As Heidegger puts it "We have *the same thing* in view, because it is in *the same* averageness that we have a common understanding of what is said" (p. 212).

In spite of the obvious irony, in Heidegger's conclusion, that "publicness proximally controls every way in which the world and Dasein get interpreted, and it is always right" (p. 165), I concluded that, for both Heidegger and Wittgenstein, the source of the intelligibility of the world and of Dasein is the average public practices articulated in ordinary language.

This interpretation still seems right to me, but I went on, mistakenly, to conclude from the *basis* of intelligibility in average understanding and ordinary language that for Heidegger, as for Wittgenstein, there was no other kind of intelligibility. I noted Heidegger's claim that "by publicness everything gets obscured, and what has thus been covered up gets passed off as something familiar and accessible to everyone" (p. 165), but I went on, nonetheless, to argue that there could be no higher intelligibility than the public, average, intelligibility provided by the social norms Heidegger calls *the one*. Any higher intelligibility, like Plato's ideas, Descartes's mathematical relations among bits of extension, or Hegel's self-transparent *Geist*, I claimed, would necessarily be metaphysical, so Heidegger would surely have rejected any such idea. Likewise, any sort of private intelligibility that was not, at least in principle, shareable would seem to be a sort of *unintelligibility*. The whole point of intelligibility is that it is shared or at least shareable, if not by all rational creatures, at least by all those brought up in a given culture or form of life. So, I simply denied that for Heidegger there could be any higher intelligibility than that in the public practices and the language that articulates them.

I have since come to see that I was wrong. Heidegger clearly holds that there is a form of understanding, of situations, on the one hand, and of Dasein itself, on the other, that is superior to everyday understanding. He calls this superior understanding "primordial understanding" (p. 212). I still hold, however, that this primordial understanding cannot be some radically different way of making sense of things, since, for Heidegger, this higher intelligibility must somehow be based on and grow out of the average intelligibility into which everyone is socialized. So, although such higher intelligibility may in fact be accessible only to the few, as a form of shared intelligibility it must in principle be available to everyone. What could such a more primordial form of understanding be?

To get a clue, it helps to recall what we learn from Ted Kisiel's researches into the sources of *Being and Time.* According to Kisiel, the book grows out of Heidegger's work on Aristotle: division I elaborates on *techne*, everyday skill, and division II on *phronesis*, practical wisdom.[5] So we would expect Heidegger to present his own version of the mastery of the cultural practices that, according to Aristotle, enables the *phronimos* to "straightway" "do the appropriate thing at the appropriate time in the appropriate way." But just what phenomena do Aristotle and Heidegger have in mind with *techne* and *phronesis*? The way to find out is to let these phenomena show themselves as they are in themselves, so I will take a moment to describe, in a very abbreviated way, four stages one goes through in acquiring a new skill in any domain, as well as what one has when one has become an expert, especially an expert in social situations, Aristotle's man of practical wisdom.

A PHENOMENOLOGY OF SKILL ACQUISITION[6]

Stage 1: Novice

Normally, the instruction process begins with the instructor decomposing the task environment into context-free features that the beginner can recognize without the desired skill. The beginner is then given rules for determining actions on the basis of these features.

The student automobile driver learns to recognize such domain-independent features as speed (indicated by the speedometer), and is given the rule, "Shift when the speedometer-needle points to 10."

The child who is learning how to act ethically in his or her culture might be given the rule. "Never tell a lie."

Stage 2: Advanced beginner

As the novice gains experience actually coping with real situations, he or she begins to note, or an instructor points out, perspicuous examples of meaningful additional aspects of the situation. After seeing a sufficient number of examples, the student learns to recognize them. Instructional *maxims* can then refer to these new *situational aspects*.

Of course, if the beginner follows the rule, "Shift at 10 miles an hour," the car will stall on a hill or when heavily loaded. So the advanced beginner learns to use (situational) engine sounds as well as (non-situational) speed in deciding when to shift. He learns the maxim: "Shift up when the motor sounds like it is racing and down when it sounds like it is straining."

Likewise, the policy of not lying will get a child into fights and excluded from important events so, with the coaching of the parents, children learn to tell their friends when leaving their homes that they had a good time, regardless of the truth. Thus the child learns to replace the rule "Never lie" with the maxim "Never lie except in situations when making everyone feel good is what matters."

Stage 3: Competence

With more experience, the number of potentially relevant elements that the learner is able to recognize becomes overwhelming. At this point, since a sense of what is important in any particular situation is missing, performance becomes nerve-wracking and exhausting, and the student may well wonder how anyone ever masters the skill.

To cope with this overload and to achieve competence, people learn through instruction or experience, to devise a plan or choose a perspective that determines which elements of the situation must be treated as important and which ones can be ignored. By restricting attention to only a few of the vast number of possibly relevant features and aspects, such a choice of a perspective makes decision making easier.

A competent driver leaving the freeway on an off-ramp curve learns to pay attention to the speed of the car, not whether to shift gears. After taking into account speed, surface condition, angle of bank, etc., the driver may decide he is going too fast. He then has to decide whether to let up on the gas pedal, take his foot off the pedal altogether, or step on the brake, and precisely when to perform any of these actions. He is relieved if he gets through the curve without being honked at, and shaken if he begins to go into a skid.

A young person learns that there are situations in which one must tell the truth and others in which one lies. Although this is daunting, the adolescent learns to decide whether the current situation is one of building trust, giving support, manipulating the other person for his or her own good, harming a brutal antagonist, and so forth. If, for instance, trust is the issue, he then has to decide when and how to tell the truth.

The competent performer, then, seeks rules and reasoning procedures to decide upon a plan or perspective. But such rules are not as easy to come by as are the rules and maxims given to beginners. There are just too many situations differing from each other in too many subtle ways. More situations, in fact, than are named or precisely defined, so no one can prepare for the learner a list of types of situations and what to do in each. Competent performers, therefore, must decide for themselves what plan or perspective to choose without being sure that it will be appropriate.[7]

Such decisions are risky, however, so one is tempted to seek the security of standards and rules. When a risk-averse person makes an inappropriate decision and consequently finds himself in trouble, he tries to characterize his mistake by describing a certain class of dangerous situations and then makes a rule to avoid them in the future. To take an extreme example, if a driver pulling out of a parking space is side-swiped by an oncoming car he mistakenly took to be approaching too slowly to be a danger, he may make the rule, never pull out if there is a car approaching. Such a rigid response will make for safe driving in a certain class of cases, but it will block further skill refinement. In this case it will prevent acquiring the skill of flexibly pulling out of parking places. In general, if one seeks to follow general rules one will not get beyond competence.

But without guidelines, coping becomes frightening rather than merely exhausting. Prior to this stage, if the rules do not work, the performer, rather than feel remorse for his mistakes, can rationalize that he has not been given adequate rules. Now, however, the learner feels responsible for his choices. Often choice leads to confusion and failure. Of course, sometimes things work out well, and the competent performer experiences a kind of elation unknown to the beginner. Thus, learners at this stage find themselves on an emotional roller coaster.

As the competent performer becomes more and more emotionally involved in his task, it becomes increasingly difficult for him to draw back and adopt the *detached* rule-following stance of the beginner. While it might seem that this involvement would interfere with rule-testing and so would lead to irrational decisions and inhibit further skill development, in fact just the opposite seems to be the case. If the detached rule-following stance of the novice and advanced beginner is replaced by involvement, one is set for further advancement, while resistance to the acceptance of involvement and risk normally leads to stagnation and ultimately to boredom and regression.[8]

Stage 4: Expertise

With enough experience with a variety of situations, all seen from the same perspective but requiring different tactical decisions, the competent performer seems gradually to decompose this class of situations into subclasses, each of which shares the same decision, single action, or tactic. This allows an immediate intuitive response to each situation.

The expert driver, generally without paying attention, not only feels in the seat of his pants when speed is the issue; he knows how to perform the appropriate action without calculating and comparing alternatives. On the off-ramp, his foot just lifts off the accelerator or steps on the brake. What must be done, simply is done.

Also, with enough experience and willingness to take risks, some children grow up to be ethical experts who have learned to tell the truth or lie spontaneously, depending upon the situation, without appeal to rules and maxims. Aristotle would say that such a person has acquired the virtue of truthfulness. Some people grow up to be experts capable of responding appropriately to a wide range of interpersonal situations in their culture. Such social experts could be called virtuosi in living.[9]

As a result of accepting risks and a commitment to being better than average, the virtuoso in living develops the capacity to respond appropriately even in situations in which there are conflicting concerns and in which there seems to those looking on to be no appropriate way to act. Pierre Bourdieu describes such a virtuoso:

> Only a virtuoso with a perfect command of his "art of living" can play on all the resources inherent in the ambiguities and uncertainties of behavior and situation in order to produce the actions appropriate to each case, to do that of which people will say "There was nothing else to be done," and do it the right way.[10]

This is obviously Aristotle's *phronimos*. Of course, there may be several wise responses. Indeed, on my account, the idea of a *single* correct response makes no sense since other virtuosi with different funds of experiences would see the matter differently, and even the same *phronimos* would presumably respond differently once he had had more experience and therefore could discriminate a richer repertoire of situations.

THE *PHRONIMOS* AS A SOCIALLY RECOGNIZED VIRTUOSO VERSUS THE HISTORY MAKER AS WORLD TRANSFORMING MASTER

We can now generalize this account of skill acquisition and return to *Being and Time* to see whether the virtuoso's increasingly refined sense of the social situation is, perhaps, the more primordial understanding Heidegger has in mind. We can do this by seeing how Aristotle's *phronimos* is related to Heidegger's resolute Dasein. Heidegger is clear that the average way of acting is to obey standards and rules. He describes "Dasein's lostness in the one" as following "the tasks, rules, and standards . . . of concernful and solicitous being-in-the-world" (p. 312). In contrast, Heidegger's resolute individual deviates from the banal, average, public standards to respond spontaneously to the particular situation. In Heidegger's terms, irresolute Dasein responds to the general situation (*Lage*), whereas resolute Dasein responds to the concrete Situation (*Situation*). As Heidegger puts it: "*for the one . . . the Situation is essentially something that has been closed off.* The one knows only the '*general situation*' " (p. 346), while "resolute Dasein" is in touch with the " 'concrete Situation' of taking action" (p. 349). The distinction between these two kinds of situation seem to come out of nowhere in *Being and Time* but they clearly have their origin in Heidegger's detailed discussion of *phronesis* in his 1924–5 lecture course. There he says:

> Dasein, as acting in each case now, is determined by its situation in the largest sense. This situation is in every case different. The circumstances, the givens, the times, and the people vary. The meaning of the action itself, i.e., precisely what I want to do, varies as well . . . It is precisely the achievement of *phronesis* to disclose the respective Dasein as acting now in the full situation within which it acts and in which it is in each case different.[11]

Given the phenomenology of skill acquisition, it should be clear that the concrete Situation does not have some special metaphysical or private kind of intelligibility cut off from the everyday. Rather, intelligibility for the *phronimos* is the result of the gradual refinement of responses that grows out of long experience acting within the shared cultural practices. Thus, in discussing *phronesis* Heidegger quotes Aristotle's remark that "Only through much time . . . is life experience possible."[12] And in *Being and Time* he is explicit that the intelligibility of the Situation disclosed by resolute action is a refinement of the everyday:

Authentic disclosedness modifies with equal primordiality both the way in which the "world" is discovered . . . and the way in which the Dasein-with of Others is disclosed. The "world" which is ready-to-hand does not become another one "in its content," nor does the circle of others get exchanged for a new one; but both one's being toward the ready-to-hand understandingly and concernfully, and one's solicitous Being with Others, are now given a definite character . . . (p. 344).

Thus, "Even resolutions remain dependent upon the one and its world" (pp. 345–6).

Moreover, as Aristotle already saw, expert response is immediate, and Heidegger agrees that "resoluteness does not first take cognizance of the Situation . . .; it has put itself into the Situation already. As resolute, Dasein is already *taking action*" (p. 347). Or, as Heidegger already put it in his 1924–5 lectures: "in *phronesis* . . . in a momentary glance [*Augenblick*] I survey the concrete situation of action, out of which and in favor of which I resolve myself [*ich mich entschließe*]."[13]

Also, according to Aristotle, since there are no rules that dictate that what the *phronimos* does is the correct thing to do in that *type* of situation, the *phronimos*, like any expert, cannot explain why he did what he did. Heidegger, of course, agrees:

The Situation cannot be calculated in advance or presented like something occurrent which is waiting for someone to grasp it. It only gets disclosed in a free resolving which has not been determined beforehand but is open to the possibility of such determination. (p. 355)

So when Heidegger asks rhetorically, "But on what basis does Dasein disclose itself in resoluteness?" he answers:

Only the resolution itself can give the answer. One would completely misunderstand the phenomenon of resoluteness if one should want to suppose that this consists simply in taking up possibilities which have been proposed and recommended. (p. 345)

All the virtuoso can do is stay open and involved and draw on his or her past experience.[14] The resulting resolute response defines the

Situation. As Heidegger puts it, "the Situation *is* only through resoluteness and in it" (p. 346).

Like the *phronimos*, the resolute individual presumably does what is retroactively recognized by others as appropriate, but what he does is not the *taken-for-granted, average* right thing – not what *one* does – but what his past experience leads him to do in that particular Situation. Moreover, as we have seen, since the Situation is specific and the *phronimos*'s past experience unique, what he does cannot be *the* appropriate thing. It can only be *an* appropriate thing. Still, unlike Kierkegaard's Knight of Faith suspending the ethical, who can only be understood by himself and others as a madman or a murderer, "Resolution does not withdraw from 'actuality,' but discovers first what is factically possible; and it does so by seizing upon it in whatever way is possible for it as its ownmost ability-to-be in the 'one' " (p. 346). Thus, in responding to the concrete Situation the resolute individual is recognized as a model; not of what *general* thing to do, but of *how* to respond in an especially appropriate way. In this way, "when Dasein is resolute, it can become the 'conscience' of others" (p. 344).

It should now be clear that Kisiel's claim – that Heidegger, in his account of resolute Dasein in division II, is working out Aristotle's phenomenology of practical wisdom – helps make sense of Heidegger's cryptic remarks about the resolute Dasein's response to the concrete Situation. But Kisiel's plausible way of understanding the passages in question is complicated by another group of interpreters who point out that Heidegger's account of authenticity is also deeply influenced by his early interest in the account of radical transformation in St. Paul, Luther, and Kierkegaard. These interpreters focus on Heidegger's use of the term *Augenblick*.

We have already seen that, indeed, in the 1924–5 lecture course Heidegger uses the term *Augenblick* to describe the *phronimos*'s instant of insight. This reading is confirmed by *Basic Problems* where the *Augenblick* is equated with Aristotle's *kairos*, the moment of appropriate skillful intervention. "Aristotle saw the phenomenon of the instant [*Augenblick*], the *kairos*," Heidegger says.[15] But *Augenblick* is also Luther's translation of St. Paul's moment in which we shall be changed in a "twinkling of an eye." So John van Buren claims that "Heidegger took this movement that concentrates itself at the extreme point *(eschaton)* of the *kairos* to be the kairological time that he had already discovered in the Pauline eschatology."[16]

Unfortunately, the evidence van Buren cites for this claim does not seem to establish it or even suggest it, but rather suggests the contrary, viz. that Heidegger uses *kairos* to refer not to *religious time*, but to secular action *in a concrete situation.*

Van Buren says that in the 1924–5 lecture course, Heidegger connected *kairos* in Aristotle with the Pauline theme of *kairos* as "the twinkling of an eye": "*Phronesis* is the glancing at the this-time, at the this-time-ness of the momentary situation. As *aisthesis,* it is the glance of the eye, the *Augen-blick,* toward the concrete at the particular time . . ."[17]

Van Buren seeks further support in a passage from Heidegger's lectures, *Phenomenological Interpretations with Respect to Aristotle,* but this passage too, supports the Aristotelian reading.

> *Phronesis* is the illumination of *dealings* that temporalizes life in its *being.* The concrete interpretation shows how this being, *kairos,* is constituted . . . It goes toward the *eschaton,* the extreme, in which the determinately seen *concrete situation* intensifies itself at the particular time.[18]

Although the translation leaves things rather murky, clearly Heidegger is here describing the cultural virtuoso's resolute dealing with the concrete Situation, not the moment of rebirth of the Christian in which he gets a new identity, nor the moment of the coming of the Messiah when the world will be transformed and the dead raised in the twinkling of an eye.

But, in spite of these blatant misreadings of the texts, the interpreters who want to give Heidegger's use of *Augenblick* a Christian interpretation are onto something important. There is a surprising moment where Heidegger introduces the *Augenblick* in a way that seems clearly to refer to the *phronimos*'s daily dealings with things and equipment. He says:

> To the anticipation which goes with resoluteness, there belongs a Present in accordance with which a resolution discloses the Situation . . . That *Present* . . . we call the *Augenblick* . . . The *Augenblick* permits us *to encounter for the first time* what can be "in a time" as ready-to-hand or present-at-hand. (pp. 387, 388)

So far, this is no surprise, but then Heidegger appends a footnote saying, "S. Kierkegaard is probably the one who has seen the *existentiell* phenomenon of the *Augenblick* with the most penetration . . ." (p. 497 iii). What can this mean?

Heidegger seems to want to describe the phenomenon of the response to the concrete Situation at a level of formality that covers any decisive moment in which Dasein, as an individual, breaks out of the banality of the one and takes over its situation, whether that be the Greek act of seizing the occasion or the Christian experience of being reborn.[19] For

Heidegger, either type of decisive moment is an *Augenblick.* In a course given shortly after the publication of *Being and Time*, the Greek and Christian views, their radical difference, and their formal similarity are spelled out together. Heidegger first speaks in general terms of "Dasein's *self-resolution* [*Sich entschliessen*] to itself . . . to what is given to him to be, this self-resolution is the *Augenblick.*"[20] He then fills this out in Aristotelian terms, explaining, "The *Augenblick* is nothing else than the *glance of resoluteness*, in which the full Situation of an action opens up and is held open."[21] But he also suggests that this Aristotelian moment of decisive action falls short of the kind of radical transformative *Augenblick* Kierkegaard had in mind. "What we here indicate with 'Augenblick' is what Kierkegaard was *the first to really grasp in philosophy* – a grasping, which *begins the possibility of a completely new epoch in philosophy* since Antiquity."[22]

Although Heidegger's view is difficult to sort out, if we hold onto the phenomena in question we can be sure that Heidegger did not simply identify the Greek understanding of *kairos* with the Christian understanding of *Augenblick*, although he did see each as manifesting a *resolute, i.e. open, way of being* which was a precondition of a *special moment of decisive action.* One thing is sure, one cannot even begin to make sense of Heidegger if, like Kisiel, one simply cites lecture-texts to argue that Heidegger's account of resolute Dasein in *Being and Time* is an adaptation of Aristotle's *phronimos*, or, like van Buren, one cites other lecture-texts to argue that *Augenblick* in *Being and Time* must be understood in the light of Christian kairological time. Without first seeing that Aristotle and St. Paul are describing two genuine, but seemingly irreconcilable, *phenomena*, the challenging exegetical questions do not even arise.

Once we focus on the phenomena, however, we can see that each interpretation has something right, but each mistakenly claims to have the whole story. A satisfactory interpretation requires clearly distinguishing two experiences of the source, nature, and intelligibility of decisive action – the Greek experience, arising from *a primordial understanding of the current Situation*, that makes possible *virtuoso coping* in the current world and the Christian experience, arising from *a primordial understanding of Dasein itself* that makes possible *a transformation of self and world.* Heidegger seems to be distinguishing Dasein's primordial understanding of the current Situation from Dasein's experience of its most primordial way of being, and yet trying to subsume them both under the *Augenblick* when he says, "Dasein gets . . . brought back from its lostness by a resolution, so that both the current Situation and therewith the primordial 'limit-Situation' of being-towards-death, will be disclosed as an *Augenblick* that has been held on to" (p. 400).

At other places in the text, moreover, it seems clear that the two different forms of understanding are disclosed by two different forms of resoluteness. The first is discussed in chapter 2 of division II. There Heidegger defines resoluteness as "*self-projection upon one's ownmost being-guilty, in which one is ready for anxiety* . . ." (p. 343). This kind of resoluteness arises from facing one's thrownness and the consequent anxiety that comes with the realization that one's average understanding with its rules and standards has no intrinsic authority. Holding on to this anxiety makes possible the openness, involvement, and willingness to take risks that, in turn, make possible the acquisition of expertise. Resoluteness thus makes possible the virtuosity of the Heideggerian *phronimos* who, because he has held on to anxiety and so no longer takes for granted the banal public interpretation of events, can see new possibilities in the most ambiguous and conflicted situations and so can do something that all who share his world will retroactively recognize as what was factically possible at the time. Such a person's understanding of his society is richer and deeper than the average understanding and so he is generally more effective. But he is not yet fully authentic.

Besides the *effective coping* of the *phronimos,* made possible by an expert grasp of the *concrete Situation,* there is a fully *authentic* way of acting made possible by Dasein's understanding of *its own way of being.* This authentic way of acting is a more complete form of resoluteness in which Dasein not only faces the anxiety of guilt, viz. the sense that its identity and social norms are thrown rather than grounded and thus have no final authority, but, furthermore, faces the anxiety of death, viz. that Dasein has to be ready at all times to die, i.e. give up its identity and its world altogether. In such an understanding, Dasein manifests "its authenticity and its totality" (p. 348).

Heidegger seems to be distinguishing and ranking the two ways of holding on to anxiety and the kind of resoluteness each makes possible by holding that only the second is authentic and whole. In chapter 5, when he turns to the "authentic historizing of Dasein" (p. 434), he says:

> We have defined "resoluteness" as a projecting of oneself on one's ownmost being-guilty. . . Resoluteness gains its authenticity as *anticipatory* resoluteness. In this, Dasein understands itself with regard to its ability-to-be, and it does so in such a manner that it will go right under the eyes of Death in order thus to take over in its thrownness that entity which it is itself, and to take it over wholly. (p. 434)[23]

Thus, anticipatory resoluteness makes possible an even more primordial form of intelligibility than the pragmatic understanding evinced by the *phronimos* or social virtuoso.

To be innovative in this religious sense requires *anticipatory* resoluteness – anxiously facing both death and guilt. The resolute *phronimos* merely experiences his thrownness and so has the sense that the social norms are not rules to be rigidly followed. He therefore gives up a banal, general understanding of social norms and responds to the concrete Situation, but he can still be understood by his peers to have effectively solved a shared problem. In anticipatory resoluteness, however, anxiety in the face of death has freed Dasein even from taking for granted the agreed-upon current cultural issues.

> Repetition makes a *reciprocal rejoinder* to the possibility of existence that has-been-there . . . But when such a rejoinder is made to this possibility in a resolution, it is made *in an Augenblick; and as such* it is at the same time a *disavowal* of that which in the "today," is working itself out as the "past." (p. 438)

Here the Augenblick does name the inception of a new creation. In the moment of decisive action, authentic Dasein can take up a marginal practice from its cultural heritage.

> [Fate] is how we designate Dasein's primordial historizing, which lies in authentic resoluteness and in which Dasein *hands* itself *down* to itself, free for death, in a possibility which it has inherited and yet has chosen. (p. 435)

Dasein can then act in such a way as to take over or repeat the marginal practice in a new way and thus show a form of life in which that marginal practice has become central and the central practices have become marginal. Such an innovator is so radical that he transforms his generation's understanding of the issue facing the culture and produces a new authentic "we." He thus goes beyond not only the banal general understanding of his peers, but even beyond the Situational understanding of the *phronimos*.[24] We could call such a fully authentic history-making Dasein a cultural master.[25]

ETHICAL AND POLITICAL IMPLICATIONS

The phenomena of the social virtuoso and the cultural master have ethical and political implications. For example, Heidegger's account of the resolute response to the factical situation offers a way out of the antinomy presented by Dworkin's and Derrida's account of legal decision making. Dworkin holds that "judges must, . . . so far as possible, regard the existing legal practice as expressing . . . a coherent conception of justice and fairness, and so are charged to uncover this conception and to make decisions in specific cases on the basis of it."[26] Thus, according to Dworkin, an explicit sense of the principles involved should actually guide a judge when she applies the law as well as when she justifies her decision.

Derrida is enough of a Heideggerian to sense that there is no theory behind a judge's practice and no single right decision, so he rightly sees that the judge's justification could not be the basis of her decision and must therefore be, at best, a rationalization. Thus he rejects Dworkin's rationalism. However, without an understanding of the phenomenon of skillful coping behind Heidegger's claim that a resolute way of being makes possible a richer more primordial kind of understanding, Derrida wrongly concludes that in making a decision the judge must be making a leap in the dark: "the instant of the just decision . . . is a madness."[27] I suspect that, three different sorts of cases are lumped together by Derrida.

(1) There is the case of extrapolating the law to new situations that are similar but never identical to previous cases and for which there is no set of features in terms of which one can justify one's judgments of similarity. Here Derrida is right, there can be no *theory* of how to proceed, but Heidegger would presumably analyze an expert judge's decisions on the basis of the phenomenon of expert coping and so hold that the judge, like any resolute *phronimos*, neither acts on principle nor makes a leap in the dark, but rather straightway engages in "*the disclosive projection and determination of what is factically possible at the time*" (p. 345). With an eye to the phenomenon, we can see that the judge would be acting as a social virtuoso, led by her past experience to respond to the subtle similarities between the current situation and situations in which she had already made what were recognized as appropriate responses. Even when such a *phronimos* reflects, she does not reflect on abstract principles but stays involved and reflects on her expert sense of the concrete situation.

As Derrida sees in such cases, there cannot be one right decision as Dworkin assumes. Two different judges, with different past experiences and different ways of having entered the current situation, may well see the situation differently. Remember, Heidegger says: "The Situation cannot be . . . presented like something occurrent which is waiting for someone to grasp it. It only gets disclosed in free resolving . . ." (p. 355). But even then, one of the several possible wise decisions need not be chosen arbitrarily. The virtuoso judges can talk to each other about the way they entered the current situation and relate the situation to other situations in the hope of getting their colleagues to see things the way they do. This may work to produce agreement, but even if it does not, the choice between the remaining candidates is not the arbitrary imposition of power; it is a choice between possible wise decisions.

Still, Derrida is right that, since similarity cannot be reduced to certain shared features, any justification that tried to explain the judge's decision in terms of *classes* of situations would have to be a rationalization that drew either on principles like those the expert judge followed when she was only competent or, at best, more refined principles the expert had abstracted from many cases. But Heidegger would want to add, I hope, that, although such principles could not capture the judge's expertise, they need not be arbitrary. That is, they could serve as convincing justifications for a *competent* decision even though they could not be used to determine what counted as the relevant similarities in the next case, and thus could not serve as the basis for a genuinely wise decision.

(2) There is the decision of a legal *innovator* who brings to bear a whole new way of looking at the role of the law in some domain. Such a decision would be even further from being rationalizable, but, if Heidegger is right, it would not be a leap in the dark but a masterful response to marginal practices. The marginal practices do, indeed, make a "leap from the wings to center stage,"[28] but the innovative master does not make a blind leap in responding to them; rather, thanks to his openness, he has a subtle sense of the marginal practices that are moving into the center.

(3) The nearest thing to a Derridian leap in the dark occurs where there are two or more conflicting sets of values. These are the kinds of cases that reach the Supreme Court, such as pornography cases in which the court must decide between the well-being of the community and the right to free speech. In such cases there does not seem to be any non-arbitrary way of deciding which way to understand the situation. Each judge will decide on the basis of his or her own set of values and past experience but the decision will be imposed by the majority. This does seem to be a case, if not of a leap in the dark, at least of an arbitrary imposition of power.

Only this third type of case fits Derrida's analysis, but Derrida mistakenly holds that *all* decisions that extrapolate to a new situation have the arbitrariness found only in type-three cases. He claims that either a decision is guided by cognitive rails and thus is mechanical but uninteresting, or else it is arbitrary. He thus misses the relevance of the two types of primordial understanding that Heidegger describes. By in effect denying the way a resolute person's past experience can feed into a sense of what is factically possible and thus make possible a wise or even an innovative decision that is not dictated by principle but is not arbitrary either, Derrida gives support to the nihilism of the legal realists.

CONCLUSION

In summary, according to division II of *Being and Time*, public, average, everyday understanding is necessarily general and banal. Nonetheless, this leveled average understanding is necessary both as the background for all intelligibility and in the early stages of acquiring expertise, and so it is both ontologically and genetically prior to any more primordial understanding. Once, however, an expert has broken out of the banal, thanks to the anxious realization of his thrownness and, by repeated risky experience in the everyday world, has mastered the discriminations that constitute his skill, he can respond to the situation in a more subtle way than a non-expert can. This primordial understanding of the concrete Situation has no special content – no source of intelligibility other than everyday intelligibility – but it, nonetheless, makes possible the social virtuoso's successful responses to the most difficult social situations. Furthermore, by facing the anxiety of death and so seeing that the issues of his culture and even his own identity could be radically changed, a fully authentic Dasein can manifest an even higher kind of primordial understanding. As a cultural master he can take up marginal possibilities in his culture's past in way that enables him to change the style of a whole generation and thereby disclose a new world.

NOTES

1 This chapter is based on a paper presented at the inaugural meeting of the International Society for Phenomenological Studies, Asilomar, California, 19–23 July 1999. I would like to thank the participants for their helpful suggestions. I would also like to thank Wallace Matson for his help in sorting out the New Testament Greek.
2 Martin Heidegger, *Being and Time*, trans. John Macquarrie and Edward Robinson (New York: Harper & Row, 1962). All parenthetical references are to this edition. Some translations have been modified.
3 Hubert L. Dreyfus, *Being-in-the-World: A Commentary on Heidegger's Being and Time, Division I* (Cambridge, MA: MIT Press, 1991).
4 Ibid.

5 Theodore Kisiel, *The Genesis of Heidegger's Being and Time* (Berkeley: University of California, 1993), Kisiel says: "The project of *BT* thus takes shape in 1921–24 against the backdrop of the unrelenting exegesis of Aristotle's texts . . . from which the *pre*theoretical models for the two Divisions of BT, the *techne* of *poesis*, for the First, and the *phronesis* of *praxis* for the Second, are derived" p. 9. Greek has been transliterated.

6 For a more detailed account see, Hubert L. and Stuart E. Dreyfus, *Mind over Machine* (New York: Free Press, 1988).

7 Such a decision as to what matters in the current situation, i.e. what sort of situation it is, requires that one share the sensibility of the culture and have the ability to respond to the similarities recognized by one's fellows.

8 Patricia Benner has described this phenomenon in *From Novice to Expert: Excellence and Power in Clinical Nursing Practice* (Menlo Park, CA: Addison-Wesley, 1984), p. 164.

9 This description poses a problem, however. How come many people grow up to be expert drivers but only a few become social virtuosi? The answer seems to be that there are at least two kinds of skills: simple skills, like crossing the street and driving, and subtle skills like music, sports, and social interaction. It makes little sense to speak of a virtuoso everyday driver, whereas one can be a virtuoso musician or a champion in some sport. Acquiring simple skills requires only that one face risks and uncertainty without falling back on rules or fleeing into detachment, whereas acquiring hard skills requires, in addition, a motivation continually to improve – then, one needs both the willingness to take risks and a commitment to excellence that manifests itself in persistence and in high standards for what counts as having done something right. One also must be sensitive to the distinctions in the relevant domain. (Such sensitivity in an extreme form in music is perfect pitch.) Such sensitivity is a component of what we call talent. Talent in this sense is a necessary condition for becoming a virtuoso in any field.

10 Pierre Bourdieu, *Outline of a Theory of Practice*, trans. Richard Nice (Cambridge: Cambridge University Press, 1977), p. 8.

11 Martin Heidegger, *Plato's Sophist* (Bloomington: Indiana University Press, 1997), p. 101. In the *Sophist* course, Heidegger has not yet made a clear distinction between *Lage* and *Situation.* In this lecture course, he uses both terms interchangeably to refer to the concrete situation. See, for example, p. 102: "out of the constant regard toward that which I have resolved, the situation [*Situation*] should become transparent. From the point of view of the *proaireton*, the concrete situation [*konkrete Lage*] . . . is covered over."

12 Ibid., p. 97.

13 Ibid., p. 114.

14 I'm following Heidegger in reading *Ent-schlossenheit* as openness not determination. See "The Origin of the Work of Art," *Poetry, Language, Thought*, trans. Albert Hotstadter (New York: Harper and Row, 1971). "The resoluteness [Ent-schlossenheit] intended in *Being and Time* is not the deliberate action of a subject, but the opening up of human being . . . to the openness of Being"

p. 67.

15 Martin Heidegger, *Basic Problems of Phenomenology* (Bloomington: Indiana University Press, 1982), p. 288.

16 John van Buren, *The Young Heidegger: Rumor of the Hidden King* (Bloomington: Indiana University Press, 1994), p. 231. The whole discussion of *Kairos* and *Augenblick* is hard to follow since, as I understand it, the term *Kairos* is never used in New Testament Greek to mean the time of transformation that later came to be called Kairological time. The term translated *Augenblick* occurs in Corinthians I, 15:52 to describe what will happen when we are raised from the dead: "We shall all be changed in a moment (*atomos*), in the twinkling of an eye (*ripei en ophthalmou*)." But the term gets extended by Kierkegaard to cover all the ways that one's identity and world are suddenly and radically transformed. Kierkegaard goes even further. The Greek for what is normally translated by "the fullness of time" when Jesus returns to transform the world is *pltroma,* while the term for the transformation in which the Christian is reborn as a "new creation" is *metanoia,* but both crucial moments are subsumed by Kierkegaard under the notion of an *Augenblick* as the moment of a decisive transformation. Finally, not too surprisingly, all the terms that refer to a total transformation of identity and/or world get lumped together and identified with the Greek moment of decisive action or Kairos. What is surprising is that those concerned with the use of these terms in Heidegger do not bother to sort out the various phenomena to which they refer. For example, van Buren blurs all distinctions when he tells us that, "Following St. Paul, as well as Aristotle, Heidegger stresses that particular *kairoi*, situations, are always 'new creations' that come 'like a thief in the night'" (p. 283).

17 Ibid., p. 229.

18 Ibid., p. 231 My addition of italics. Unfortunately, van Buren does not give a page reference to the source of this quotation.

19 Which Kierkegaard calls becoming a new creation, see Søren Kierkegaard, *Fear and Trembling* (New York: Penguin, 1985), p. 70.

20 Martin Heidegger, *Gesamtausgabe*, vol. 29/30 (Frankfurt a.M.: Klostermann, 1983), p. 224.

21 Ibid.

22 Ibid., p. 225 (my italics).

23 It is hard to reconcile this claim that *only anticipatory* resoluteness reveals Dasein authentically and fully with the claim in the earlier discussion of the resoluteness of facing guilt that "we have now arrived at that truth of Dasein which is most primordial because it is *authentic*" (p. 343). I think Heidegger was simply confused as to how he wanted to relate the two kinds of resoluteness. Generally, he sticks to the view that anticipatory resoluteness is the most complete kind of resoluteness because it involves facing death.

24 Heidegger sensed that such an authentic Dasein's reinterpretation of what his generation stands for – how the shared social practices hang together and have a point – allows him to transform his culture, but in *Being and Time*

Heidegger could not yet see how radically a culture could be transformed. Only when he had understood that the style of a culture – its whole understanding of being – could change, could he fully grasp what it would be like for a cultural master to disclose a new world. Heidegger presumably would include such cultural masters among the statesmen, gods, and philosophers who disclose new worlds. They are all instances of "truth establishing itself." See "The Origin of the Work of Art," pp. 61, 62.

25 The most extreme form of the transformation such a history-making Dasein brings about is a cultural version of the *Augenblick* of Christian conversion. This, for Kierkegaard, is the *Augenblick* as the fullness of time. The whole culture is reborn into a new world. Since the new world has new standards of intelligibility, the cultural master, like Kierkegaard's Abraham, cannot explain himself and so cannot be recognized by his peers as having done something appropriate as the *phronimos* can. But, unlike Abraham suspending the ethical, who is totally repulsive to his contemporaries and even himself, the history-maker, because he draws on a shared heritage, is not totally unintelligible. He is a charismatic figure who can *show* a new style and so be *followed*, like Jesus was followed by his disciples, even though they did not understand the meaning of what they were doing. He will not be fully intelligible to the members of the culture, however, until his new way of coordinating the practices is articulated in a new language and preserved in new institutions. The phenomenon of world disclosing is described and illustrated in, Charles Spinosa, Fernando Flores, and Hubert L. Dreyfus, *Disclosing New Worlds* (Cambridge, MA: MIT Press, 1997).

These accounts of the special way the social virtuoso can seize the moment and the way the historical innovator can transform the culture seem to be correlated with Heidegger's two-stage account of the present dimension of Dasein's authentic temporality. *Primordial* temporality makes possible world-time and thus the *phronemos*'s experience of being solicited, on the basis of past successes, to respond to the current Situation so as to open up new possibilities for dealing with available and occurrent entities. (Heidegger's account of how primordial temporality makes possible pragmatic temporality has been analyzed by William D. Blattner in his excellent book, *Heidegger's Temporal Idealism* [Cambridge: Cambridge University Press, 1999].)

Authentic temporality, by contrast, is a secularization of the Kierkegaardian account of Christian temporality in *The Concept of Anxiety* in which the temporal structure makes possible the decisive instant of individual conversion and world transformation. Heidegger seems to have wanted to recover both the Greek and the Christian understanding of temporal transformation, but did not have time to work out how the two kinds of non-successive temporality (primordial temporality and authentic temporality) were related to each other and to his ontological project.

26 See Gerald J. Postema, "Protestant Interpretation and Social Practices," *Law and Philosophy* 6 (1987), 283–319. Postema presents a critique of Dworkin

based on Bourdieu and Wittgenstein which is similar to the one I am suggesting here.

27 Jacques Derrida, "Force of Law: The 'Mystical Foundation of Authority,'" *Cardozo Law Review* 11, part 2 (1990), 967.

28 Michel Foucault, "Nietzsche, Genealogy, History," in *Language, Counter-Memory, Practice,* trans. Donald F. Bouchard and Sherry Simon (Ithaca, NY: Cornell University Press, 1977), p. 150.

CHAPTER II

Another time

John Sallis

What would be required in order to suppose *another time*? What would be required in order to suppose and even in some measure to establish that there is another time, assuming that one can appropriately say of time that it is or at least that there is time, that there is this time and perhaps another time? What could warrant setting aside the assumption – seldom challenged in the history of philosophy – that time is singular? What could warrant setting aside even the assumption that, if there are multiple times, they are nonetheless in the final account all gathered into a single time, so that in the end the singularity of time would still be preserved? Can one be assured of the efficacy of such a gathering? Can one be assured that the time of a dream, the time of imagining, and the time of madness can all be reclaimed and reintegrated into a single all-encompassing, all-governing, time? Can one be assured also that the times of elemental nature can be gathered and integrated into this single time? Can one be assured that the time of day and the time of year, that is, the times told by the most natural of clocks, the sun, can be brought to coincide, without remainder, with the times of the soul and of history? Or would there perhaps remain outside any such singular time as such, outside any time regarded as constituting time as such, an irrepressible trace of another time?

The question of the singularity of time is thus linked to the question of the *as such* of time, to the question whether there is an *as such* of time and hence a time as such. By putting in question the *as such* of time, one destabilizes in advance the question "What is time?" For in opening the question of the *as such* of time, one opens the possibility that time may be such as to have no single, coherent *what*, that there may be no such essence of time. Within such an opening, one cannot but prove already to have gone astray in posing the question of time in the form of the question "What is time?" One would not simply have posed a completely neutral question, but rather – as perhaps always – one would in the very formulation of the question already have responded to a certain preunderstanding, which could also involve misunderstanding, errancy.

And yet, the question cannot merely be put aside, if for no other reason than that it is precisely the question western philosophy has almost always put to time. If the question is limited, if the project of delimiting time as such, of determining its essence, is bound by certain limits, then those limits can be exposed only – or, at least, most effectively – by entering into the question and following it through in the most radical way, thus forcing to the limit the singularity and identity that philosophy has ascribed to time.

I

What, then, is time?

The question comes much too late. It is of course a citation from a text handed down across an enormous expanse of time, a text thus itself peculiarly entangled in that about which it poses this question. It is not only a text that was written a long time ago but also one that has been taken up time and time again, repeatedly appropriated in and to another time.

Augustine does not take the question for granted. Even if he never openly puts the question in question, he does attest to its force, to its recoil upon the questioner. For Augustine the question is disturbing. His first response to it in the *Confessions* is to express how disturbing, how baffling a question it is: "What, then, is time? I know well enough what it is, provided that nobody asks me; but if I am asked what it is and try to explain, I am baffled."[1] Thus the posing of the question attests to the strangeness of the sense of time, that one has a sense of time, which, on the other hand, remains elusive and resists being drawn out and expressed as such.

But what, then, *is* time? What can it be said *to be*? Can it be said to be? It seems not, at least not without restrictions so severe as to reduce its sense of being almost to that of not being. For that part of time called past is no longer, and the part called future is not yet. Neither past nor future can be said to be. But the other part, the present, is a part of time rather than eternity only because it moves on to become the past. But, Augustine writes: "How can we say that even the present *is*, when the reason why it *is* is that it is *not to be*? In other words, we cannot rightly say that time *is*, except by reason of its impending state of *not being*" (XI.14).

One cannot even say that time *is* in part. For of its three parts, none simply *is*. The one part that cannot be declared nothing at all falls short of being nothing at all only by the very slightest of differences. Instead of not being, it is not to be. It is (not nothing) only by virtue of its impending not being. Its being borders on not being; its being is determined as such by reference to not being, to its impending not being.

The present would thus be constituted as *being* (in some small measure) only by being set back upon the double void of past and future. As if the present were nothing but that which in the future (which is nothing) will have become past (which is nothing). As if the present were nothing but the double bond to nothing.

As if it were not also the moment of presence, the moment in which things are present to one's vision.

In the *Confessions*, indeed in the very passage in which the present is linked constitutively to the not-being of past and future, there is an indication, slight but unmistakable, that the value of presence remains in force. Augustine writes: "As for the present, if it were always present and never moved on to become the past, it would not be time but eternity" (XI.14). For Augustine the difference between time and eternity is all-decisive, and indeed he takes up this difference well in advance of the passage on the parts of time. In other words, he first expresses what fundamentally determines the difference and then, in the later passage and on the basis thus provided, explicates the constitution of time.

The difference is a difference of presence, a differentiation with regard to presence. Augustine writes: "In eternity nothing moves into the past, but all is present [*sed totum esse praesens*]. Time, on the other hand, is never all present at once" (XI.11). Even eternity is determined by the present, by the value of presence. Eternity is an absolutely unlimited present, a present that does not move into the past; it is a present that will not in the future have become past and that has not in the past been still future. Eternity is present, and what differentiates the present from eternity is only that the present *of time* is constitutively bound to the not being – that is, the non-presence – of the past and the future. Thus, to say that "the present is time only by reason of the fact that it moves on to become the past" (XI.14) – that is, only by virtue of its impending not being – is *not* to say that the present (and, hence, time as such) is constituted solely by the bond to the not being of past and future. Rather, it is to say that the present is a present *of time* – rather than the present of eternity – by virtue of its bond to the not being (that is, the non- presence) of the past and the future. Even if the present of time is submitted constitutively to its impending not being (present), it is still – decisively, constitutively – *present.*

The constitutive value of presence, not only for eternity, but also for the temporal present and even for the future and the past, is unmistakably attested by the way in which all these modes are brought back to *praesens* and accorded their being, at least to some degree, on this basis. And what of *praesens* itself? To what is it brought back? What is its locus? Where is it that everything present becomes present?

It is from this question – the question of the *where* (ubi) – that Augustine proceeds: "If the future and the past are, I want to know where they are" (XI.18). Deferring the question of the *where*, Augustine declares that future and past, if they *are* in any measure, are present. Wherever they may be, "they are not there as future or past but as present," for the future is not yet and the past is no longer. His conclusion: "Wherever they are and whatever they are, it is only by being present that they *are*" (XI.18). Only insofar as the *future is present* can it be whatsoever (whatever it be) and be somewhere; and likewise for the past. Yet how can the future and the past be present without the very differentiation of time into three parts being effaced? And in this case would not the very distinction between time and eternity be abolished? For what distinguishes time from eternity is precisely that its present is constitutively bound to the not being of the future and the past.

How can the future and the past be present while remaining, respectively, future and past? This is possible only by virtue of what could be called the intentional or apertural structure of the present (gathered in the word *praesens*, in what for us is its double meaning): the present is a moment of presence, a moment in which vision is opened upon things present. But how can things not present – namely, the future and the past – nonetheless be somehow present? Only if, while not being present as such, they are held in a place that accords them a certain presence, a place that shelters them from not being, a place that is such that to be there in that place, in that receptacle, is to be present. Then it can be said that, though the future and the past are not, there are nonetheless three times: a present of the past (*praesens de praeteritis*), a present of the present (*praesens de praesentibus*), and a present of the future (*praesens de futuris*). Or, since no differentiation is inscribed between, for instance, the past and what is past (that is, those things or events that belong to the past), nor of course between present and presence, the three times can also be delimited as: a presence of what is past, a presence of what is present, and a presence of what is future.

Augustine is thus brought back to the question of the *where* of time, that is, of the place where each of the parts of time would be sheltered from not being and so would be present. Augustine takes this place to be the soul, and this means also that he takes the soul to be the only such place. As a way of securing the differentiation of times (and hence of time from eternity), Augustine takes the soul to be the place of time, its *where*. This setting of time in its *where* cannot have the sense of a mere subordination of time to place, but rather its sense must be such as to erode this very distinction in the direction of a reception and a receptacle that, with a precedence neither spatial nor temporal, would precede all determination of places and of times. Even if this sense of precedence never becomes manifest or thematized in Augustine's text.

Whatever its precedence, Augustine is assured that the place of time is the soul: "Some such different times do exist in the soul [*sunt . . . in anima*], but nowhere else that I can see. The present [presence – *praesens*] of what is past is memory [*memoria*]; the present of what is present is beholding [*contuitus*]; the present of what is future is expectation [*expectatio*]" (XI.20).

Different times are (present) only in the soul, Augustine thus insists, "but nowhere else that I can see."

How is it that, for Augustine, it is in the soul – "but nowhere else that I can see" – that time has its place? How does the soul provide time with its *where*, with a place where it is sheltered from not being? By way of what operations does the soul grant to time a place to be?

The future has its place, its presence, in expectation, through this operation and the power that makes it possible. Likewise with the past: it has its place in memory, is granted its presence through this operation and its enabling power. What, then, about the present? Must it, too, be sheltered from not being? Must it, too, be granted its presence by an operation of the soul? Or is it not, precisely as present, itself inalienably present? Does it not suffice that the present is the very opening to presence? Is there need to submit even the present to an operation of the soul in order to assure it its presence? Is there need to double the present into a presence of the present? Is there need to double its opening upon presence, to double it by reference back to an operation of the soul, an operation *in* the soul, that would shelter the present from not being?

Augustine is convinced that there is such a need. Why? Because the present has no space, no extent – a thesis that he is confident no one would deny: "Again, no one would deny that the present has no extent [*spatium*], since it *is* only at the point of its passage [*in puncto praeterit*]" (XI.28). It would be difficult to exaggerate the force of this thesis, the force of its consequences of course, but also the force with which it is made to exclude a certain *spatium* that the present could otherwise be taken to have: the space of its opening upon presence, the extent of its extendedness to the things that nature sets before one's vision. One would presume even that it is by virtue of this *spatium* that the present is so akin to eternity that the latter is determined by the value of presence, determined as unlimited presence ("In eternity . . . all is present"), determined as a present to which absolutely unlimited *spatium* belongs.

But if, as Augustine is convinced, there is no *spatium* of the present, then an operation of the soul must come to shelter it from the not being of being only at the point of its passage. An operation of the soul must come to supply the present with a *spatium* of presence in order that it can *be*, in order that there be presence of the present. Augustine calls that operation *attentio*, and not, as in the previous passage (XI.20), *contuitus*: "Yet, [the soul's] attentiveness persists [*perdurat attentio*], and through it that which is to be passes toward the state in which it is to be no more" (XI.28). It is as if Augustine were concerned that merely beholding (*contuitus*) might not suffice to give a *spatium* and so a presence to its present. Or rather, at least, such beholding would need to be redoubled so that one not only beheld something but held that very beholding in mind, held it in a perduring attentiveness capable of granting it a *spatium*. In the end, the present would have no extent other than that of the soul's operation of perdurant attentiveness.

Augustine broaches this end when, translating Plotinus' διάστασις[2] into *distentio*, he ventures to identify the extending, the stretching out, denoted by this word, to identify it as constituting the very *what* of time. Augustine writes: "It seems to me, then, that time is merely a distention, though of what it is a distention I do not know" (XI.26). And yet, if *distentio* designates the movement through which intervals of presence are installed within the otherwise incessant flight of what is to be into what has been, if *distentio* names not just this flight but its presence, that is, the presence and extent granted it by memory, attentiveness, and expectation, then this *distentio* will be inseparable from these operations of the soul. It will perhaps be even *of the soul*: "I begin to wonder whether it is a distention of the soul itself" (XI.26).

Transformed into the distention of the soul, withdrawn into the soul as the only place thought capable of sheltering it from not being, time will be deprived of its direct engagement with things. Thus withdrawn from things, time will no longer be taken to impart itself to their comings and goings; or, at best, it will seem to do so only secondarily, only subsequent to its proper constitution, in an order of precedence that would no longer be that even of time itself. For Augustine time can be sheltered from not being only through being doubled in the soul, only through being doubled by the three dyadic forms: presence of the past, presence of the present, and presence of the future. Once the time in which things come to pass has been doubled by this other time within the soul, the reversal is inevitable: as the time sheltered from not being, as the time that can be said to be, this other time within the soul will be taken, not as the mere double or doubling of another time, but as the original, as time itself, as originary time.

II

It is Heidegger who has radicalized to the limit the sheltering of time within the soul, its being of the soul. Thereby he has also forced to the limit the singularity and identity that philosophy has ascribed, if only tacitly, to time. Most transparent in this regard is Heidegger's 1924 lecture *The Concept of Time*: referring explicitly to the *Confessions* and to the question that Augustine pursued concerning the identity of time with the soul, Heidegger renews the interrogation and comes finally to a conclusion that radicalizes to the limit the placement of time in the soul. Setting aside the classical determination of that being that we ourselves are, redetermining it as Dasein, Heidegger declares that time is Dasein, that Dasein is temporality. Correspondingly, Heidegger traces the displacement undergone by the question "What is time?" – its transformation into the question "Who is time?" and finally into the question "Am I my time?"[3] *Being and Time* carries through in a thorough and rigorous way the identity declared in the lecture: in *Being and Time* all the existential structures and even the opening of the world are brought back to their ground in temporality, which is the meaning of the being of Dasein. The question is whether, in forcing the singularity and identity of time to the limit, Heidegger also initiates their disruption. And whether, following Heidegger to this limit, one could at least warrant opening the question of another time.

In any case Heidegger's project could not but have a significant bearing on the Augustinian sheltering of time from not being and on the consequent installing of time in the soul, its determination as of the soul.

For both the need to shelter from not being and the appeal to the doubling of time as the means of sheltering it proceed on the basis of an understanding of *being as presence*. Since Heidegger's project in its most global parameters is to put in question the meaning of being, indeed, above all, to put in question the understanding of being as presence that has governed western philosophy since the Greeks, his project cannot but recoil upon and begin to erode that very Augustinian analysis that, on the other hand, he carries through to its completion.

Being and Time was not simply to have ended with the temporality of Dasein. On the contrary, the analytic was to have advanced beyond Dasein and temporality to time and being. Even though this final analytic would have been developed from the temporal interpretation of Dasein, it would nonetheless have constituted an advance by bringing to light time "as the horizon for all understanding of Being" (*SZ* 17).[4] The final move would, then, have been from temporality as the meaning of the being of Dasein to time as the horizon for all understanding of being. Set within this horizon, understood from it, being would be exhibited in its temporal character. In order to indicate that such a temporal character could not consist merely in being in time as beings can be said to be in time, Heidegger designates it by the Latin cognate *temporal*, in distinction from *zeitlich*. Indeed, he marks the advance as such by differentiating between *die Zeitlichkeit des Daseins* and *die Temporalität des Seins*. He writes:

> The determination of the meaning of being and of its characters and modes on the basis of time we call its *temporal* determination [*seine* temporale *Bestimmtheit*]. Thus the fundamental ontological task of interpreting being as such includes working out the *temporality of being* [Temporalität des Seins]. In the exposition of the problematic of temporality [*Temporalität*] the question of the meaning of being will first be concretely answered. (*SZ* 19)

This advance from *Zeitlichkeit* to *Temporalität* was of course never carried out. In its published form, *Being and Time* breaks off at the end of the analysis of Dasein and *Zeitlichkeit*, breaks off with a series of questions about this very advance that has not been carried out: "Is there a way leading from originary *time* to the meaning of *being*? Does *time* itself reveal itself as the horizon of *being*?" (*SZ* 437).

From these indications it is difficult to determine the precise character of the advance from *Zeitlichkeit* to *Temporalität*. In the recently published "Aufzeichnungen zur Temporalität," Heidegger indicates, but only very cryptically, that the question of the apriori would be addressed in the account of *Temporalität.* But he says little more than the following: "Auch im Apriori: Zeit als *Temporalität.* Das Apriori selbst ein temporaler Begriff."[5] Nor is much clarification provided by the new elaboration of the missing division of *Being and Time* that Heidegger undertakes in the 1927 lecture course, *Basic Problems of Phenomenology.* For the course consists largely of a reconstitution of the problematic of *Being and Time* beginning with four historical theses on being, and, though briefly venturing to develop the question of the meaning of being in general, it breaks off without having advanced more than a few steps toward an answer to that question. The few general indications given tend, if anything, to reduce somewhat the extent of the advance. In one passage, for instance, Heidegger reformulates the question of the meaning of being as a question of the condition of possibility and then adds: "When *Zeitlichkeit* functions as such a condition, we call it *Temporalität.*"[6] Here it is as though only an alteration of function differentiated *Temporalität* from *Zeitlichkeit.* In another passage he says: "*Temporalität* is the most originary temporalizing [*Zeitigung*] of *Zeitlichkeit* as such."[7]

Yet, whatever its specific character, the move to an analytic of *Temporalität* would be an advance to a form of time that would be more originary than the originary time of Dasein. It would be an advance beyond the time that the existential analysis establishes in its identity with Dasein, an advance beyond the time that would be sheltered in what was once called the soul, an advance toward another time. It is the question of such an advance that needs to be pursued in order to drive Heidegger's analysis to the limit where perhaps a first glimpse of another time may be offered; and though the advance will turn out to proceed along a way different from that to which Heidegger alludes in his all too brief discourses on *Temporalität,* it will be broached largely on the basis of certain particular indications found in Heidegger's text.

If there is another time that, like *Temporalität,* is beyond – or rather, before – Dasein's temporality, then this other time will also be anterior to Dasein's historicity, which is founded on Dasein's temporality. This other time, this time before time, could, then, appropriately be called prehistorical time. But in this designation everything depends on determining what the *pre-* signifies, that is, what the sense of anteriority must be.

In a sense Dasein's temporality is prehistorical, is anterior to history. In this regard anteriority refers to the order of founding: temporality is what makes possible Dasein's occurrence (*Geschehen*), and the latter, in turn, is what founds history in all its various senses. Yet, precisely by being in this sense prehistorical, temporality as such is thoroughly historical. Dasein's time is historical time.

Heidegger's analysis in this regard focuses on Dasein's occurrence (*Geschehen*). To Dasein there belongs a certain extending (*Erstreckung*): Dasein extends itself or is itself extended from birth to death, or, perhaps better, there is an extending of Dasein from birth to death; this extending is what constitutes the connectedness of life. This specific movement of extending is what Heidegger calls the occurrence (*Geschehen*) of Dasein. The structure of Dasein's occurrence (*Geschehen*) is called historicity (*Geschichtlichkeit*). In the most rigorous terms, it is historicity that is founded on, made possible by, temporality. This relation is perhaps most evident in Heidegger's description of the originary mode of Dasein's occurrence, which he calls fate (*Schicksal*): Dasein's occurrence in this mode is geared to its being freed, through authentic being-toward-death, so that it chooses to choose among the possibilities that, as thrown, it finds handed down to it, so that, in Heidegger's words, "Dasein, free for death, hands itself down to itself in a possibility that it has inherited and yet has chosen" (*SZ* 384). In being-toward-death there lies the future, in being thrown amidst handed-down possibilities there lies having-been (*Gewesenheit*), and in taking over and choosing there lies the present. Heidegger's conclusion: fate – and, more generally, Dasein's occurrence as such – "requires as the ontological condition of its possibility, the constitution of being of care [*die Seinsverfassung der Sorge*], that is, temporality" (*SZ* 385). In short, temporality is the condition of the possibility of Dasein's occurrence, that is, of historicity. And, as Heidegger also shows, everything to which the word *history* – the two words *Geschichte* and *Historie* – is extended comes back finally to Dasein's historicity.

On the one hand, then, Heidegger sets temporality before history by exposing it as the condition of the possibility of history. But, on the other hand, Heidegger also closes the gap that might otherwise be taken to separate condition from conditioned. The analysis of historicity, he says, "merely reveals what already lies enveloped in the temporalizing of temporality" (*SZ* 376). Thus, historicity is not anything other than temporality. As Heidegger says, still more directly: "Historicity as the constitution of the being of existence is 'fundamentally' temporality [*Geschichtlichkeit als Seinsverfassung der Existenz ist 'im Grunde' Zeitlichkeit*]" (*SZ* 404). Therefore, while temporality is the condition of the possibility of historicity (and hence of history), it is nothing other than historicity, nothing set apart from and in this sense anterior to historicity. Dasein's time is as such historical time. And, since Dasein's time is originary time, there would be, in the final analysis, no prehistorical time.

And yet, there is something that would seem to limit the coincidence of temporality and historicity, something that, while also stemming from temporality, must be differentiated from historicity. Heidegger mentions the need and use of calendars and clocks, that is, a certain reckoning with time that is turned toward things and only remotely, if at all, linked to Dasein's historicity. Heidegger mentions too that whatever occurs along with it Dasein experiences as "in time." Heidegger singles out those things belonging to nature: the processes of nature, whether living or lifeless, are encountered as "in time." This time within which natural things occur is, to some extent at least, other than the time of history, even if this other time also has its origin finally in temporality. The analysis of this other time is thus coordinate with and independent of the analysis of historicity, so that, as Heidegger remarks, the analysis of how this time of within-timeness (*Innerzeitigkeit*) originates from temporality could just as easily be placed before, instead of after, the discussion of the connection between historicity and temporality. Heidegger declares even that, insofar as the time of within-timeness also stems from temporality, historicity and within-timeness are equally originary (*gleichursprünglich*) (*SZ* 376f.). This other time in which things occur and with which Dasein reckons is another stem of temporality, irreducible to historicity even though linked to it through the common root, temporality. The question is one of gauging the withdrawal of this other time from the time of history and of determining its capacity to resist assimilation to Dasein's historicity. Can this crack in the hegemony of history be opened to such an extent as to expose a time that is prehistorical in the most radical sense?

The final chapter of *Being and Time* opens with another reference to Dasein's reckoning with time, this reckoning now being characterized as an elemental comportment, which, Heidegger insists, must be clarified before it can be determined what is meant in saying that beings are "in time." It is not just that a dimension of the phenomenon of temporality remains unconsidered; rather, the analysis of temporality remains, says Heidegger, incomplete specifically because it has not yet shown how "something like world-time [*Weltzeit*] in the rigorous sense of the existential-temporal concept of world belongs to temporality itself" (*SZ*

405). Heidegger already alludes to what will become evident in the course of the analysis to come: world-time is the time *in which* beings occur; it is the time by virtue of which they have their within-timeness (*Innerzeitigkeit*). The question to be addressed is, then, that of the relation between Dasein's most elemental reckoning with time and the constitution of world-time.

Heidegger does not, however, address this question directly. Instead of an analysis of world-time as such, what Heidegger proceeds to develop is an analysis of what he calls *die besorgte Zeit*. This time, another time to be distinguished both from that of historicity and from temporality, is a time of concern in two senses. It is, first of all, the time that belongs to the sphere of circumspective concern, the time constituted, as it were, within this sphere. But, secondly, it is also the time with which Dasein can be concerned, the time to which Dasein's concern can be directed, as, for instance, in reckoning with time.

Heidegger's analysis undertakes to show how the time of concern arises from – is constituted on the basis of – temporality, which by this demonstration, says Heidegger, would thus also be shown to be *originary time*, granted, as Heidegger will easily show, that the ordinary concept of time as a sequence of nows arises, in turn, from the time of concern. Granted, too, that no other time becomes manifest, no other time that would fall outside the order of founding: now-time founded on the time of concern, and the time of concern founded on temporality, thus shown to be originary time. Granted, then, that world-time also can be accommodated to this order of founding.

How does the time of concern arise from temporality? Heidegger's answer is explicit: by self-interpretation. In other words, the time of concern is self-interpreted temporality; it is temporality set interpretively before itself, an interpretive doubling of temporality.

The contours of Heidegger's analysis in this regard can be readily sketched. In circumspective concern Dasein is engaged with the things at hand (*das Zuhandene*) within the world. Dasein understands these things, that is, projects them upon their world-horizon; Dasein interprets them, exhibits them *as* something in relation to the meanings granted them by the horizon; Dasein discourses about them, articulating the context of meaning, and expresses this discourse in language, addressing itself to these things. Yet these things at hand are not objects over against Dasein such that in speaking of them Dasein could leave entirely out of its account its own comportment to them. On the contrary, in interpreting and speaking of the things at hand, Dasein cannot but also interpret and express its own being-alongside them. In Dasein's comportment to them, in circumspective concern, there is always self-interpretation and self-expression; that is, in such comportment Dasein is always disclosed to itself with some degree of transparency, disclosed to itself in a self-interpreted form, that is, as a form of temporality. The time of concern is precisely the form in which temporality is set before itself through the self-interpretation and self-expression that occur in circumspective concern. The time of concern is the form that self-interpreted temporality assumes in the sphere of circumspective concern.

What is this form of time? How does the temporality of circumspective concern interpret itself, that is, within what horizon, within what context of meanings? Heidegger's answer is not entirely univocal: in circumspective concern Dasein interprets its temporality, interprets itself as temporality, by reference to the world *or*, as Heidegger's actual descriptions bear out, by reference to the things and events at hand within the world. For example: *now that* I reach for the right tool so that what I am making will be finished *when later* someone comes for it, I find the tool just where it was *when formerly* I used it. In this interpretation there is operative what Heidegger calls an assigning or giving of time (*Zeitangabe*): Dasein assigns its temporality to its concrete, factical being-alongside things at hand, transposes temporality into a time of its concern with things at hand. Furthermore, by setting temporality – that is, itself as temporality – into the field of things at hand, Dasein gives time to itself, gives itself a time with which it can be concerned, with which it can reckon. There is, then, a *double giving of time*: Dasein gives, assigns, time to the things and events at hand within the world so as thereby to give to itself the time of concern. Thus, the reckoning that would be a genuinely elemental comportment would have the character of a double giving of time.

Yet the time of concern, constituted in and through this double giving, is not yet – not quite – world-time. Heidegger says that in order for world-time to arise from the time of concern the latter must have been made public (*SZ* 414). This being made public cannot consist simply in others' coming to share the time of concern; for other Daseins will always already have been there all along (Dasein as *Mitsein*), and accordingly, the time of concern would never have been a solitary time that an isolated Dasein would then come to share with others. But what is it, then, that makes time public? What is it that brings about the advance from the time of concern to world-time?

Although the time of concern can arise through self-interpretation simply in reference to the things and events at hand within the environing world (*Umwelt*), Heidegger indicates that there is a further horizon that comes into play, a horizon that bears on time's becoming public, its becoming world-time. This other horizon is that of the kind of concern with time that we are familiar with as astronomical and calendrical time-reckoning (*SZ* 411). Orientation to this other horizon Heidegger links to Dasein's thrownness, to such an extent that he declares thrownness to be the reason why there is time publicly.

Heidegger's analysis proceeds from the need for sight. Circumspective concern needs the possibility of sight; its double giving of time, one may add, likewise is submitted to this need, so that in the giving of time this need for sight must be taken into account. Above all, this means that in its thrownness Dasein is submitted to the alternation of day and night, the brightness of day giving this possibility of sight, night taking it away. Hence, the double giving of time, which operates within circumspective concern and constitutes the time of concern, cannot take place without reference beyond the environing world of that concern; it cannot take place without also referring – or rather, submitting – to the gift of light bestowed by the heaven, preeminently by the sun. Designating the assigning of time as a matter of dating, Heidegger declares: "The sun dates the time that is interpreted in concern." He continues: "From this dating arises the 'most natural' measure of time – the day." In turn, he says, the dividing up of the day is "carried out with regard to that by which time is dated – the journeying sun" (*SZ* 412f.). It is this dating – carried out from the heavenly bodies and their distinctive places in the sky – that makes time public, that makes it assignable in a way that we can share, as Heidegger says, " 'under the same sky' " (*SZ* 413). Thus, only in coming to be dated from the sky does the time of concern become world-time. Whereas Dasein gives time to environmental things and events, the sky gives time to Dasein and to its entire sphere of circumspective concern. Whereas, giving time to things at hand in circumspective concern, Dasein gives itself this time, sets itself before itself as this form of time, this double giving of time is submitted to the sky, is bound by that other time that the sky and, preeminently, its sun give to Dasein and its restricted, not-yet-public, indeed narrow sphere of circumspective concern.

In Heidegger's discussion of world-time, one finds the following, very remarkable declaration: " 'Time' first shows itself in the sky, that is, precisely there where one comes across it in directing oneself naturally *according to it*, so that time even becomes identified with the sky" (*SZ* 419).

First showing itself in the sky, time – this other time, this uranic time – is anterior to the time that Dasein gives itself in circumspective concern, anterior to such a degree that it is from the sky that time is first given to this narrow sphere. Little wonder that this other time from above has even, as Heidegger says, been identified with the sky. For instance – the most compelling instance, though it is unlikely that Heidegger had it in mind – in Plato's *Timaeus*, in which the moving image of eternity, identified as time, is nothing other than the starry heaven.

There is little reason to suppose that this other time, uranic time, could be assimilated to Dasein's historicity. One might rather suppose that its circling gives the time within which the time of history would arise, that it gives the time within which Dasein hands itself down to itself, just as it gives the time for Dasein's self-interpretation in circumspective concern.

The more difficult question is whether this uranic time can be appropriated to temporality, to its order of founding, so that temporality could still be declared originary time and the identity and singularity of time still preserved. Or whether uranic time is another time, whether it is a time that escapes the founding order, whether it is a time other than the temporality of Dasein, a time even that commands that temporality, a time other than human time, a time to which human time cannot but submit. An inexorable time.

Above all, it will be a question of whether the region that gives this other time can be assimilated to the existential structures, all of which lead back, in the founding order, to temporality. Yet one cannot but wonder whether it could ever suffice phenomenologically to regard the sun as no more than something at hand in a world delimited by human goals and possibilities or as something rendered objectively present (*vorhanden*) only by being deprived of the referential significations it would in the first instance have had in such a world. Is the inexorability of the sun as it traverses the sky not more insistent than any such things could ever be? To say nothing of the sky, which is not a thing at all, which shows itself in a showing in which the profile-structure belonging to all self-showings of things is completely effaced. Could the sheer radiance of the sky, its pure shining, the radiant shining that *is* the sky, ever be mistaken for something at hand in the narrow human world? Then, neither could the time it gives be assimilated to Dasein's temporality. And then, one would need to say that the time given by the sky, this uranic time, is, in a way both remote and wondrous, an other time.

NOTES

1 St. Augustine, *Confessions*, XI.14. I have used the Latin text of book XI (with German translation) in Kurt Flasch, *Was ist Zeit?* (Frankfurt a.M.: Klostermann, 1993). For some passages I have adapted the translation by R. S. Pine-Coffin (St. Augustine, *Confessions* [Maryland: Penguin Books, 1961]). Subsequent references to the *Confessions* are given by book and chapter numbers alone.

2 "The spreading out [διάστασις] of life involves time" (Plotinus, *Ennead* III.7.11).

3 Martin Heidegger, *Der Begriff der Zeit* (Tübingen: Niemeyer, 1989), pp. 26–8.

4 All references to *Being and Time* (indicated by *SZ* followed by page number) are to the ninth German edition: *Sein und Zeit*, 9th, unaltered, edn. (Tübingen: Niemeyer, 1960).

5 Martin Heidegger, "Aufzeichnungen zur Temporalität," *Heidegger Studies* 14 (1998), 21.

6 Martin Heidegger, in *Die Grundprobleme der Phänomenologie, Gesamtausgabe* vol. 24 (Frankfurt a.M.: Klostermann, 1975), p. 389.

7 Ibid., p. 429.

CHAPTER 12

Intentionality, teleology, and normativity

Mark Okrent

According to Heidegger, all human activity involves a double teleology. One acts in order to accomplish some end, but one also acts for the sake of being a certain sort of person. Engaging in an act of philosophical interpretation is a paradigmatically human activity. So if Heidegger is right regarding human action (and I believe that he is), any act of interpreting a philosopher's work must not only be an act that is performed in order to achieve some goal, but also an act in and through which the interpreter acts for the sake of realizing some possibility of human existence.

I have spent a substantial portion of my life attempting to interpret the work of Martin Heidegger. This activity has had, in general, the goal of my coming to understand his work. But human activities rarely have such general goals. Rather, one acts in order to accomplish something in particular. In the case of acts of interpretation such particularity is usually achieved by the interpreter approaching the texts to be interpreted with a leading question in hand, a question that specifies what is to be found out in the interpreting. And for my interpretation of Heidegger this leading question has been specified by my understanding of what it is to be a philosopher. For, while the "in order to" of my interpretation is to understand Heidegger, that for the sake of which I carry out the interpretation, the possibility of human existence that I thereby embody, is that I be a philosopher.

Heidegger himself teaches us that it is the task of the philosopher to raise the question of being. And in this age, to raise the question of being also involves raising the question of human being, the question of the meaning of the being of Dasein. Since Descartes, human being has been understood in terms of mentality, and since Brentano, that mentality has been understood in terms of intentionality. But Heidegger suggests that intentionality itself depends upon being-in-the-world. So the leading question with which I approach the work of Heidegger is just the question of how we should understand the most characteristic claim of his early philosophy, that being-in-the-world is a necessary condition on the possibility of intentionality. If one could understand this assertion one would also understand Heidegger's answer to the question of the meaning of Dasein's being, and also, one hopes, come closer to answering that question for oneself.

Heidegger typically formulates the dependency of intentionality on being-in-the-world in the traditional language of transcendental philosophy. According to Heidegger, Dasein's being-in-the-world is a necessary condition on the possibility of intentionality. "The Dasein exists in the manner of being-in-the-world, and this basic determination of its existence is the presupposition for being able to apprehend anything at all."[1] Now, if Heidegger is right, and we are warranted in asserting that Dasein's being-in-the-world is a transcendental condition on the possibility of intentionality, then there must be a transcendental argument that supplies the warrant for this claim. And the particular form that my leading question in interpreting Heidegger has taken has been how best to understand this implicit transcendental argument.

One might think that it would be relatively easy to articulate Heidegger's transcendental argument concerning the way in which being-in-the-world is necessary for intentionality. After all, Heidegger was thoroughly familiar with the transcendental tradition stemming from Kant, and acutely conscious that his claim has the form of an assertion of a transcendental condition on the possibility of intentionality. So Heidegger must have realized that he needed a transcendental argument to warrant the claim that intentionality is only possible for an entity that has being-in-the-world as its mode of being. Nevertheless, the structure of this argument is anything but transparent.

The reason for this is that Heidegger's philosophical practice was heavily influenced by Husserl's. According to Husserlian phenomenology it is possible to simply intuit categorial structures, such as the being of Dasein or the essence of the intentional as such. If this is possible, then it is also possible to simply *see* (in some extended sense of "see") that intentionality is impossible without being-in-the-world. And, in that case, an *argument* which infers this conclusion from the necessary features of intentionality is unnecessary. So, given the centrality of categorial intuition to his philosophical practice,[2] Heidegger seems to have assumed that he did not need to provide an explicit argument which had as its conclusion that being-in-the-world is a necessary condition on intentionality.

Unfortunately Heidegger's work itself raises several serious doubts regarding the claims of Husserlian phenomenology in general and concerning the doctrine of categorial intuition in particular. To mention just one of these doubts, the possibility of categorial intuition depends upon an assumption regarding the character of our access to our own intentional life that Heidegger's own work seems to undercut. Phenomenology is an essentially "first personal," introspective enterprise. As such, it depends upon our ability to reflectively distance ourselves from our own first-order mental life by having second-order mental intentions directed towards this life. In the Transcendental Deduction in the B edition, Kant had formulated this ability by claiming that it must be possible to attach the "I think" to each of our intentions. But when Heidegger discusses this passage he specifically rejects this understanding of our primary relation to ourselves.[3] And it is anything but clear that his alternative account of our reflective nature, in terms of the way in which we find ourselves in our practical dealings with things, could serve as a ground for claims regarding the intuitive apprehension of categorial structure. So, given Heidegger's own understanding of reflection, it seems that Heidegger's self-understanding of his philosophical practice in terms of phenomenological intuition must be taken with a grain of salt. Rather, many of the assertions that Heidegger presents as being warranted by categorial intuition are in fact warranted, if at all, by transcendental *arguments*.[4]

Every transcendental argument proceeds in two stages. First, one identifies some feature of intentional states without which they would not count as intentional. Second, one argues that states could not have those features unless certain other conditions were met. So it is of cardinal importance for any attempt at transcendental philosophy that one correctly identify the conditions under which a state, event, or entity counts as intentional.

In the Transcendental Deduction in the B edition, Kant started a tradition which took a certain notion of self-consciousness, that it must be possible for "an 'I think' to accompan[y] all representations,"[5] as the basis for transcendental arguments. In saying this, Kant is following a Cartesian and Lockian tradition for which it had seemed self-evident that all mental states, and thus all intentional states, are conscious states. Heidegger has an ambivalent place within this Kantian transcendental tradition. He certainly does not accept the claim from the B Deduction in the form in which Kant makes it. On the other hand, he does accept a cognate claim, that every directing itself towards concomitantly involves a self-unveiling of Dasein.[6] This might be true of Dasein, as Heidegger thought. And there are indications that Heidegger understood this to be an appropriate starting point for a transcendental argument.

It has never seemed to me, however, that the possibility of self-consciousness or the "I think," or the concomitant unveiling of self *is* necessary for intentionality. That is, it seems to me to be possible for there to be intentional states that lack the possibility of being conscious or becoming self-conscious.

I have a number of reasons for thinking that there can be intentional states that are not capable of becoming self-conscious. I will not pause to detail those reasons here. In a preliminary way, however, it is fair to say that all of these reasons turn on the priority, when it comes to intentionality, of action over self-understanding. There seem to be a whole variety of human *actions* that must be understood in intentional terms, as involving goals, even though the agents of those acts appear entirely incapable of recognizing that they *are* the agents of those acts or of recognizing that they act as they do because they themselves are motivated by reasons. Examples include not only the standard Freudian cases, but also a wide range of situations taken from experimental psychology and neurology. Certain actions undertaken by patients with various brain lesions and split-brain patients, for example, seem to cry out for understanding in terms of the agent's goals, or her beliefs and desires, although the agent herself is entirely incapable of intending these goals, beliefs, and desires as her own in the normal way. And once this fact is recognized about human action, a second fact becomes evident. It seems to be necessary to understand many acts of animal agents in teleological terms even though there is no reason to think that those agents are capable of intending themselves *as* the agent of those actions. And while not all teleology involves intentionality, the phenomena are close enough in structure and closely enough related in the human case to raise interesting questions regarding whether or not certain animal agents are capable of intentional states even though they lack an unveiling of self. So, as I said above, for these reasons and others, it has never seemed to me that the possibility of the "I think" or the unveiling of self is a suitable starting point for transcendental arguments that are designed to determine the necessary conditions on *all* intentionality.

There are interesting differences between the sorts of intentionality that demand the possibility of the self being unveiled and those that do not, however. For example, any language user or any being that is capable of rationally evaluating her reasons for acting must have intentional states that are capable of becoming self-conscious. So transcendental arguments that take the possibility of the "I think" accompanying intentional states as their base step are not without interest. But insofar as it is possible for there to be intentional states that are not capable of becoming self-conscious, the unveiling of self is not a suitable base step for a transcendental argument designed to show that all intentionality rests on being-in-the-world.

But there are other elements of Heidegger's analysis of intentionality that do provide such a suitable starting point. Here, it seems to me, is a condition on intentionality that is highlighted by Heidegger and which *is* necessary for all intentionality. Every intentional state has a content. When one says that some state is intentional one means at a minimum that that state is about or directed towards something and that there is a way in which that state is directed towards what it is about. Beliefs, perceptions, and goal-directed actions are paradigm cases of states, events, or entities that exhibit intentionality. Each of these types exhibit some variety of what is now often called "attitude," which helps to individuate those states. It is one thing to believe that P and quite another to want that P. But intentional states are also individuated by what they are about or directed towards. My wanting to eat vanilla ice cream is different from wanting to eat chocolate just insofar as one is a desire for vanilla and the other for chocolate. *What* an intentional state is about or directed towards is, in a broad sense, the content of that state. When Jane believes that there is a door knob on the door, or wants there to be a door knob on the door, or perceives that there is a door knob on the door, or acts in order that there is a door knob on the door, the content of each of these states is that there is a door knob on the door. Similarly, when Jane simply takes a door knob as a door knob by using it as such, what she does is a taking as, and as such it has the content that this thing is a door knob.

But *what is it* for any event, state, or entity to have content? If one starts from the standpoint of first-person attribution, it might initially seem self-evident and unproblematic that many of our states have content. Descartes defines the term "thought" "to include everything that is within us in such a way that we are immediately aware of it." So insofar as each of us thinks, each of us is aware *of* something about ourselves. And *what* we are aware of about ourselves is frequently that there is a state in us which is different from other states just insofar as it embodies a different idea, a different "form" from other such states ("I understand this term [idea] to mean the form of any given thought, immediate perception of which makes me aware of the thought"),[7] a form that has "objective reality" just insofar as it "represents" something. So it is built into the very nature of our being, on this view, that there are states in us of which we are immediately aware, that have content, and that we are immediately aware of as having content. So what could be problematic?

This view gets problematized from several distinct perspectives. The perspective that probably most influenced Heidegger was supplied by Kant, who recognized the instability of the Cartesian picture from within the first-person perspective. On this picture our thoughts have two features: they are immediate presentations of *ourselves* that are about something else. So there is some fact about me, presented to me, which at the same time refers to the not me. But not all of my self presentations have this additional feature of content. Pains, tickles, mere sensations as opposed to perceptions, lack content. So what, Kant implicitly asks, do intentional states have that these others lack, given that both types involve self-presentation?

Kant also supplied the answer to this question. States with intentional content are states that have objective reference, they refer to objects. This is just to repeat that such states do have content. But states that have objective reference are also objective in the sense that they can be right or wrong depending upon the state of the object to which they refer. That is, any intentional state is *normatively evaluable* and the *standard* against which it is to be evaluated is supplied by the content of that state.

Beliefs are the most obvious examples of the normative evaluability of intentional states, and of the way in which the content of the state also supplies the norm for evaluation of that state, but beliefs do not supply us with the most general characterization of the feature in question. Husserl picked out this most general normative feature of intentional states when he spoke of the fact that intentional states can be fulfilled or empty. Heidegger emphasizes this same normative feature of the intentional in his discussion of fulfillment, evidence, and acts of identification in the Introduction to the *History of the Concept of Time*, for example. I prefer to put the point by saying that all intentional states have satisfaction conditions, and that those conditions are specified by the content of those states.

Any belief, as a belief, can be true or false. That is to say, any belief is normatively evaluable regarding its truth. Whether the belief is true depends upon whether or not a certain set of conditions actually obtains. These are the truth conditions on the belief. For any belief, the conditions under which it would be true are the conditions specified in the content of the belief. Similarly, any act that has a goal can be successful or unsuccessful at reaching that goal. Whether the act is successful or not depends upon whether a certain set of conditions come to actually obtain. These are the satisfaction conditions on the act which are specified by the content of the act. Beliefs are different from overt acts just insofar as they have different sorts of satisfaction conditions which determine how they are to be normatively evaluated. Beliefs are true just in case their satisfaction conditions actually obtain, so those conditions are truth conditions. A goal-directed act is successful just in case its satisfaction conditions come to obtain. For any overt, goal-directed act, the satisfaction conditions are specified by the goal of that act, which is the intentional content of the act, or what it is directed towards. These are the most obvious cases, but other intentional states are also normatively evaluable in similar ways with their contents playing similar roles. When I take a door knob as a door knob by actually using it as such, for example, I am doing something that could be right or wrong, depending on whether or not my taking as a door knob actually reveals a door knob.

This coordination of the content of intentional states with the norms against which these states are to be evaluated gives rise to two deep philosophical problems. First, intentional states are states with objective reference. States with objective reference have satisfaction conditions that are supplied by their contents, which allow for their normative evaluability, which is essential for their objective reference and thus for their intentionality. Now, intentional states are individuated by their contents. So what it is to be any particular type of intentional state is determined by its content, and that content is identical with the norm against which that state is to be evaluated. That is, it is intrinsic to any intentional state that it is *to be evaluated* in light of its content. But how is it possible for a state to contain the conditions for its normative evaluation intrinsically? Ordinarily, we think that things can be normatively evaluated only extrinsically. As Heraclitus would have it, salt water is both good and bad: Good for fish, bad for us. But it is not evaluable in itself, for to be salt water does not supply a norm for evaluation. Intentional states, however, are not like that. They are, and must be, intrinsically evaluable. How is this possible?

The fact of the normativity of intentional content gives rise to a second deep problem. Because intentional content both fixes the objective reference of an intentional state and also has an intrinsically normative character, the object referred to by an intentional state need not exist. It must be possible for norms, as norms, to fail to be satisfied. So it must be possible for intentional states to refer to or be about objects or states of affairs that do not exist. And, because of the surface grammar of our ordinary way of talking about intentional states and the logic of relations, this presents us with a formidable problem, a problem which is central to both Heidegger's philosophical development and my appropriation of Heidegger.

In ordinary language we usually assert the presence of an intentional state by specifying an agent that has that state, the content of that state, and by using a verb that takes a grammatical object to express how that agent stands vis à vis that content. I *believe* that $2 + 2 = 4$; I *am attempting* to open the door. This syntactical structure suggests that when an agent is in an intentional state, that agent stands in some sort of relation with the content of that state. But what sort of object is the intentional agent related *to*? There seems to be something wrong with each of the candidates for the role of second relata, the content relata. It is a necessary feature of any attribution of a relational property that all of the relata involved in the relation must exist. If Valerie is taller than Anna, both Valerie and Anna exist. But I can think about my sixth child, even though she does not exist, never did, and never will. So the *object* implicated in the content cannot be the entity involved in the relation. Nor, for similar reasons, can the actual state of affairs that in normal contexts is involved in intentional content be the second relata. I can believe that it is raining even when it is not raining, that is, even though there is no state of affairs that is the raining. Nor can the relata be the thought or representation of the object or the thought of the state of affairs involved in the content. If some representation were the object about which I think when I think, then it would be literally false to say that unicorns do not exist, and if what I am related to were the representation or thought of the state of affairs, then whether or not some state of affairs actually obtained would be irrelevant to the truth of the belief that it did. Finally, one can think of the second relata involved in content as an abstract object, such as a proposition. But this option just reiterates the initial problem. The belief that p is supposed to involve a relation to the proposition p, and that proposition is a real, but abstract entity. But that proposition *means* that p. That is, it is related in a particular way to the *possible* state of affairs p. But what is it for an abstract object to be related to some possible, but not necessarily actual, state of affairs?

The early Heidegger was centrally aware that it is necessary to any intentional state that it appear to have a relational structure but that it is not necessary that both of the relata of this "relation" need exist. Indeed, there are numerous indications that Heidegger took this relational structure, in which an intentional agent seems to be related with an object that need not exist, to be the central fact about intentionality that needs to be understood.[8]

The difficulties involved in understanding the second relata of intentional "relations" led Heidegger to reject the supposition that being in an intentional state involved any real relation. Rather, he tells us, the "relation" involved in such intentional states is not a relation between two actual entities, but "intrinsic" to the intentional state itself. He says of perception, for example, that "the expression 'relation of perception' means, not a relation into which perception first enters as one of the relata and which falls to perception as in itself free of relation, but rather a relation which perceiving itself is, as such."[9]

But this account by itself is incomplete and unsatisfying. It is best seen as a way of understanding intentional states rather than an account of how such states are possible. Question: what sort of relation does my having a desire for an ice cream cone involve between me and ice cream cones? Answer: it is just intrinsic to my desire, as the desire that it is, that *it is a desire for an ice cream cone*. Well I knew *that*: that is just to say that it *is* a desire for an ice cream cone, that is, a desire that is evaluable regarding satisfaction by whether or not I come to have an ice cream cone. But what is it for a desire to be *that* desire? Intentional states are partly individuated by their contents, and those contents pick out particular objects and states of affairs. What is involved in that "picking out" if it is not a real relation? In order to understand intentionality we must see how to answer this question.

But if this is the case then we have finally encountered a suitable base step for a rational reconstruction of Heidegger's transcendental argument to the conclusion that being-in-the-world is a necessary condition on all intentionality. According to Heidegger, all intentional states are such that they intrinsically involve a being related to an object in such a way that that object provides for the possibility of the intrinsic evaluability of the intentional state, even though the intentional object need not, in fact, exist. So, whatever is necessary for the possibility of this sort of relatedness to entities, is a necessary condition on intentionality. And, Heidegger tells us, being-in-the-world is such a condition.

How are we to understand this claim? Why is being-in-the-world necessary for the intrinsic normative evaluability and peculiar relational structure of intentionality? To answer this question one must first understand the structure that Heidegger names "being-in-the-world."

There are a number of different ways of gaining access to the structure that Heidegger identifies as being-in-the-world. For me, the most suggestive has always been by way of the examples that he gives of "being-in." For Heidegger, only an entity of a certain type, one that has being-in-the-world as its mode of being, can have intentional states. And any entity that is in-the-world must *be in* the world, in the sense of being-involved-with the world, or so Heidegger informs us. But when is it the case that an entity is "being-in"? Well, here are some of the modes in which an entity can be-in in the sense of being involved with: "working on something with something, producing something, cultivating and caring for something, putting something to use, employing something for something, holding something in trust, giving up, letting something get lost, interrogating, discussing, accomplishing, exploring, considering, determining something."[10]

Different readers read this list from different perspectives, and different features of these states are salient depending upon which of those perspectives one occupies. From my perspective, what is salient about the activities on this list is that they are *activities.* It is a necessary condition on "working on something with something," for example, that the one who does this *does something*, that is, engages in some overt action, and that it be true of that action that *it has some point.* The central fact about the items on this list is that they are all overt activities that are correctly describable as fitting the teleological category of having a goal. And if these activities are paradigmatic examples of being-in, and only entities that have being-in-the-world as their mode of being can have intentional states, then this suggests the thesis that only agents that act for ends can have intentional states, that is, the thesis that intentionality rests on a bedrock of teleology. That is, if being-in-the-world is necessary for intentionality, as Heidegger claims, and the ability to act teleologically in order to achieve goals is necessary for being-in-the-world, as Heidegger's examples suggest, then an agent's having the ability to act teleologically in order to achieve goals is necessary for that agent to have intentional states. This, I take it, is the most plausible way to understand the transcendental argument that stands behind Heidegger's claim that being-in-the-world is necessary for intentionality. An agent's being-in-the-world is necessary for the possibility of that agent having intentional states because only agents that can act for goals can have intentional states.

Here is how to flesh out the connections. Consider, for example, the act of "producing something," say a cake. Insofar as what one is doing is properly described as [trying to] produce a cake, what one does has a content. What one does is directed towards there being a cake of such and such type. There would seem to be only two possibilities concerning how we understand that in virtue of which this activity has a goal, and thus a direction and a content. Either what the agent does is directed towards the possible state of affairs of there being a cake, and has the content that there should be a cake, in virtue of it being caused in the appropriate way by internal states of the agent that have the appropriate content (she *desires* that there be a cake and *believes* that acting in this way produces the cake), or the action *itself* has the direction and content that it does somehow independently of the agent's beliefs and desires. But Heidegger insists that being-in-the-world is necessary for the intentionality of any states, so it would seem that he cannot explain the directionality of paradigmatic modes of being-in, goal-directed acts, by appeal to the intentionality of the states for which the directionality of the modes of being-in are necessary, mental states. That is, for Heidegger, the goal-directedness of producing a cake cannot depend upon the mental content of the agent's beliefs and desires. For Heidegger, the goal-directed teleology of involved being-in-the-world cannot rest on the mental content of conscious or unconscious internal states.

So let us assume that Heidegger is right in this view. We are left with the alternative hypothesis regarding action, that the directional content of the paradigmatic modes of being-in, of goal-directed activity, is primary and the intentionality of mental states is secondary. But the adoption of *this* hypothesis shows how it is possible for there to be a state that is apparently relational but does not imply the existence of that to which it is related. For overt, goal-directed actions have the remarkable property of being directed towards possible states of affairs that do not currently exist and perhaps never will. And they have that property in virtue of their relations to *other* states of affairs that *do* exist, but which are not the state of affairs towards which they are directed.

Consider the conditions under which we would feel ourselves warranted in saying that someone was acting in order to achieve some goal, say producing a cake. We would say that someone was attempting to produce a cake only if she engaged in a series of actions which were related to each other and to the environment in which they occur in such a way that, taken together, they would tend to result in there being a cake were each of them "successful." The agent opens the refrigerator, gets the eggs, cracks them in a bowl, beats them, adds milk and flour, pours the mixture in a pan, etc. Each of these steps in the process is described in terms of what it is "in order to" bring about, the eggs being cracked, being beaten, etc. Now, were all of these discrete acts to achieve the result in terms of which they are described, the cake would be produced. That is, they are all "in order to" produce a cake. On the other hand, taken by itself, none of these acts physically described need have the goal that it has. My moving my arm in the direction of the refrigerator handle need not be in order to open the door, let alone in order to bake a cake. The goal of that motion is no intrinsic property of that motion. It is only because that motion took place within the context of the overall production of a cake that it counts as instrumental to that goal. So, it would seem that an act having a goal is a holistic property in the sense that no event can have a goal unless it is appropriately related to other events that also have goals, in virtue of *their* relations.

But it is also the case that no act can have a goal unless it involves relations with the real environment. Each of the component acts of producing a cake might fail, in the sense of not bringing about the state of affairs that it is interpreted as having as a goal. The egg might fail to crack, for example. But unless the agent did *something* in the real world which would result in the egg cracking under some conditions, the act could not count as occurring in order to bring about a cracked egg. And this is true both of each of the component acts of the activity of producing a cake and of the overall activity as a whole.

So "acting in order to" involves, at the least, both a complex set of relations among a series of real overt actions and a complex set of relations between the agent of those actions and its real environment. But it would not seem to require any real relation between the agent or her acts and any cake, concrete, abstract, or representational. That is, producing a cake is an activity that counts as "in order to" produce a cake in virtue of real relations among real but non-cake entities.

And here is the answer to the question of how it is possible that intentional states have the peculiar relational character they have. Intentionality is in some way modeled from and piggybacks on the teleological "relation" of an activity having a goal. Saying that an activity has a goal, say, producing a cake, is not saying that there is some relation between that activity and some ghostly state of affairs, the cake having been produced, which is the goal. Rather, to say that an activity has the goal of producing a cake is to describe that activity as relating to its environment in such a way that it would bring about a cake under some definite conditions. So, having goal G is a holistic, relational characteristic of an act, but it does not involve any relation to *G*. Activities have goals, but there is nothing that is a goal. To say that intentionality is modeled on teleology, then, is to say that for an intentional state I to have a content C, is for I to have a holistic relation of a certain sort with other states of the agent of I and with that agent's environment, but that I need not have any real relation with the possible state of affairs, *C*. And to say that intentionality piggybacks on teleology is to say that no agent can count as having intentional states unless it also counts as overtly acting for goals, for what it is for any agent to have intentional states must be understood in terms of the relation between those states and what the agent does in order to accomplish its goals. This, I take it, is the essential core of Heidegger's claim that being-in-the-world is a necessary condition on intentionality. We understand what it is for a Dasein to have intentional states by way of understanding how those states are related to what the entity does in order to bring about results, rather than understanding what it is for an agent to act in order to bring about results by way of those acts' relations with the agent's intentional states.

The reason we *specify* intentional acts, overt and mental, through an identification of the content of the act is also evident on this view. There are lots of ways to act in order to crack an egg, physically described. But all of these physical events share one feature which is salient when one is trying to figure out what an agent is up to. They all would result in an egg being cracked were they successful. That is, the feature of overt physical events which serves to type acts as "in order to crack an egg" is *a possible state of affairs*, a state of affairs that would result from these acts under certain possible conditions. So it is intrinsic and essential to any act directed towards the goal of cracking an egg, *so described*, that it has that goal, even though what it is for the act to have that goal does not involve any real relation with any actual egg having been cracked, but merely real relations with other acts and entities in the agent's environment.

That overt actions that are performed in order to achieve some goal are typed and thus individuated by their goals shows how it is that intentional states can be intrinsically normative. For the goal of an act is no actual state of affairs. Rather, it is just that possible state of affairs which would come to exist were the act successful. That in virtue of which an act is typed as in order to G is intrinsically normative: G, which is both the goal of the act and that in virtue of which the act is typed, is just that norm that is to be used in evaluating this class of acts for success. So if one could give an articulation of what it is for an act to have a goal, one would also at the same time show why it is that such acts stand under intrinsic norms. And if, as I suggested above, mental intentionality piggybacks on overt teleology, then one must understand the normativity of the intentional in terms of the normativity of the teleological.

There is a sense in which this Heideggerean suggestion looks as if it is "behaviorist," but it really is not. The behaviorists tried to understand the content of mental states in terms of the input and output conditions on dispositions to act, *those inputs and outputs described in non-teleological terms.* That is, the behaviorist project is essentially reductive. This understanding of the claim that being-in-the-world is necessary for intentionality, on the other hand, is holistic: one is asking how a set of actions which each have a goal must be related if any of them is to have a goal. It goes on to interpret the *intentional* states of the agent in terms of their relations with the activity of the agent described in *teleological* terms. Instead of the behavioristic reduction of intentionality to dispositions to behavior physically described, one places intentionality in the context provided by the real goal-directed activity of an agent in the world.

It also looks as if this view is almost identical with Davidson's project, but once again it really is not. For Davidson thinks that overt actions have a goal only if they are caused in the right way by states of the agent which have the appropriate content. On the current Heideggerean inspired view, on the other hand, agents can have states with intentional content only if they act in the world in ways that admit of teleological descriptions, but *agents can act in ways that are correctly described teleologically, even if they have no mental states with intentional content.* That is, being-in-the-world is a necessary condition on the intentionality of mental states.

This, then, is the character of my appropriation of Heidegger. I took it to be the case that Heidegger needed a transcendental argument that led to the conclusion that being-in-the-world is a necessary condition on intentionality. I was led to the view that Heidegger took the key features of intentionality to be the fact that intentional states are related to their objects in such a way that those objects need not exist and that the content of an intentional state provides an intrinsic norm for the evaluation of that state. What I appropriated from Heidegger is the suggestion that both of these essential features of intentional states are possible only for a being that is capable of overt, goal-directed activity, that is, that is capable of teleological behavior.

This way of describing what I learned from Heidegger also serves to highlight the nature of my differences with Heidegger. Where I disagree with Heidegger is only on the issue of whether or not Dasein's mode of intentionality is the only possible type of intentionality. Heidegger is right in thinking that Dasein's mode of intentionality always involves a concomitant unveiling of self. In teleological terms, this fact shows up in the fact that Daseinish being-in-the-world always involves a relation between "the in order to" of acts (or, perhaps more properly, the "in order to" of *tools*) and the "for-the-sake-of" of the agent of the act or the user of the tool. What any Dasein does is always for the sake of some possible way of being Dasein, rather than being done merely in order to realize some possible overt state of affairs. And Heidegger correctly sees that the "for-the-sake-of" is not reducible to or analyzable in terms of the "in order to" relation. It is not so reducible because what *Dasein* does always arises out of a self-conception that the Dasein is always already attempting to embody. I did write this paper in order for it to be the case that I could publish it. But, and this is an important but, this is not the sort of goal this act could have unless I understood myself as a philosopher and was acting for the sake of my being a philosopher. So whatever conditions there are on understanding oneself as being some possible type of Dasein in and through acting for the sake of being that possible way of being Dasein are necessary conditions on acting in order to realize Daseinish sorts of goals.

Now, if Dasein's mode of intentionality were the only possible form of intentionality, then these conditions on acting in terms of a practical understanding of one's own mode of being would be conditions on any agent having intentional states. And Heidegger makes this limiting assumption. He holds the modified Kantian view that I articulated above that a concomitant unveiling of self is a necessary condition on all intentional states. Heidegger, in essence, is producing an extended transcendental argument which takes a version of the Kantian starting point as its base step: All intentional states are possible only in light of an existential self-understanding, so whatever is necessary for existential self-understanding is necessary for our type of intentionality.

Heidegger thus takes the Daseinish form of intentionality as *basic*. And since for Heidegger human intentionality is basic, so is human teleological behavior. And if this is the case, then the sorts of normativity associated with this behavior, acting for the sake of realizing socially prescribed ways of being Dasein and acting with tools as they are to be used in a culture, are the basic forms of normativity. If animals can be understood as having intentional states it is only as a kind of deficient case of Dasein. In taking this stand, Heidegger does not break with modernity; he continues the tradition that stretches from Descartes and

Kant through Wittgenstein, Sellars, and Robert Brandom. But it is not a tradition in which I place myself.

Rather, I place myself in an older naturalistic tradition that starts with Aristotle and runs through Leibniz and Dewey, that sees human intentionality and teleology as *species* of animal intentionality and teleology. I accept the profoundly anti-Heideggerean views that we are rational animals, and that to understand what is necessary for our teleological behavior and our intentional life one must first understand the simpler teleological behavior and intentional life of non-Daseinish animals. Agents can act for goals even though they never can become conscious of themselves, and never act in terms of any self-understanding, and to understand us we must understand them.

Thus, I can only appropriate from Heidegger the suggestion that teleology is necessary for intentionality, not Heidegger's own specific analysis of teleology, which presupposes that human goal-directed action is basic. On the other hand, Heidegger has many valuable insights regarding the distinctively human form of intentionality and its relation to the distinctively human form of action. And these are insights that I fully intend to appropriate, beginning now.

NOTES

1 Martin Heidegger, *The Basic Problems of Phenomenology*, trans. Albert Hofstadter (Bloomington: Indiana University Press, 1982), p. 164.
2 See, for example, Martin Heidegger, *History of the Concept of Time*, trans. Theodore Kisiel (Bloomington: Indiana University Press, 1985).
3 Heidegger, *The Basic Problems of Phenomenology*, pp. 158–61.
4 See my *Heidegger's Pragmatism: Understanding, Being, and the Critique of Metaphysics* (Ithaca, NY: Cornell University Press, 1988).
5 Heidegger, *The Basic Problems of Phenomenology*, pp. 158.
6 See, for example, *The Basic Problems of Phenomenology*, pp. 158–73.
7 Descartes, *Objections and Replies*, in *The Philosophical Writings of Descartes*, vol. 2, trans. John Cottingham, Robert Stoothoff, and Dugald Mordoch (Cambridge: Cambridge University Press, 1984), p. 113.
8 Ibid., pp. 154–8.
9 Ibid., p. 61.
10 *History of the Concept of Time*, p. 159.

Index

Abraham 95, 173 n. 25
absolute, the 119
absolute being 106, 120
absolute domination 11
absolute future 129
absolute obligation 68
absolute Other 119, 30
absolute subjectivity 60, 120
absolute unity 18
absolutism 141
action 13, 16, 22, 23, 115 n. 5, 122, 123, 147, 148, 157, 158, 160–8, 172 n. 16, 191, 194–7, 200–6
address of being 29, 88, 90, 92, 98
Africa 74
African 51, 98
agents 194, 198–206
aletheia 20, 90, 99
analytic philosophy 1–5, 9–11, 16, 118 n. 37, 145, 155
Anaximander 25, 129
ancient philosophy 105, 120
animals 45, 58, 59, 127, 128, 194, 305, 206
answer a call 87, 90, 92, 94, 148, 149
anthropologism 120, 127
anthropology 71, 72 119–27, 131
anti-semitism 53, 57, 65
anticipatory resoluteness 166, 167, 172 n. 23
Antigone 47
anxiety (*Angst*) 121, 141, 149–51, 153 n. 26, 166, 167, 170
appropriation (*Ereignis*) 35, 42, 45, 50, 88, 89, 104, 121, 124, 126, 130, 132, 176, 189
apriori, the 102, 103, 113, 182, 183
Aristotle 25, 69, 85, 88, 95, 97, 104, 105, 111, 113, 157, 160, 161, 162, 163, 164, 165, 171 n. 5, 172 n. 16, 206
articulation 14, 20, 22, 147, 156, 173 n. 25, 186, 203
at hand 186–9
attunement 31
Augustine 25, 86, 87, 95, 176–82
Austin, J. L. 44
authenticity
  account of 163
  authentic reality 55
  authentic resoluteness 166
  being 155, 166
  being-toward-death 184
  Dasein 167, 170, 172 n. 23
  disclosedness 162
  historizing 166
  language of 68
  understanding 131, 166
  we 167
average everydayness 155–7, 161, 163, 166, 170

background understanding 10–25, 114, 170
Baeumler, Alfred 66
becoming 15, 42, 70, 129, 171 n. 9, 172 n. 19, 188
beginning (*Anfang*) 16, 87, 105
behaviorism 204
being (*Sein*) 10, 11, 13, 32, 42, 48, 89, 99, 103, 104, 121, 124, 126, 127, 129, 145, 183
  absolute 106, 120
  call of (*Seinsanspruch*) 12, 21, 23–5, 72, 76, 87–90, 96
  of beings 10, 23, 60
  being-alongside 146, 187
  care, being of 184
  comportment, being as 185
  concealing of 147
  crossing out of 130, 131
  Dasein, being of 102, 150, 166, 191, 192, 205
  desertion of 127
  dispensation of 70, 114, 126
  epoch of 23, 87
  event of 128, 130, 132
  existence, being as 125, 126, 184
  existential analytic 32, 54
  finitude of 131

being (*Sein*) (*cont.*)
  fourfold, being of the 130
  forgetfulness of 118
  givenness of 105
  ground of 128
  history of 10, 11, 13, 18, 21, 24, 25, 26, 63 n.3, 69, 88, 89, 90
  historical 54
  human 3, 4, 13, 15, 16, 24, 31, 32, 36, 38, 41, 42, 45–7, 50, 53, 54, 55, 58, 59, 75, 93, 97, 99, 104, 106–9, 119, 121–9, 141, 142, 144, 146–8, 171 n. 14, 181, 191
  -in-the-world 97, 121, 129, 145, 147, 150, 161, 192, 195, 196, 199, 200, 201, 203, 204, 205
  indigence of 147
  intentional 106, 107, 108, 109, 199
  life, being of 164
  lightness of 72, 76, 79
  language of 88, 89
  letting-be of 87, 132
  movement of 18
  name of 129
  narrative of 89, 130
  not-being 176, 177, 180, 181
  object, being as 131
  oblivion of 10, 23, 25, 29 n. 55, 127
  otherwise than, the 147
  openness to 125, 126
  people of 88, 89, 90, 99
  phenomenological seeing, being as 103
  postmodern 72
  presencing, being as 87, 104, 105, 178, 182
  question of 3, 32, 99, 101, 103, 104, 105, 121, 125, 126, 182, 183, 191
  refusal of 147
  response to the call of 76, 87, 88, 90, 147
  sending of 87
  shelter of 178, 179, 180, 181
  social 112
  subject, being of the 147
  subjectivity, being as 106
  temporality of 3
  thought of 12, 21, 22, 23, 76, 86, 132, 146
  throw of 127, 184
  toward death 128, 154 n. 28, 166, 184
  truth of 76, 101, 104, 127, 128, 144
  unity of 13
  unconcealment of 13, 69, 147
  understanding of 4, 10, 11, 12, 13, 14, 15, 16, 17, 19, 20, 21, 22, 23, 24, 25, 27 n.10, 125, 173 n. 24, 182
  withdrawal of 54, 73, 114, 129, 130
  world, being of the 144, 145
beings (*Seiende*) 13, 14, 22, 120, 123, 125, 127, 129, 148, 182, 185, 186
belief 20, 195, 196, 197, 201
belonging (*Gehören*) 39, 54, 88, 104, 127, 129, 130, 149, 164, 189
Bennet, William 69
Bernasconi, Robert 18, 104, 153 n. 25
Biko, Stephen 62
biology, racial 50–67
biologism 129
Blattner, William 173
Blochmann, Elisabeth 56, 58
Boas, Franz 53
body 51, 53, 54, 55, 58, 72, 73, 77, 78
Borgmann, Albert 29, 68, 117 n. 35
Boulainvilliers 152 n. 11
Bourdieu, Pierre 160, 174 n. 26
Brandom, Robert 112, 206
Brentano, Franz 191

calendar 185, 188
call of being, *see* being
call to justice 92, 93, 99
call of duty 68, 69, 77, 78, 79
Caputo, John 28, 72, 85, 117 n. 35, 118 n. 37
care (*Sorge*) 97, 119, 124, 142, 146, 151, 184, 200
Carnap, Rudolf 9, 10, 11, 16, 22, 24, 111, 118 n. 37
cause 113, 114, 118 n. 37, 124, 144
Cavell, Stanley 4, 30, 48
Christ 94, 95
Christian 14, 39, 48, 85, 86, 87, 88, 93, 95, 96, 98, 131, 164, 165, 172 n. 16, 173 n. 25
Cioffi, Frank 118
Clausewitz, Carl 142
Clauss, Ludwig 66
clearing (*Lichtung*) 13, 23, 30, 99, 112, 119, 132, 145
Climacus, Johannes 94, 95
cogito 119
cognition 19, 93, 169
Coleridge, Samuel 39
competence 158–60, 169
concealment 3, 36, 41, 42, 73, 74, 90, 99, 131
concern 5, 161, 162, 186, 187, 188
  circumspective 186, 187, 188, 189
conscience 163
consciousness 102, 106, 107, 109, 147, 193, 194, 201, 206
constitution
  of the absolute future 129
  of action 13
  of care 146
  of Dasein 140
  of events 18–20
  of experience 120
  of foreground 13

of human being 130
of human finitude 125
of interpretation 85
of knowledge 35
of metaphysics 122, 124–6
of objects 19
of the present 16
of a people 89, 96
of a problematic 15
of pure consciousness 106
of the question of being 126
of skill 170
of time 175–89
of the transcendental ego 120
the West 88
of world-formation 123
context 20, 43, 157, 186, 187, 198, 202, 204
correspondence 104, 145
Critchley, Simon 2, 4, 5, 101
culture 12, 13, 14, 15, 24, 25, 34, 51, 53, 60, 70, 74, 77, 79, 90, 91, 114, 156, 157, 160, 162, 164, 167, 170, 171, 172–3 n. 24, 205

Darwin, Charles 58, 67
darwinism 58, 62, 65 n. 17, 67
Dasein 32, 42, 43, 45, 55, 104, 119, 121, 123, 14, 125, 126, 127, 129, 140, 145, 146, 147, 148, 149, 150, 151, 156, 161, 162, 164, 165, 167, 181, 182, 183, 184, 186, 191, 192
analytic of 102, 107, 120, 126, 142, 182
at-home character of 47, 48, 127
authenticity of 166, 167, 170, 172 n. 24
becoming of 87
and being-in-the-world 192, 205
and being-with 187
essence of 126, 147
extension of 184
finitude of 125, 128
historicity of 54, 183, 184, 185, 189
intelligibility of 156, 157, 165, 166, 186, 187, 189, 205
neediness of 125
and nothingness 121, 149, 150
rationality of 127, 130, 206
self-unveiling of 194, 195, 205
structure of 140, 148, 203, 204, 205
solitude of 141
temporality of 5, 182, 183, 185, 186, 187, 188, 189
thrownness of 126, 188
transformation of 31, 173 n. 24
uprootedness of 139, 149, 150, 153 n. 26, 161, 165
world and 123
Dastur, Françoise 4, 119
David, Pascal 53, 56, 65
Davidson, Donald 145, 204
death 33, 35, 43, 128, 129, 130, 131, 149, 150, 154 n. 28, 166, 167, 170, 184
deconstruction 18, 34, 104, 105, 127, 140, 153 n. 26
Deleuze, Giles 101, 142
demythologizing 85, 98, 99, 118 n. 37
Derrida, Jacques 26, 32, 34, 41, 44, 46, 48, 55, 56, 60, 61, 66 n. 24, 93, 114, 167, 168, 169, 170
Descartes, René 14, 15, 23, 25, 55, 103, 156, 191, 195, 205
desire 37, 194, 195, 199, 201
destruction 3, 24, 36, 104, 105, 131
Dewey, John 76, 206
dialectic 17, 49
Dilthey, Wilhelm 104, 107, 115–16 n. 10
disclosure 31, 69, 71, 112, 113, 123, 143, 147, 149, 161, 162, 164, 166, 168, 170, 187
distantiality (*Abständigkeit*) 49, 72, 77, 139
divine, divinity 37, 39, 42, 79, 119, 129, 131, 133 n. 39, 173 n. 25
Dreyfus, Hubert L. 16, 27 n. 23, 117 n. 28, 155, 170
Du Bois 62, 63
Dummett, Michael 10, 27
dwelling 18, 33, 38, 40, 41, 42, 44, 144, 145
Dworkin, Ronald 167, 168, 173, n. 26

earth 30, 41, 63 n. 3, 119, 129, 130, 131
ecstatic 48, 126
ego 108, 119, 120, 132
embody 191, 195, 205
Emerson, Ralph W. 34, 36, 41, 42, 44, 45, 49
empirical 9, 10, 11, 52, 113, 118 n. 37, 120
enigma 3, 25, 58, 117 n. 35
environing world (*Umwelt*) 112, 121, 188
epistemology 58, 68, 88, 108, 111
epochality 60, 62, 69, 87, 94, 114, 165
equipment 121, 156, 164
equiprimordial, 143
errancy 38, 76
eschatology 163, 164
essence 131
of an age 22
of being 87
of Dasein 47, 126, 147, 148
of finitude 124
historical 16
of home 47
of human being 23, 50, 55, 73, 127, 144
of intentionality 192, 204
of language 50
of life 58

essence (*cont.*)
of mental experience 102
originary 92
of spirit 48
of time 175, 176
of thinking 23, 86, 94
of metaphysics 10
eternity 37, 128, 176–80, 189
ethics 62, 68, 69, 73, 74, 85, 92, 99, 100, 108, 109, 111, 144, 145, 146, 151, 157, 160, 163, 167, 173 n. 25
Euclid 88
Europe 1, 51, 53, 55, 72, 98
event 10, 18, 19, 20, 22, 23, 25, 39, 40, 42, 63, 104, 122, 127, 128, 129, 130, 132, 166, 178, 187, 188, 193, 195, 202, 203
everydayness 3, 5, 13, 17, 20, 30, 40, 41, 44, 68, 70, 107, 117 n. 28, 138, 139, 151 n. 3, 153 n. 26, 155 156, 157, 161, 162, 170, 171 n. 9
existence 42, 68, 70, 92, 97, 106, 108, 120, 121, 124, 125, 126, 127, 130, 131, 141, 146, 147, 148, 149, 150, 151, 153 n. 26, 155, 156, 157, 161, 167, 184, 192
existential 13, 32, 54, 87, 107, 111, 113, 119, 120, 121, 123, 125, 126, 129, 146, 147, 181, 183, 185, 189, 205
existentialism 65, 120, 121
existentials 103, 113
existentiell 125, 147, 164
experience 10, 13, 14, 19, 22, 23, 44, 55, 73, 85, 86, 91, 92, 97, 102, 106, 107, 108, 109, 110, 111, 112, 113, 120, 121, 132, 153 n. 26, 158, 160, 161, 162, 163, 164, 165, 167, 168, 169, 170, 173 n. 25, 185
expert 157, 160, 162, 166, 168, 169, 170, 171 n. 9
expertise 149, 160, 166, 169, 170
expropriation 30

facticity (*Faktizität*) 85, 86, 87, 104, 107, 112, 123, 124, 125, 140, 141, 146, 147, 148, 149, 150, 151, 154 n. 27, 163, 166, 167, 168, 170, 187
faith 14, 25, 31, 86, 88, 89, 90, 93, 94, 95, 97, 98, 110, 117–18 n. 35, 163
falling 140, 146, 148
Fanon, Frantz 62
Farias, Victor 64, 65
fate 40, 47, 70, 75, 167, 184
Faulconer, James E. 29
Fichte, Johann 119, 120
field 19, 106, 187
finite 122, 124, 125, 126, 131, 132, 139, 140, 144, 150
finding-oneself (*Befindlichkeit*) 123, 145
Fink, Eugen 122, 123
fleeing 149, 171 n. 9
folk (*Volk*) 50–5, 61–3, 90
forgetting 91, 93, 94, 118 n. 37, 147, 149
formal 43, 85, 92, 96, 101, 102, 104, 105, 113, 115 n.1, 164
Foucault, Michel 114, 142, 143, 144, 145, 152 n. 11
fourfold 119, 129, 130
Fournier, Susan 74
Freud, Sigmund 75, 194.
Fukuyama, Francis 71
fulfillment 36, 196
future 16, 37, 63, 93, 129, 151, 159, 176, 177, 178, 179, 181, 184

Gadamer, Hans-Georg 112
gathering 93, 175, 178
genealogy 97, 142, 143, 144, 152 n. 11
Gibson, William 72
givenness 13, 16, 22, 40, 41, 46, 93, 103, 105, 106, 107, 110, 129, 131, 132, 147, 148, 149, 161, 187, 188, 189
goodness 68, 73, 77, 79, 159, 197
grasp 93, 149, 162, 165
Greek thought 13, 16, 17, 39, 85–96, 98, 104, 105, 164, 165, 172 n. 16, 173 n. 25, 182
ground 10, 13–17, 19, 50, 55, 56, 59, 61, 62, 66 n. 36, 103, 113, 121–9, 131, 132, 143, 166, 181
Guattari, Félix 101

Habermas, Jürgen 109
Hacking, Ian 144
hearing 88, 89, 90, 92, 93, 145
Hebrew 89, 90, 91, 92, 94, 95, 96, 98
heed 78, 89, 90
Hegel, G. W. F. 95, 109, 111, 112, 156
Heraclitus 25, 79, 96, 128, 197
hermeneutics 17, 85, 86, 104, 107, 109, 110, 112, 113, 148, 149
hidden 10, 114, 140
historicity 112, 183–6, 189
historiography 12, 19, 20, 24, 25, 29
history 2, 4, 12–26, 42, 47, 51, 54, 59, 61, 63–5, 69–73, 75, 80 n. 7, 86–91, 104, 108, 112, 114, 131, 141, 167, 173 n. 25, 175, 183–6, 189
of being (*Seinsgeschichte*) 10, 11, 13, 18, 21, 25, 26, 63 n. 3, 69, 88, 89, 90, 96
of philosophy 12, 15, 17–20, 22, 25, 175
of salvation 88, 89, 93, 94, 95, 96
Hölderlin, Friedrich 30, 31, 33, 34, 38, 40, 41, 42, 43, 45, 95, 131
holiness 89, 99

home 42, 47, 48, 149, 153 n. 26
horizon 119, 123, 186, 187, 188
of being 125, 182
human being, *see* being, human
human condition 70, 77
humanism 32, 56, 62, 68, 74, 76, 120, 121, 122, 127, 128, 129, 133 n. 39, 144, 146
humanity 92, 93, 127, 128, 130
humbleness 47, 99, 140
Husserl, Edmund 25, 46, 97, 101–11, 114, 119, 120, 123, 192, 193, 196

ideas, history of 21
idealism 55, 96, 119, 130
image 20, 34 36, 39, 44, 189
imagination 33, 97
immanence 102, 106, 132
inauthenticity 116
instancy (*Inständigkeit*) 126
instant (*Augenblick*) 73, 163, 168, 173 n. 25
intelligibility 14, 17, 19, 156, 157, 161, 162, 165, 167, 170, 173 n. 25
intentionality 20, 24, 102–9, 114, 115 n. 5, 178, 191–206
normativity of 196–7, 203–4, 205
interpretation (*Auslegung*) 2, 17, 20, 21, 22, 85, 88, 103, 109, 140, 149, 165, 166, 182, 186, 187, 188, 191, 192, 202, 204
interpreter 17, 163, 164, 191
intuition (*Anschauung*) 97, 103, 115 n. 6, 123, 125, 160, 193
categorial 102, 103, 104, 105, 114, 115 n. 6, 192, 193
involvement 3, 123, 147, 159–68, 172 n. 23, 176, 194, 196, 198

Jaspers, Karl 96
Jesus 87, 172 n. 16, 173 n. 25
Jewish 89, 94, 96
Jews 89, 90, 93, 94, 95, 96, 98
judgment 68, 122, 137, 144, 145, 167, 168, 169
justice 92, 95, 99, 168, 100

kairos 86, 97, 163–4, 165, 172 n. 16
Kant, Immanuel 25, 102, 119, 124, 125, 126, 192, 193, 196, 206
Kierkegaard, Søren 87, 95, 97, 163, 164, 165, 172 nn. 16, 19, 173 n. 25
Kisiel, Theodore 157, 163, 165
knowledge 45, 93, 112, 142
Kundera, Milan 72

Lacan, Jacques 142
land 33, 34, 49 n. 15, 94, 99
Lang, Berel 56, 57, 61, 66 n. 29, 67 n. 45
language 9, 43, 44, 50–1, 54, 88, 90, 91–2, 93, 96, 99, 112, 115 n. 6, 143, 144, 173 n. 25, 186, 194, 198
German 25, 98
ordinary 45, 156, 198
law 143 n. 11, 152 n. 11, 168, 169
Lefort, Claude 142
Leibniz, Gottfried Wilhelm v. 206
Levinas, Emmanuel 26, 90, 92, 108, 109, 114, 131, 143, 146, 147, 149, 151, 154 nn. 27, 29
liberalism 55, 75
light (*Licht*) 5, 23, 47, 145, 148, 188
Locke, John 33, 113, 193
logical analysis, method of 9–10, 15, 155
Luther, Martin 87, 95, 97, 163
Lyotard, Jean-Françoise 92, 143

Makkreel, Rudolf 115 n.
marginal practices 17, 167, 169
margins of philosophy 138, 139, 140
McDowell, John 111, 112
meaning, linguistic 9, 20, 34, 43, 91, 92, 198, 199
meaningfulness (*Bedeutsamkeit*) 121
memory 90, 92, 93, 179, 180
mental states and experiences 102, 118 n. 35, 191, 193, 201, 203, 204
Merleau-Ponty, Maurice 109, 110, 111
metaphysics, metaphysical, metaphysicians 3, 10–11, 13–17, 19–25, 27 n. 22, 32, 34, 44, 48, 54, 59, 62, 86–7, 91, 103, 120, 122, 124–31, 146, 156, 161
Milton, John 41
modern age, modernity 4, 13–15, 19, 23, 55, 68–70, 106, 127–8
mood (*Stimmung*) 39, 48, 55, 73, 121, 123, 132, 138, 145
moral, morality 33, 62, 68–9, 73, 74, 75, 76, 77, 78, 79, 90, 124, 144
Mourelatos, Alexander 17, 22, 28 n. 25

nationalism 65 n. 17, 98
National Socialism 50–2, 57–8, 60, 61, 64 nn. 6, 11, 86, 91, 98
natural attitude 4, 105, 106–8, 109–10, 116 n. 15
naturalism 56, 111–12, 143, 206
natural sciences, *see* science
nature 32, 33, 40, 46, 55, 78, 111, 121, 123, 165, 175, 180, 185
Nazi, *see* National Socialism
Nothing, the (*das Nichts*) 9, 13, 43, 121, 129
Natorp, Paul 115
neo-Kantianism 96, 97, 103
neo-Schellingianism 110, 117 n. 27

Neurath, Otto v. 111
Nietzsche, Friedrich 22, 23, 25, 30, 57–8, 59, 60, 62, 66 n. 35, 119, 128, 142
nihilism 170
norms 19, 34, 112, 116
  ethical 68, 69, 74
  social 166, 167
nows, *see* temporality
Nozick, Robert 137, 138, 144, 145, 150

object 3, 13, 19, 20, 45, 102, 107, 108, 151, 186, 196, 197–8, 199, 204
  subject–object relation 76, 111, 122
objective reference 196, 197
objectivism 104, 111
obligation 4, 68, 124, 141, 143
oblivion (*Vergessenheit*) 10–11, 13, 16, 23, 25, 29 n. 56, 90, 127, 148
occult 113–14
Okrent, Mark 5, 115 n. 5, 153 n. 25
ontic, ontical 144, 145, 147, 149, 150, 153
ontology 11, 138, 151
  and anthropology 72, 124, 125
  and background 12, 20, 24
  in *Being and Time* 4, 108, 112–13, 119, 120, 121, 143, 145, 149, 170, 173 n. 25, 182
  and Dasein 147–8, 184
  fundamental 108, 112, 113, 122, 126, 150, 153 n. 26
  history of 3, 104–5
  Husserlian 120
  and racism 57
  and technology 71, 76
ontological difference 142, 145
onto-theo-logic 94, 95
openness (*Entschlossenheit*) 92, 112, 126, 129, 147, 166, 169, 171 n. 14
origin (*Ursprung*) 43, 90, 96
originary
  call 90
  essence 91–2
  thought 94, 99
  time 181–6, 189
Overbeck, Franz 86, 97, 99–100 n. 2
own, owning 4, 26, 42, 45, 88, 132, 148–9, 166

Parmenides 17, 25, 96
past, the, *see also* temporality, 18, 20, 93, 167, 176–8, 179, 181
St. Paul 86–7, 95, 97, 163–5, 172 n. 16
perception 115 n. 6, 123, 195, 196, 199
people (*Volk*) 40, 47, 50, 51, 52, 53, 54, 55, 61, 62, 63 n. 3, 65 nn.15, 19, 20, 88, 89, 90, 96, 98, 99, 100 n. 6
phainaesthetics 99
phenomenology 92, 94, 97, 123, 193
  in *Being and Time* 24, 101–14, 155, 163
  Husserlian 4, 46, 97, 101–14, 119–20, 192–3
  of skill acquisition 157–61
philosophy 11, 31, 33, 34, 39, 45, 73, 79, 96–7, 101, 108–9, 119–20, 138, 139–40, 148–9
  continental and analytic 1, 2–3, 9–10, 12, 16, 24, 26, 44, 46, 111–12, 118 n. 37, 155
  history of 12, 15, 17–18, 19, 21–2, 25, 86–7, 104, 182
  and religion 85–6, 92, 94, 99
philosophical concepts 43–4, 86, 97
phronimos 157, 160, 161, 162, 163, 164, 165, 166, 167, 168, 173 n. 25
phronesis 157, 161, 162, 164, 171 n. 5
phronetic 102
phusis, *physis* 13, 88
place 18, 38, 41, 132, 178–9
Plato 25, 32, 34, 68, 88, 97, 104, 105, 113, 156, 189
platonism 112
play 4, 130
Plotinus 180
poetizing 34, 38, 42, 43, 90, 94
poetry (*Dichtung*) 37, 38, 39, 41, 94, 95, 96, 131
poets 42, 43, 48, 98, 100 n. 9
politics, political 14, 46, 56, 57, 62, 63, 65 n. 20, 68, 72, 80, 106, 142–3, 144, 167
postmodernism 70, 71, 72, 74, 75, 76, 78, 79
practices, practical activity 2, 3, 4, 5, 14,15, 16–17, 19, 23, 102, 109, 111, 112, 113, 156, 157, 162, 167, 169, 172, 173, 193, 205
preconceptual 85, 97, 125
pre-givenness 103, 125
pre-ontological 149
pre-scientific 112, 113
pre-theoretical 85, 102, 107, 110, 113
presence, being as 182
presencing 87, 105
present, the, *see also* temporality 16, 20, 37, 40, 93, 151, 164, 173, 176–81
  praesens 177, 178, 179
present-at-hand (occurrent, *Vorhandensein*) 55, 97, 107–8, 109, 110, 111, 112, 143, 162, 164, 168, 173 n. 25, 189
Putnam, Hilary 137, 138, 144, 145, 149, 150

question of being (*Seinsfrage*) 3, 32, 99, 101, 103, 104, 105, 106, 121, 124, 126, 147, 182, 191–2

race, racism 50–67
  metaphysical 56–7, 59–62

Ranke, Leopold v. 141
ready-to-hand (available, *Zuhandensein*) 108, 111, 112, 121, 162, 164, 173 n. 25, 186
realism 96, 117 n. 28
  legal 170
  moral 76
reality 35, 37, 39–40, 69–70, 71, 72, 73, 77–9, 92, 108, 109, 129, 196
Rectoral Address 51, 52, 55, 57, 72
reflection (*Besinnung*) 16, 51, 140, 193
relativism 137, 141, 145, 151
religion 4, 37, 41, 44, 78, 85–9, 93–4, 97–8, 99, 131, 133–4 n. 39, 146, 164
repetition (*Wiederholung, also* retrieval) 3, 90, 104, 105, 146, 167
representation 14, 19, 91, 92, 102, 127, 193, 196, 198
resoluteness (*Entschlossenheit*) 68, 161, 162–3, 164, 165–6, 167, 168, 170, 171 n. 14, 172 n. 23
resource (*also* standing reserve) 13, 69, 70, 71
retrieval *see* repetition
Richardson, William J. 122
Robinson, John 74
Rockmore, Tom 57
romanticism 39, 70
Rorty, Richard 18, 19, 22, 75, 76, 92
Rosenberg, Alfred 52, 56
Rosenthal, Alfred 57
rules
  ethical 68
  practical 157–8, 159–60, 161, 162
  social 166, 167

Sallis, John 5, 104
salvation 14, 88, 89, 94, 95, 96
Sartre, Jean-Paul 62, 120–1
saving power 25, 70, 76, 87, 131
Scheler, Max 107
Schelling, Friedrich W. J. v. 119, 127
Schopenhauer, Arthur 36
Schor, Juliet 74
science 4, 9, 10, 11, 14, 34, 59, 61, 94, 113
  natural 61, 110, 111, 113
  race 50, 60
  social 74, 76
scientism 4, 110–11, 113–14, 117–18 n. 35, 118 n. 37
scriptures 89, 92, 94, 95, 96
Searle, John 1, 26
self-alienation 148
self-consciousness 60, 115, 193, 194, 195
self-interpretation 121, 186, 187, 189
self-overcoming 128
self-preservation 36, 58
self-understanding 194, 205, 206
signification 92, 143, 189
skepticism 15, 46, 112, 141
skills 69, 78, 156–61, 163, 168, 170, 171 n. 9
soul (*Seele*) 34, 53, 54, 55, 56, 175, 179–81
Sophist (Plato) 104, 171 n. 11
space 42, 72, 179, 180
spatium 180
Spengler, Oswald 141
spirit (*Geist*) 34, 48, 50–2, 53, 54, 55–6, 60, 61, 62, 98, 128, 156
style 3, 5, 15, 19, 26, 150, 153 n. 25, 170, 173 nn. 24, 25
subject 14, 31, 55, 107, 119, 120, 122, 123, 127, 129, 130, 145, 147, 150, 171 n. 14
subjectivism 103, 104, 121, 122, 123 127
subjectivity 54, 60, 62, 106, 119, 120, 122, 124, 147
supererogatory 68, 69, 77

Taminiaux, Jacques 103, 105, 122
Tanach 89, 92, 93, 96
Taylor, Charles 76
techne 157
technology 4, 11, 13, 16, 23, 24, 25, 69, 70, 71, 72, 74, 76, 77, 79, 147
teleology 56, 191, 194, 200, 201, 202, 203, 204, 206
temporality 3, 5, 54, 173 n. 25, 178, 181–7, 189
temporalizing 54, 164, 183–4
theology 85, 86, 87, 95, 112, 124
thinking (*Denken*) 2, 10, 11, 15, 21, 22, 23, 25, 40, 44, 59, 60, 76, 86–7, 88, 89, 90, 91, 92–4, 95, 96, 97, 98, 104, 122, 124, 128, 132, 140
thinkers 10, 12, 14, 16, 21, 22, 23, 25, 43, 48, 63, 85, 87
Thoreau, Henry David 30–49
thrownness (*Geworfenheit*) 123, 126–7, 140, 148, 150–1, 166–7, 170, 184, 188
time 5, 18, 37–8, 74, 77, 86, 97, 141, 163–4, 165, 172 n. 16, 173 n. 25, 175–90
totality of equipment (*Zeugganzheit*) 123, 156
traces 87, 91, 93, 99, 114, 149
Trakl, Georg 41, 48
truth
  of being 10, 15, 76, 101, 104, 127–8, 131, 143
  of beings 59–60
  of history 42
  and power 142–3
  propositional 145, 196, 197, 198
  of salvation 14

transcendental
  argument 192, 193, 195, 199, 200, 204, 205
  ego 120
  idealism 119
  ontology 121, 122, 123, 125
  phenomenology 106, 110
  subject 120, 123
turning (*Kehre*) 24, 104, 121, 122, 143
twinkling of an eye (instant; *Augenblick*) 162, 163, 164–6, 167, 172 n. 16, 173 n. 25

uncanniness 47, 48
unconcealment, *see also* truth, 13, 90, 99
understanding
  average 156, 166, 167, 170
  of being 10–25, 32, 125, 149, 173, 182
  everyday 44
  primordial 157, 161, 165, 166, 168, 170
  self 103, 194, 205, 206
  theoretical 108, 109, 110
unsaid (*Ungesagte*) 85, 89, 90
unthought (*Ungedachte*) 20, 85, 89, 90, 91, 94, 110
untruth 140, 143, 149

van Buren, John 116 n. 20, 163, 164, 165, 172 n. 16
violence (of understanding/interpretation) 17, 21, 45
Visker, Rudi 5, 29 n. 62

Wacker, Otto 51
Walton, Sam 78
Weinert, Hans 64
whiling 43
withdrawal
  of being 73, 90, 114, 129, 130
  of god 87, 132
Wittgenstein, Ludwig 26, 34, 44, 45, 46, 156, 206
Wordsworth, William 39, 41
world (*Welt*), *see also* being-in-the-world, environing world
  life-world 112, 113
  and fourfold 119, 129–30
  man as world-forming 45, 121, 122, 129
  spiritual world 51–2
world-time 173 n. 25, 185–6, 187–8
Wrathall, Mark 1, 4
Wuthnow, Robert 74

Young, Julian 52, 66 n. 24

Zarader, Marlène 89, 90, 91, 92, 93